By Padraic Fiacc

Poetry
By the Black Stream
Odour of Blood
Nights in the Bad Place
The Selected Padraic Fiacc
Missa Terribilis
Ruined Pages: Selected Poems
Red Earth
Semper Vacare
Sea: Sixty Years of Poetry

As Editor
The Wearing of the Black

MY TWENTIETH-CENTURY NIGHT-LIFE

My Twentieth-Century Night-Life
A Padraic Fiacc Miscellany

Lagan Press
Belfast
2009

Published by
Lagan Press
Unit 45
Westlink Enterprise Centre
30-50 Distillery Street
Belfast BT12 5BJ
e-mail: lagan-press@e-books.org.uk
web: lagan-press.org.uk

ARTS
COUNCIL
of Northern Ireland

ISBN: 978 1 904652 60 1

first published 2009
reprinted with corrections 2009

Author: Fiacc, Padraic
Title: My Twentieth-Century Night-Life
A Padraic Fiacc Miscellany
2009

Set in Meridien

Contents

Preface

... We
Chat about the 'troubles' and/or

The weather, and, like, horse laugh:
'What has murder and torture to do
With us? There is no war.'
                    —'Foetus Papyraceous'

Padraic Fiacc has been a presence in Irish letters for over sixty years.

While there is a disturbing and intimidating unity to Fiacc's poetry, it would be reasonable to say that his work falls into two broad categories: poems of the Celtic Twilight (whilst at the same time challenging and renewing that tradition with a bracingly modernist/experimental poetic aesthetic) and, spurred by the political, social and moral collapse around him, poems of 'the troubles'.

Indeed, his work—along with others—has acted as a catalyst for an ongoing (and, at times, seemingly endless and somewhat vitriolic) debate on the role of poetry in times of civic conflict, attracting both passionate supporters and fierce critics in equal measure.

Indeed, the hostile reception in the north of Ireland of his anthology of 'troubles poetry', *The Wearing of the Black*—along with Seamus Heaney's *North* and Thomas Kinsella's *The Butcher's*

Dozen—and to Fiacc's poems generally was to prove an imaginative, cultural and political faultline, an aesthetic dividing line, if you will, sorting out the sheep and the goats. Attacked as journalistic, vampiric and exploitative by critics such as Edna Longley, James Simmons and others loosely gathered around the *Honest Ulsterman* magazine, the savaging of the anthology was to prove, for good or for ill, a turning point in Northern Irish letters.

But this gathering—in some ways to be read as an addendum to Gerald Dawe and Aodan MacPoilin's near-definitive editon of Fiacc poems, *Ruined Pages*—stands unashamedly in the supporters' corner.

The aim of this miscellany is two-fold: to preserve—and to bring to a wider audience—some of Fiacc's critical and biographical writings which may help the reader to have a more complete understanding of the personal, aesthetic and socio-cultural impulses behind the poetry and to act as a 'mini-study guide' by providing a variety of critical/personal responses to his work by others.

The first section, 'Cuckoos With Me ... ', collects together Fiacc's critical/journalistic offerings. As a gathering, it is by no means definitive. Much has been lost and awaits rediscovery. But it *is* indicative of Fiacc's concerns over the years. Beginning with his rather precocious reviews of, and reveries on, the work of such figures as Padraic and Mary Colum, Austin Clarke and Michael McLaverty, the collection establishes his personal and aesthetic connection with the figures of the late Celtic Twilight. Later pieces show Fiacc's response to the onset and onslaught of 'the troubles' both in terms of defending *The Wearing of the Black* and, by turns tentatively and then rumbustiously, setting out his belief that poetry has a moral duty to report on and respond to the violence both outside and, by implication, inside ourselves. Furthermore, these pieces from *Hibernia* and other magazines, illustrate Fiacc's belief in the dictum 'semper vacare' (which was to feature as the title to his 1999 collection) which he loosely translates as 'make space' or 'give way'—that not only is it the poet's role to create imaginative space for his own self-expression but also to give space to the younger or more marginalised voices. Several of the pieces here, for instance, are promotions of the then-in-its-infancy 'Ulster Renaissance' with features on the work of Seamus Heaney,

Michael Longley and Derek Mahon or even younger, less established, poets of the period.

We also have included a selection of his jobbing review work to indicate a more day-to-day aspect to Fiacc's journalistic endeavours. These pieces—a few of which were sub-edited almost beyond sense—provide occasional insights into the man: his praise for now largely forgotten novelist Ulster novelist, Jack Wilson, for example, or his *Honest Ulsterman* article 'Three Holy Blue Flower People' and its implicit support for the counter-culture of the period.

The second section, 'Our Little Boat is Too Small ... ', consists of more substantial pieces: two critically-praised radio memoirs of his New York childhood and autobiographical montages/extracts. Both these montage pieces have been drawn from much more extensive autobiographical fragments which Fiacc has been orchestrating for many years under the provisional title of *Dead Trees*.

Finally, as already outlined, the final section of this miscellany, 'It is I Who Left You .... ', gathers a variety of critical responses and encounters in an attempt to highlight various aspects of Fiacc's poetry and career: the 'troubles' poet; the American Fiacc; the religious sensibility underlying the poems; the poet of 'failure'; the poet standing almost counter-intuitively against the prevailing orthodoxies of Northern Irish poetry; the poet as 'encourager' of the talent of others. Providing a centre and commentary to this section are two interviews with Fiacc which pick up on many of recurring aspects of the poetry.

Some of the responses are non-critical appreciations with the inclusion of much-needed biographical material. Others, like Brendan Hamill's 'The Troubles He's Seen' and the visual artist James Millar's studies of Fiacc, attempt a more personal and intimate approach, in some ways attempting to explore the intermeshing of personality and the times. Also included is Paddy Scully's one-man show on Fiacc, *Darker Than Sundown*.

Much remains to be written about Patriac Fiacc. Hampered, to put it politely, by the incorrigibilty of the poet himself, the poems have not received the critical attention they deserve.

It is hoped that this miscellany will be a modest step in helping to rectify that situation.

Today is my birth
-day. I am seventeen.

My home town
Has just bin
Blown up:

Dead feet in dead faces,
Corpses still alight,
Students helping kids
And old people out of

Still burning houses.

I have nothing to write
Poems about.

This is my twentieth-century

Night-life.

Patrick Ramsey
Lagan Press

Publisher's Note
As outlined above much of Padraic Fiacc's critical/journalistic work has been lost. If readers wish for any other articles/materials not included in this selection to be considered for inclusion in future editons, please send photocopies to Lagan Press or contact us by e-mail.

CUCKOOS WITH ME
REVIEWS AND CRITICAL WRITINGS

Good and Evil
Prolegomenon to a study
of Michael McLaverty's work

IT IS SO FACILE TO MENTION the name of Chekhov and to end it there, or in going from McLaverty to the whole school of northern artists: the music of Richard Strauss, the dry poetries of Auden and T.S. Eliot, the anti-expressionistic experiments of Stravinsky and Picasso; one cannot help but shiver at the new cold turn. Willy Pogany, the Hungarian artist, rose up in the back of the room when I was giving a small talk on Jack Yeats in New York. He said: "But these young artists,"—that was me!—"they are so scientific!"

I met Michael McLaverty as I went forth to meet Mr. Colum and Mme. Undset. The melody of Dr. Lonnrot's *The Kalevala* singing in my ear from the violins of Sibelius:

> Foreign food I do not relish,
> In the best of strangers' houses.
> In his land a man is better,
> In his home a man is greater.

And

> Then they went to seek a minstrel,
> One whose voice was of the strongest.

I had come from the dry purity of the French mould, pausing for moments at the Alhambra de la Granada where one could escape the mincing daintiness of the civilised in the national barbarism of de Falla. From Spain where everything Byzantine met with the song of Dante, Thomas Aquinas and the Arabs, I turned my perspective north.

In England they speak today of Søren Kierkegaard. It is not without meaning that I began at once a series of talks with Michael McLaverty on 'Irish novelists and the Concept of Evil'.

He has in his 'The Prophet':

> In water and out of water, in sheughs and out of sheughs; 'tis them things, Brendan, that'd make you feel it.

The study of any northern writer today is the study of two forces. We find it everywhere we turn, a daring quest which is the need of the times; and how they are falling everywhere, these gods who tell us with Patrick Kavanagh:

> Child there is a light somewhere
> Under a star,
> Sometime it will be for you
> A window that looks
> Inward to God.

We have fallen into the sadness of Austin Clarke at the sight of the tragedies of Wilde and Joyce:

> Forever sinning without end:
> I pity in their pride
> And agony of wrong, the men
> In whom God's likeness died.

We are the two brothers in Frank O'Connor's story, 'Uprooted'. Mankind, on the whole, has lost, with these wars, much of its old spirit and wonder. The artist is almost banished from western society. Music saved itself in nationalism, and poetry and painting will have to remember today, also, Keidrych Rhys's cry:

> Lightning
> Is different in Wales.

There is much of the thing in Yeats' 'Under Ben Bulben' (but perhaps the worst is not):

Cast a cold eye
On life, on death.
Horseman, pass by!

It is, too, natural that the Germans under Nietzsche revolted
with their idolatry against the hatred of nature. Yeats is most
interesting because he has both idolatry and hatred in his excesses:

Swear by those horsemen, by those women
Complexion and form prove superhuman,
That pale, long-visaged company,
That air of immortality,
Completeness of their passions won;
Now they ride the wintery dawn—

It seemed hundreds of years ago since he, himself, predicted his
own coldness and the coldness of our generation ('The
Unappeasable Host'):

For they will ride the north when the ger-eagle flies,
With heavy whitening wings, and a heart fallen cold.

John Hewitt's 'The Splendid Dawn' tells us where we are now
(and he is another Ulsterite with his eye on Robert Frost).

Daybreak began with colour in the sky
That colder yet had held itself aloof
From the raw, wind-whipped and unkindled earth,
And all at once a marvellous dawn appeared
Angry with sailor's warnings, spears of gold,
And burning clouds that set the wood afire,
A dawn too splendid and too vast for one
Lonely and cold in an unfriendly place.

If one would go to the works of McLaverty, unaware of the dark
consciousness of modern society seething today in the potent state
of regret, one would be taken aback at the duality, the great
mystery under the visible things, this gentleness, this sternness. It
may go as far back as the father of lies who said: "You will be like
gods, knowing good and evil." We find it in Plato, surely, who said
man was cut in halves, in Dun Scotus who said the individual is the
complete sum of twos, the ideal and the real, and isn't he talking
about genius? To Jacob Bohme to whom it was a religion that a

thing which was not the union of two opposing forces was dead; Christ would vomit from His mouth the lukewarm, the indifferent. We find it in that mystery of books, Dostoyevsky's *The Brothers Karamazov*:

> The sense of their own degradation is as essential to these reckless, unbridled natures as the sense of their lofty generosity ... They need continually this unnatural mixture. Two extremes at the same moment or they are miserable and dissatisfied and their existence is incomplete.

With the Irish philosopher, Berkeley, there was a demand for unity to overcome the dualism of things, and for him to think a thing with the whole person made it be. Rimbaud and Verlaine married the precise with unprecise, and at Paris, where extremes are always meeting, the east and the west, the north and the south, there is a school of Catholic writers professing what is called *surnaturalisme*, in which the point is, in expression, to present the revolting and the sublime together. It is enough to mention the name of Julian Green and Bremond's saying: "Those profane states of nature which trace the mystical states of the soul."

The fact that when one reads McLaverty at first one is beset with two opposing reactions is a proof of the completeness of the man. I could have said with Roy McFadden in his 'Elegy':

> O Look, he lies
> Cold in the shallows of the ebbing light.
> A tree grown through his heart.

But because, today, Adam is poor Verlaine in gaol, I had to exclaim:

> Mon Dieu, mon Dieu, la vie est
> Simple et tranquille.

Yet, if Adam was not always poor Verlaine in such a state of regret, one could speak of McLaverty as Rouault's friends spoke of Rouault: with devotion but nonetheless mercilessly; for the man is obeying, as Maritain might say, all this, the necessity of growth, and there are moments in him, in Stravinsky, Hopkins, Sibelius, in all the northerners when the cold purity of their style is cruel.

Griffith and Padraic Colum had, at the beginning of this century, what was criticised as sordid materialism. The socialism of contemporary English writers has a tendency to leave the person out in its realism.

McLaverty has set seed as all northern minds do with their love for detail, their Byzantine unities, in the naturalistic and material worlds. He evokes for us intimate pictures of God in His creation:

> 'He's in great condition. We should cut his comb and wattles any time and have him ready for Easter.' And he'd put him down on the tiles and listen to the scrape of his claws. Then he'd feel the muscles on the thighs, and stick out his beard with joy. 'There's no coldness about that fella, Mick. He has shoulders on him as broad as a bulldog. Aw, my lovely fella,' feeling the limber of him as his claws pranced on the tiles.
> —'A Game Cock'

It is a wholesome, a healthy joy of living things, beinghood, the positive asserting of combined forces which mankind has too horribly taken for granted.

In McLaverty there is that same sense of informing nationalism with the cosmopolitan, that rich taste of deep rejecting all that does not make for the lawful mating of opposites in nature as there is in the work of Sigrid Undset. Her great saga, *Kristin-lavransdatter*, is the health of a world, is both ugly and beautiful. There is, as a matter of following nature, none of the shallow delineations which slanted Mauriac's *La Pharisienne*: there is nowhere in any of the northern Catholic writers the Manichean faith or angelism of the later Yeats:

> That this pragmatical, preposterous pig of a world,
> Its farrow that so solid seems,
>   Must vanish on the instant if the mind but change its theme.

Fr. D'Arcy's study, 'The Mind and Heart of Love', sheds a profound light, by the use of modern research into behaviour, upon the mannerisms of an artist with McLaverty's seemingly evangelical outlook, though it might be enough to say of most of his early work that it was written in Greece before the death of Alexander, that it is free from the ornamental erudition which was the ignominious mark of the Hellenistic age. He is already making a slow but long transition with his short story, 'The Mother', and his novel, *In This Thy Day*, into what Mme. Undset used to tell us in New York: "The theme of all literature is sin." Yet when a child dies into manhood something is gone, as from all the early poetries. Goethe went back to his own Grecian gold-youth when he was able to write:

Über allen Gipfeln
Ist Ruh,
In allen Wipfeln
Spürest du
Kaum einen Hauch;
Die Vogelein schweigen im Walde.
Warte nur, balde
Ruhest du auch.

There was no rhetoric in the beginning. These documents of little lives are a work that make us come across art as a plough would hit up against a jewel. The world after all is the lusty woman in *Ulysses*: "I'll sing that for him ... if he's anything of a poet."

The poetic illumination of McLaverty is the best of buttermilk. Where he can have a child say in 'Pigeons':

My eyes would be very gluey and I would rub them with my fists until they would open in the gaslight. For a long while I would see gold needles sticking out of the flame, then they would melt away and the gas become like a pansy leaf with a blue heart.

He can also describe:

Wet days with the rain sizzling in the lake.

And:

Under the closed door stole the night-wind, the bits of straw around the threshold rising gently and falling back again.

One would have to quote his entire short story 'Look at the Boats' for an ample example of the humanity of McLaverty. It is in such a story, I think, that he shows bare the vein of his terrible pity and undercurrent of strong love for his strong people.

If he is going to make a deeper turn as the process of intellectual evolution forces every artist to, at one time or another, if he is going to draw the line between his early works and later studies, one will surely justify the early charity of his poetic illumination in the achievement of Francis of Assisi. D'Arcy writes in 'The Mind and the Heart of Love':

> Scheler depicted Saint Francis of Assisi as the most moving and perfect example of human living, just because he combined an intense interest in all objects and persons around him and at the same time was completely self-denying.

Irish Bookman, vol. 1 no. 5, December, 1946

Padraic Colum

"BUT THERE ARE NO MORE GREAT Irish writers," said Mary Colum. It seemed to me at that moment her words had the proud glimmer of an autumnal dynasty, such an ethos as would trail after it the thousand eyes of a peacock's tail: all that went, for instance, buried with Yeats in France. And there she sat under her portrait of Æ, and you could feel the drafts in between of the vent of years of fire that had put snow on the wild redness of her hair.

We talked awhile that night in February, 1946, until she got bored and rose up to go down to get some beer.

When she went out Colum settled himself more deeply into a large throne-like chair and asked me to recite one of my lyrics. I could only remember the first parts of 'To a Tug Horn':

> The sound of the boats on the river
> Is an old call and a long call
> In me going forever
> Till the stars fall.
>
> Break my heart with your moan and your cry
> The heartful moan and the low sound.
> My heart is in the rainy sky;
> My heart is drowned ...

He suggested an idiomisation of the first line in the second stanza to: "My heart with your cry *break* with your cry."

Immediately, I saw the lovely austerity of the Gaelic saving me again from the hackneyed: how it accented the verb, how much more poignant the effect by repetition and limit.

All at once Colum began to chant Frank O'Connor's translation 'To Tomaus Costello at the Wars' ...

"But there's a grandeur about the thing, a grandeur!" He had in his hand Donagh MacDonagh's *Poems from Ireland*:

> Your father's trade take up anew
> And magnify the northern blood—
> The light of poetry are you,
> The stirring of the coals of love ...

Whether it was the beer or the fact that I felt I owed so much to the man and had no words in which to thank him (for I was taking a boat in the morning to leave the US forever) I became a little drunk, so towards midnight I made some shape to get up to go.

Coming out to the elevator he said: "Always remember, Padraic, the words of Berkeley: that to perceive is to create."

Riding down the lift, dizzy with the beer, maxims and hints stirred in my brain like a spell: "Limits are good for you."

The words of Tagore in *The Mason*:

> But if you ask me why I live in a hut covered with straw while I can build big houses of brick and why my house should not be the biggest of all, I am sure I cannot tell you.

The words in *The Kalevala*:

> While the young are standing round us
> Let them learn the words of magic
> And recall our songs and legends.

The words of Goethe:

> Superstition is the poetry of life; so that it does the poet no harm to be superstitious.

The words of Guérin:

> I want to be a man in my poems, or nothing at all.

Lines from Colum himself:

> Stride the hill, sower
> Up to the sky ridge
> Flinging the seed,
> Scattering, exultant ...
> Give to the darkness and sleep
> To gladden the world
> Who is fain to being
> To build day by day
> To raise up his house
> He shall go forth alone.

When I reached my apartment I opened up his *Collected Poems* and somehow I was able to turn just to those grains of line which put into art the sum of all that he wanted me to understand:

> 'Uncunningly made—even so
> —close to the ground are reared
> The wings that have widest sway
> And the birds that sing best in the wood,' he said
> 'Were reared with breasts to the clay.'

***

> You've wildness—I've turned it to song;
> You've strength—I've turned it to wings.

***

> —Sons of the Dust behold—
> Your malice becomes my song!

***

> —they strive for this—
> the fullness of passionate nerve.

***

> The franchise of one
> without kith or kin
> —only the pauper's
> single mind.

***

O impotent, bare things
You give at last the very cry of earth!

***

I who hear the hedge sing
Will fare with all the rest
With thoughts of lust and labour
And bargain in my breast.

Somehow it all came to what motivated, according to de Vogüé, 19th-century Russian literature: "And God made man out of the slime of the earth."

Colum after all was a link to me, a young writer, with an Ireland that has already withered, that passionate of all times when Griffith was able to get up and say:

> I have an unshaken faith in the innate strength of our people's soul, sir.
>
> It has its backers already among men and women of faith and vision, and among the intellectuals. Their opinions will infilter the masses of the nation in time.
>
> The digger and ditcher, hewer and stitcher, are as human as the soldier, and only to boys, novel readers, and sham statesmen is the rifle a whit more heroic than the spade. The purpose is the grand thing, and when the spade shines for a noble end, it out-glitters the flashing of the sword, and the spade-man will obey you, conquering back this island as no swordsman ever feared and obeyed any Geraldine or O'Neill in the old fighting days ...

It seems strange that only a few months ago [May 1947] did the mayor of New York award Colum on behalf of the American Irish Historical Society a medal 'in tribute to his eminence in literature'. It seems a somewhat trivial and tardy recognition of a man who has devoted his entire life to something as rare as the heroic spirit in a dead world.

About the man himself is always the boy that stood at the workhouse window and watched and watched the wandering, restless Ireland of the generation of the famine:

> —men who followed decaying trades, and ballad-singers with tramp-

fiddlers and pipers. As I watched them taking a road of a morning, going I knew not into what mysterious region, the romance of the road was brought home to me, and I think it has never quite left my mind ...

I can only think of a quatrain of Seumas O'Sullivan's 'Mantra' which could word the impression I first received of Colum:

Towards the westward beacon light
He flies across the foam,
This is the path he knows by sight.
And the far land is his home.

In his play, *The Land*, Matt Cosgar is pulled into this wanderlust, symbolising almost a generation. In *The Fiddler's House*, who could ever forget Hourican's passion and the words that end up:

Well, here's Conn Hourican the fiddler going on his travels again. No man knows how his own life will end; but them who have the gift have to follow the gift. I'm leaving this house behind me; and maybe the time will come when I'll be climbing the hills and seeing this little house with the tears in my eyes. I'm leaving the land behind me, too; but what's land after all against the music that comes from the far, strange places ...

There is something of Conn Hourican in Padraic Colum; I was the one who could see that. In his play, *Thomas Muskerry*, it is the blind piper, Myles Gorman, who strikes perhaps the deepest note in all Irish literature, the skirl of the pipes as Gorman wanders off in freedom from the workhouse while the ill-fated Muskerry dies into a deeper freedom.

It is this power of Colum's to recreate the more ancient and more poignant Ireland and to inspire others to go on from where he left off that has made the man a more than significant figure.

In a letter of December 1946, Michael McLaverty wrote to me the following:

All those writers have what many of the moderns lack—poignancy: and I must confess that the art where that quality exists is the art which affords me permanent satisfaction ... I think of Hopkins' sonnets, Higgins' poem on Padraic Ó Conaire, Colum's *Garadh*, *Thomas Muskerry*, and his unsurpassable *Journey*; Synge's *Riders to the Sea*; Tolstoy's *Death of Ivan Illiych*. I could go on enumerating! It is only as one feels deeply—a feeling engendered by complete immersion and contemplation—that one can write with that precision that achieves intensity and durability: a writer devoid of feeling usually degenerates into a cloudy verbalism and no amount of literary artifice can conceal his debility.

> My cries heave, herds-long;
> huddle in a main, a chief
> woe, world-sorrow; on age-old
> anvil wince and sing
>
> O the mind, mind has mountains: cliffs of all
> Frightful, sheer, no-man fathomed ...
>
> I wake and feel the fell of dark, not day.
> What hours, O what black hours we have spent
> This night! What sights you, heart, saw; ways you went!
> And more must, in yet longer light's delay.

There you have writing that is as sharp and clear as the white ice on a ploughed field: writing that pierces to the bone—writing that has made the exact words surrender themselves. Or go back to Virgil: "Ah hard-hearted one, alone and far from me thou beholdest the snows and frosty banks of the Rhine: Ah, may the frosts not harm thee, may no rough ice cut thy tender feet!" The direct cry of the heart is in all these lines. And somehow when poetry lacks this spontaneous utterance—a failure to sing of 'summer in full-throated ease'—one feels that either the poet is sick or the world that makes him is sick. Perhaps we have too many theorists—too many people writing out of a study of technique and not from the compulsive quality of their themes, the sincerity that will conquer words and make them do its bidding. We are losing the poise and beauty and surety of men like Herbert:

> Sweet day! so cool, so calm, so bright,
> The bridal of the earth and sky:
> The dew shall weep thy fall tonight—
>   For thou must die.

Perhaps, the importance of both McLaverty and Colum lies in their humanity, but what is deeper is what lies embedded in their artistic consciences. That is perhaps why they are able to teach as well as to write.

Colum, like McLaverty, is from the midlands, and as one thinks of Ledwidge, Higgins, Michael Walsh, and Goldsmith, one could imagine the midlands to symbolise that country between extremes: where as it was written over the Greek temple there is nothing too much. As a realist Colum is not just always a prophet or a priest, nor, I think, does he wish, as his friends do, that he be. But of recent date he has gone up into, as you might say, the eyrie. Not for nothing is his latest play called *Balloon*. Here for instance is a headline in a Boston newspaper: PEOPLE FIND IT HARD TO UNDERSTAND PADRAIC COLUM'S BALLOON, BUT MANY CALL IT A MASTERPIECE.

It was in the October of 1945 when I was in New England that Colum mentioned the play with an air of 'Well, it will happen any day now'. He wrote me a letter, which is a thing momentous in itself; as a matter of fact, had I known in the beginning his hatred of writing letters, I wouldn't have torn up in a fit of rage the letters that he did write to me. He used to cut the lining out of me right to my face, and I used to pretend I wasn't that vain to take any notice of him but when he would pass a remark in a letter like: "I curse the day I set into the reading of—! What were you driving at? And your use of words. Oh!"

Or: "Your poems read like translations, very poor translations."

It used to give me the loveliest pleasure to take his letters and tear them into the smallest little pieces. In this letter which he did write I thought it of portent that he should have apologised in this matter:

> Dear Padraic Fiacc,
> It must be the influence of Saint Francis that makes me write a letter ...

The pertinence of these words is much more than the surface facts that he and his wife, Mary, used to stay at the Saint Francis Health Resort in New Jersey, or that I, his annoying pupil, was studying under the Franciscans in college. Indeed, when Colum had written me that letter he had completed arrangements for the future production of a very Franciscan play ... a play called *Balloon*. He had spoken to me about it in New York and from what he had told me of it at the time, I rather lifted an eyebrow. In the letter he said:

I haven't an idea when the play is going on; we haven't yet got a cast and it may not be until spring.

My suspicions were intensified for the play appeared to me to be highly out of taste, that is, his orthodox taste. He had told me of his ramblings in the cafés to find the girls he was looking for, how in the quest he found his way into Dinty Moore's where he tasted, probably for the first time, the American's proverbial idea of an Irish dish: corned beef and cabbage, and indeed, relished it.

Yet, when we met on occasion again in New York he mentioned the name (quite carelessly) of the occult clown who is, it appears, the figurehead of *Balloon*. He mentioned the name of Dun Scotus.

In the same year, 1943, when I was busy with the production of one of my own plays based on words from his 'The Sower', he himself had just completed a script of fifteen thousand pages. This he brought to Michael Meyerberg in New York, notorious for handling the out-of-the-way. Meyerberg took an option, though now I fear the worst; my friends in the U.S. tell me the play has dwindled down to normal size. It received production for the first time anywhere in the world in August, 1946, at Ogunquit in Maine. There is talk, too, of London, New York, and Paris performances.

It was ten years ago here in Dublin when his *Mogu of the Desert* was done by the Gate Theatre with Orson Welles, when, at that time, Colum began to obey the instinct to create a drama for an American audience. He discussed the idea with Norman Bel Geddes, designer and producer, at the time.

This latest of his plays is a criticism of modern disintegration, a cry for reverence of the individual spirit, catching the cry from Paris: 'Save, save the person in man.' Colum once said to me:

It is said that the nations are dying out and that the states are coming in.

More than a Gaelic hatred of states is behind the portentous warning of a poet with a medieval mind, who can see what few bridges we have left to traverse the gaps of not only the famine of a hundred years ago but also the famine not one hundred years ago that has withered the earth with guns.

As he read to me his new novel, which is more massive, I think, than anything Colum has ever attempted before, I was taken aback at the continual unfolding discovery that he was truly under the influence of Saint Francis, a saint who is called, even in profane places, 'the Greek model'. He said he wanted to do in it what Gogol did in *Dead Souls*.

The play, *Balloon*, is to be properly done in ballet with masks, but for its first performance this was excluded. Nevertheless, the music of the hurdy-gurdy and the balloon ascension, symbolic of creative power and wonder lowered with mechanisms, are there. The story of the play is baffling them over in the new world; and perhaps it would baffle us here—for this is a new Padraic Colum, a man who is making a great joke, and who is infinitely pleased that no one can see the point of it but himself; he is making foreshadowing mockery when other men like O'Neill are savagely silent. The Americans are finding it incredible that the Hotel Daedalus (the setting) is a symbol of their over-material, specialised city of technique, that it is full of all the confusion the countryman in Colum has created, that it is full of all the noise of forty-seven speaking actors and more who do not speak, who do not dare to speak; just as Paras Veka, the gypsy princess, is the eternal woman in it, the victim, perhaps, of a civilisation of hotels and cafés, who does not seem to be able to escape, like Kafka, the entanglement of civilisation; who, nevertheless, retains her mystery despite the all-knowing who have no reverence for her mystery who is Eve beckoning to the boy Casper (symbol of Adam in the play) as the animal in the heart of man luring him to spiritual reality. Casper seeks not only to know her but to know the great ones of the hotel also, and to become one of them. Glock, the clown (the wise fool), who philosophises, is Dun Scotus, is a Franciscan, a kind of sacred clown, living and loving nature as God created it. The boy, Casper, desirous of heroic being, finds out that he can only attain it by being true to himself, by being the person God made him, rather than the type man would make of him.

Certain New England critics are attributing Colum's assertion of personality to Emerson, but they are not looking as far back, into the middle ages, as they should. But then, they might not know what we know, that Colum has made the transition from poet to philosopher as did Claudel in France, and nobody can tell whether it is a good thing or not. He has certainly refrained for a long time from making this mockery that was always in his heart for those that build Babel.

Of his earlier plays *Thomas Muskerry* is perhaps the most poignant, though some say it is less satisfying than the two other long plays *The Land* and *The Fiddler's House*; but surely, in *Thomas Muskerry*, never was Colum nearer to his own peculiar genius and to the ideal of the perfect detachment of art. When one considers the type of petty kitchen play that is filling our theatres today, a revival, or at least a reprinting of Colum's earlier plays is found to be in order.

The man himself has perhaps wandered and strayed from the time he was a boy looking out of the workhouse window into the romance of the road, till now, when over half a century later, he can take a pin and stick it into the balloon of the world. But perhaps, Colum, like the Gogol that he so admires, can be seen only in a latter-day significant light, and will be known as the one who can afford to say in *The Kalevala*:

I have shown the way to singers,
Cut the branches, shown the pathways,
Here the path lies newly opened,
Widely open for the singers,
And for the greater ballad singers,
For the young who now are growing.

Irish Bookman, vol. 1 no. 12, August 1947

Mary Colum

HERE IS A BOOK* THAT IS UNDERCURRENTLY sad. That it is written by a woman of salt makes it direct and a little icy. That it is written by a woman at all makes it of portent.

> The great facts of the world of my mature years have been wars and destruction ... They have crushed everything else out of sight.

Three futile wars in the lifetime of Mary Colum. Perhaps only a woman, or a Dostoyevsky, or a poet could afford to vomit the platitudes that the boy in man dares to boast of outside of the garden of Eden ... pure races, common brotherhoods, one wide world and so on.

> Then the craze for conformity, for uniformity, the passion to make people all have the same religious or political principles, the same social habits, has always been a great cause of trouble.

Here is a book that is not merely the memories of a woman who has taken up the cross of becoming a critic of letters, but the story of a woman, who in receiving the vision of futility, can now turn a critical eye on life itself. Edna Millay in her 'My Spirit Sore From Marching' uttered woman's exasperation:

> Man with his ready answer,
> His sad and hearty word

For every cause in limbo,
For every debt deferred,

For every pledge forgotten,
His eloquent and grim,
Deep, empty gaze upon you:
Expect no more from him.

Here is a book where the sigh of a woman transcends any feeling for style, and the style, not being conscious, suits the wariness and the sadness. It is saved from pomp by this, but not always saved from feline wit. As a result, the male reader can have a chance to stick out his tongue and say: 'I told you so.'

The one thing that marred the book to me was the airing of a catty session between Mrs. Colum and a woman-poet. It's too much of a trend in modern autobiography to tell other people's sins instead of our own. Women, for any amount of fact-knowing, never seem to reach man's charity, and charity, after all, is what creates literature. For all my fondness for Mary Colum, I found myself taking the side of that person she sharpened her nails on.

Apart from this one contrariness on my part, *The Life and The Dream* touched an undercurrent chord that is universally felt these days. I thought, here is the life of a woman with a virile and fine mind. I remember when first meeting her, comparing her to Mme. Undset. They seemed to have that something inexplicable in common: aristocracy. One can only hint at it, but out there in the new world, it seemed something precious-old-world.

The seventeen chapters up to 'Departure' make all the rest of the book seem unimportant. But in a quicker and deeper look one can see threads of comparison that make meaning. The US is a *state*, and Ireland is a *nation*. Something seems hidden in opposition there, as if for all the petty localism of the individual, the individual has more humanity than the mass. It surely is telling the number of suicides that seem to burn holes in the pages of the section devoted to America. A society that is too en-masse is often that desert of loneliness that Tolstoy sought.

Mary Colum first woke to art in: "A sort of whirling ecstasy that was not all pleasure," inspired by a soulful old woman, her grandmother, a queenly type of the women of two generations ago, who carried to their graves a manner and generosity that is almost lost to us now ...

> If she gave away something she could not afford, she would cheerfully say, as if that explained everything, 'It is for others.'

The racy parts here at the beginning of the book, which deal with 'The Neighbours', 'Strolling Musicians', 'Ballad Singers', 'Travelling Men', 'The Land and the People', and 'The Life of the Countryside', have about them a sense of permanence that is lovely because it is real and good.

Writing about an attractive aunt with whom she lived, for instance:

> I was as happy as she was once, when a strange man called at the house about a horse. He did not know her, and taking her to be the daughter of the house instead of the wife of the man he had come to see he remained cheerfully to drink tea with her. She slipped her wedding ring, as I had often seen her do, into the drawer of the tea table and engaged in happy and whimsical conversation, talking rapidly.
> 'You are beautiful,' he said to her. 'I never met anybody like you!'
> I listened from a córner entranced, to every word he said, and thought it was wonderful to have men talk like that to you. On this occasion she really wanted me around, because she could have sent me out of the room if she had wished. Like all Irishwomen she did not want things to go beyond a certain point, past laughter and hand-kissing. She seemed a little alarmed I remember when the horsey strange at parting, lifted a lock of her hair at her neck and said, 'It is spun gold.'

Mrs. Colum's early adjustments to boarding-school life saved her from becoming too precious on the one hand and too tomboyish on the other. In the sections marked 'Boarding-School Days', and 'An Old World Training', one's own boarding-school days are liable to drift back through the pages. Catholic schools of this sort vary little over the world ... the same insistent accent on ordered behaviour, the ordinary problems of individual-versus-institution; also, which is interesting, our first try at human relationship (which because it is our first, may leave that 'immortal hurt'). Goethe's *Erster Verlust* comes to mind:

> Oh who brings back the beauteous days—
> Those days of earliest love ...

Mary Colum's friendship with the haunting young girl, Finda, a singer:

> She gave to many of us then in the morning of life, one of those thrills, which when received in impressionable adolescence, one never forgets ...

and the hurts that sometimes come:

> —as the slight scar on my foot, left by an accidental cut in playing hockey, still remains, so there are also scars on my mind, some that healed something beneath, some that were but the ever-aching remains of a wound.

The Abbé Dimnet wrote to her about this old-world schooling: "You and I have the same background."

That tradition with its over-accent on the spirit (in Ireland and France, etc), the worst criticism of which is that it ill-prepares its students for a practical life. But *le bon sens* in a world of little self-suffering, little conscience, based on howsoever involved a psychology which seems to transform guilt into fancy and sin into instinct, is that form of sanity which is based on a belief in absolutely nothing at all. The great contribution of an old-world training is that it instils into young people what is ceiling and what is floor, that is, outside of the walls that encompass the garden of paradise. When Joyce threw up this sort of moral sense of responsibility he killed his only chance for maturity. The myth of amorality is a peculiarly adolescent one.

In the reading of this book I found out the explanation of things about Mrs. Colum that I once thought odd, and had attributed to different sources. For instance, I thought her liking for beer was a substitute in the US for stout (stout isn't the same there; the taste goes out of it in crossing); but actually she developed a liking for beer in her German school. It set me in mind of my own boarding-school days in the US when we were served as students a hard, beerlike cider at our meals which the monks made out of a surplus apple-harvest. Always in such a book as this one enjoys being touched into associations and tripping over little familiars.

Mrs. Colum's humanity comes out in the part mentioning 'The Neighbours'—

> The people I was born among, and everybody I knew around for miles and miles ... the most civilised, the most kindly that I had ever known ...

This may be a bias, but it could be quite true. Manner is something from the past and the people in the remotes of Ireland who are close to the past could teach the rest of us civilisation ... these kindly people who were not

> ... scraping and grasping about money ... but who lived by a sort of barter and exchange ... What people in Ireland inherited was something inside of themselves.

The west of Ireland is so bare, so poor, so much of an understatement in the olden tones that whenever or wherever it is written about it is something that tugs and wrenches, that makes us suffer to remember the suggestion that the unpowerful alone can make of soul.

Mrs. Colum's portrait of the melancholy Bartley is as memorable as meeting any of the shiftless people of life, who, by their very detachment from self, work themselves into our hearts like a thorn. What a pain is left in our mind when finishing the entire book to have to feel that Bartley's life—this semi-barbaric peasant of a man who has returned from prison to an Ireland already withered—is no less futile than the life of a Childers, or a Pearse, or a Casement, that men are no more able to shield their fellow men from the fierce hunger of life (even by martyrdom)than they are able to force into reality the boyish myth of a pure race.

> When Bartley died, she did shortly afterwards, I felt as if a whole section of my life were gone. He had, in the end, sunk into a state of extreme sadness.

The whole theme of this book is sad. Well may it be.

Great figures pass through it, men like Yeats and that noble group who were executed, not to mention a whole school of American intellectuals who took their own lives. One thinks of a quatrain from Patrick Kavanagh's 'Beech Tree':

> It is August now, I have hoped
> But I hope no more—

My beech tree will never hide sparrows
From hungry hawks.

The modern mood is futility, a dangerous mood, bordering on the edge of despair: the Dead Land. We are Ana in Kate O'Brien's *That Lady*:

> She laughed at him and said that time often showed the great adventure of not getting things done.

I really think Mary Colum should have prefaced this piece by Solomon to the front of *The Life and The Dream*:

> I turned me to another thing, and I saw that under the sun the race is not to the swift, nor the battle to the strong, nor bread to the wise, nor riches to the learned, nor favour to the skilful: but time and chance to all.

But no matter if the dream fails. We may have fallen into a deeper reality, more mysterious and sweeter than the dream, in order, it may be, to help us readjust our sense of values, which, from a bit of too-much myth-making, has become out of focus.

Irish Bookman, vol. 2 no. 1, September 1947

* Mary Colum, *The Life and the Dream*

Austin Clarke

THE INHABITANTS OF THE WEST HAVE become jaded, weary. A whole class of people has slipped into the temple as buyers and sellers. Only from far off like the reiterating drums of the Basque Ravel's Bolero laughs the sly laughter of profound joy that is both austere and tragic. From Salamanca, Miguel de Unamuno intones with the quiet but barbaric grace of de Falla: "In me I feel the medieval soul."

It could be said that Russia, Ireland, and Spain are not in Europe. By some peculiarity of temper they are Byzantine and gates to the east. Contemplative. Fiery. Arrogant.

I say all this before I say that the poems of Austin Clarke are classic in mode. (And what young writer, writing in English, dare use the word 'classic' without thinking of T.S. Eliot and the Roman tradition, a thing a little highly overestimated, and too big to be true.) Apart from the Catholic religion, the imperial sense and all those dull gods which the boy, Alexander, tried to steal out of Greece and re-plant in Rome, went un-at-home enough to try to rest in peace in the snows of Siberia, the rains of Ireland, or the hot sun of Spain. I use 'classic' in the more inclusive sense, and I say that Mr. Clarke is a classicist because he uses a tradition outside of his moods: either to write of by itself, or make myth with, or costume his moods in. One could mention here the influence of the Spanish Arabs through Thomas Aquinas on Dante, just as much an influence as Aristotle! Dante also turned earth to the fresh side by the use of people-speech. Eliot seems to think the classic is anti-inner-voice:

> Why have principles, when one has the inner voice? If I like a thing that is all I want.

Or again:

> Listening to the inner voice which breathes the eternal message of vanity, fear, and lust.

However anti-romantic Eliot is, he might be a little one-sided. The cactus flower that blooms in the desert is no more, no less reality than the moon to an Italian herd-boy or a man's sons. There is enough room in the major poet for the three elements: romanticism, realism, classicism. Which brings me to the highly regional poet: Austin Clarke, who at the same time as having an inner voice, has 'principles'. On the other hand, I wouldn't wish in this essay to defend Clarke for his strict adherence to Irish classicism. Poets ought to write about what they feel, and this is just what they do.

There's Pushkin's *Eugene Onegin*, Eliot's *The Wasteland*, Egil Skallagrimsson's elegies on his sons, Kavanagh's *The Great Hunger*, or Po Chu-I on politics, not to mention Ovid's wisecracks, Baudelaire on the beauty of Satan, Villon's so-what's?, Rimbaud's fascism, or Saint Brigid on a whim, (an 'inner voice') of giving beer to God. And so on.

It's only that Clarke is interesting as a writer of joy. And Ireland seems to be 'The House in the West':

> Where low rains are heavier
> Than the sail in haze
> And the cold sea is spread
> On the soil to raise harvest ...
>
> In a bare land that halves every cloud,
> There is a great house.
> Men with the crowbar,
> Breaking a road
> From the spar of the dark land,
> Have seen those far windows,

While unyoking a cart-load,
Take fire and a star ...

But like the strong joy that it is, it is rooted somewhere in hell.
The difference between the medieval mind and the modern is the
difference between Dante and a modern poet. Dante stands in the
marketplace and goes home and writes about Beatrice, a girl that
passed through it. She was beautiful. The modern poet stands in
the marketplace and goes home and writes about the marketplace.
The modern poet is incomplete and literal-minded. Things to him
are specks of dust that get in his eye. If he has the tragic sense at
all he goes to the gates of hell and enters them like a Joyce, and
even touches the floor. But that's as far as he gets. Dante, on the
other hand goes to hell, through it, to purgatory, through it, and
then to joy, joy, joy, tears of joy.

The tragedy, if I may dare to guess, that induced Clarke to make
such a fertile transition from the highly sensual myth-tales to the
medieval dramas of 'conscience' and of 'inner conflict' must have
something to do with the words:

The thousand tales of Ireland sink: I leave
Unfinished what I had begun nor count
As gain the youthful frenzy of those years;
For I remember my own passing breath ...

And, if I may dare to believe, with the Civil War of 1921 which
must have hit his generation a hard blow:

Yet, knowing I would never see him,
I gave my hand to Liam Mellowes ...

There immediately flashes into my mind, upon those words, the
picture of a Capuchin lay brother bidding farewell to one of the
gentlest of men. I remember the friar going over the whole ethos
of the Irish war only to stop there, an abrupt pause of
bewilderment, and then, suddenly, to rise up and go out as if to
chop some wood. He finished his story by saying that he shook
hands with Liam Mellowes and they took him away. Concurrently,
an Irish Carmelite priest in New York, spoke of Mellowes, whom
he knew well as one of the men who left a gap never to be filled—
'mockery to any semblance of a gain' ...

Yet, to leave the less speculative ...

Clarke, like Ravel, is an evolutionist, rather than a revolutionist. He returns to the old forms like Stravinsky to the styles of Handel. He is more well known for this interesting use of assonance. At the same time one could not separate his innovations in music from the thought-content. He is too organic, integral.

'The Vengeance of Fionn', written when he was very young, has all the spice and plenitude, surety, lineament and loveliness of the early Yeats' 'Patrick and Oisin'. In fact, I'm inclined to think its birth might have made W.B. shiver a little.

> What have the old to do
> With dreams the heated sinews of youth ...

How vaingloriously joyful, a lad-song in places! One could feel that he loved the boast of his voice:

> I am of that old breed
> That's gone, begotten from the fire that's hid
> In the loins of the cold rocks. Like a boy
> Stubbornly courag'd this grew—this that's my own—
> This Fianna sprung fiercely from my joy
> Of generation ...

One feels, too, that the half-boy who wrote this epic song is Diarmuid and that he has a brazen animal confidence, that he has youth enough to steal the Grainne of poetry away from the older man. In a way he did. Yeats grew sour, sour as Fionn, aye, in his last book, sour as Oisin.

> I sit
> Mumbling at a turf fire half blind with rheum ...

And how well the young Clarke seems to know:

> Thou! Sweetly human, dream-strange yet to be hurt
> By a chance nettle, hast known inalienable tears
> And stumbled with a noon's hunger. Yet, Love, to be
> Piteously human is sweetest!

'The Fires of Baal' was also written in the blood of youth. Here is a poem that is Byzantine in the flair, almost lust, for detail. Here one can see the Gael-mind's closeness to the east. It is as rich and flavoured as a Siamese ballet done in gold masks over the ruined temples of Bangkok. Such lines as:

As lions whelped amid the burning sands ...
... With sun-struck limbs
Dripping, the luscious bough of pomegranate ...

The spectacle of:

... luxurious Sodom and Gomorrah,
With smell of cooking, noise of gun and dish,
Until God's patient anger broke angelic,
In burning brimstone, thunder and in night.

The whole sensual dance of modern and ancient man-city:

In pride and hate until all vengeance came—
Swept down headlong as heaven and the ages,
Unpeopled, dropped in flame and flaming, lit
The abyss ...
                         So the Promised Land
Was hidden and each city knew a cry ...

Against those early works highly coloured, Clarke's later works take on an aspect of apparent paling, but in a closer look one can perceive a tighter contract of passion giving it that characteristic austere intensity, that shining ripeness. His dramatic poems, for instance, 'The Son of Learning' and 'The Flame', are a peculiar blend of contraries, a thing that Blake felt, but as Eliot points out, didn't have the tradition beyond himself to express adequately what he felt. Clarke, however, listening to both his tradition and his inner voice, finally evolved and developed his own mode. As Padraic Colum writes in a preface to his *Collected Poems*:

I believe that the mid-Ireland, the Ireland between legend and modern history, is for Austin Clarke the country native to his mind which every poet turns to, the country that gives a landscape to his people and a background to his situations.

In this meditative, contrast-loving turn of mind, Clarke shows himself, in his recent work in the *Dublin Magazine* and elsewhere, to be not only the leading writer of Irish passion since the death of

Yeats and Higgins, but also a lighthouse to the young writer in quest of his own place in that tradition. As he was fathered by Æ, in a way, we who are young are fathered by him.

Irish Bookman, vol. 2 no. 3, December 1947

Contemporary Irish Poetry

BLANAID SALKELD'S POEM, 'EVASION', KEYNOTES many another in this collection*: a changing Ireland like a changing Spain: a split personality in the act of splitting—anything rather than to wrestle or struggle with the personality.

> The old woman has forgotten her face:
> a chance mirror met, to avoid disgrace
> she blinks her glance with lightning wit;
> no recognition reflects in it ...
>
> casting off and losing that thing was I.
> she turns objective, for shame—in case
> she might have to acknowledge her latest face.

The general run of verse is poor—and it is verse! If the old woman is turning objective it is not for shame but probably because she no longer has a subject to be subjective about; no use in blaming anyone but ourselves. Even 'ourselves alone' is vague compared to the 'I'.

In this collection dramatising the 'main trends' of present-day Irish poetry you can see for yourself what way the wind blows—if you even want to take it seriously. The Northern group is there just to show no hard feelings but many a name could be left out and there would be even less hard feelings. A lot of it has no agony or remorse but a great deal of naming Ireland and the Irish by their names and that's all if you don't mention the Hopkinsesque icing; but to attack any one writer bit by bit would be like attacking a child not come to age.

Kavanagh's criticism of the late Higgins could cover this whole study. About three poets in this survey would escape by the skin of their teeth. Why name names except to remark that the verse I myself have had published is on the same immature par as much of this—if not worse.

We will simply have to accept what only appears to be the curse of the taboo—those limits which will force us to dig into reality rather than either to sing with a talky-throated Al Jolson or make our quill so collective it dissolves. Talent can be a little beast and devour its own substance. It is a sin for us to make the reader feel the intermediation of contraceptives between the poet and life.

In the words of Donagh MacDonagh:

Years of counter and office, the warped mesh
Of social living, dropping on stones,
Wear down all that was rough and worthy
To a common denominator of dull tones.

Farren on the one side and W.R. Rodgers on the other show the Christmas-tree effect of a too brilliant rhetoric—which is, after all, only verse in its very thought. Notice also how significant C. Day Lewis becomes when he abandons the sing-songy, or compare Donagh MacDonagh's poem on Dublin with that affair of MacNeice's on Dublin. Roy McFadden and Clarke seem to be almost alone as writers who are in any pain. All the rest are charm and cheer, geography, opinion, and a great desire, like myself, to listen to their own voices.

Poetry Ireland, No. 7, October 1949

* Greacen & Iremonger (eds), *Contemporary Irish Poetry* (Faber, 1949)

Kings and Fools

HENRY VI WAS ONE OF THOSE souls who by always being off somewhere in a dream world and letting others make their decisions somehow manage to leave a trail of anarchy wherever they go. A "devout kindly simpleton" he "looked more like a child than a man" and was capable, when he could come-to at all, of sudden 'unguarded' remarks in the thick of a diplomatic session when a word out of turn could spark off a war.

Dr. Storey's fascinating *The End of the House of Lancaster* proves by a cumulative presentation of as-yet-unpublished historic records that, rather than "hereditary claims to the throne", the true cause of the War of the Roses in a society made up of a "parasitic bastard form of feudalism" was this very psychological disadvantage of Henry as a reluctant (if not quite absent) father figurehead.

In spite of the demoniacal forces at work in the "aberrant, pathological end of the trance scale" (and some of them sickening enough) in order to appease this or that phallic or hermaphrodite idol we, victims ourselves to the abject Rat Race and other less colourful idols of a blue-nosed Mannon, can still find something worth our scrutiny in each section of *Trances* (this probing study of semi-mystical states of mind in primitive peoples). But in the section devoted to Spirit Laughter what could be more heartening than when the much belaboured tape-machine defeats its own pretentious competence by playing back enormous magnificent belches?

In *The Faulkner-Cowley File* we are in debt to the fool poet in Malcolm Cowley no less than to the "distinguished critic" that he was able to recognise a kindred soul in a much begrudged foolhardy genius and at a time too when US 'academic critics' together with a "deafening frogpond croak" of book reviewers had prematurely written Faulkner off as 'finished', seventeen books and all! The publication of this file will also encourage other writers who may drop out of favour or come upon bad days of adverse criticism for these letters and memories are an historic proof that critics, like doctors, can sometimes be more than mistaken.

Robert Shaw's Goldman enigma which outshines even his last three novels is the story of a sudden switch in personality to what Yeats called the 'anti-self' where the empty pit in man's being yawns wide open to let the Holy Fool, *The Man in the Glass Booth*, make his (howsoever hopeless) breakthrough to all us "friends brothers hypocrite-mirrors"!

"I was a fool to come back," Michael Marler tells his real or anti-self (or both) in Patrick Hall's *The Harp That Once*. The split widens for sons of Irish immigrants expected to be dialectically bilingual and capable of space-walking from one planet to another from a shaky cliff-edged affluence to the vendetta of the native ghetto. Here is a bright disenchanted witty successful first novel by that best of all combinations—an English Irishman!

Richard Powell farcically tilts at the genius for stupidity of the 'I want to save others' type of fool in his *Don Quixote, USA* and by some contrary quirk of fate, probably to confound the proud, the Goodpastures not only exist but usually 'survive and prevail'! Alas, writer and publisher could do well to ponder that with humour, like beauty, the rule always is 'less is more'.

In *The Centre-Piece*, Harriet Visser Long, expatriate American in Paris, rich idle fool in a vin rose-coloured trance, emerges as a whipping boy to a crew so motley that we must give Peter de Polnay credit for writing about them all.

Leslie Butler renders the irony dense enough in *The Man Who Crawled Away*, a thriller that has to be absorbed by a slow process of osmosis. Half slave of a Master Beggar, the seeming fool this time, with a gift for making simple souls have "uncomfortable feelings", is the Stricken One, and his brain is indeed, tellingly (*mot juste*) "bemused".

Hibernia, February 1967

R.L. Storey, *The End of the House of Lancaster*
(Barrie & Rockliff, 1966)
Stewart Wavell, Audrey Butt and Nina Epton, *Trances*
(George Allen & Unwin, 1966)
Malcolm Cowley, *The Faulkner-Cowley File. Letters and Memories,
1944-1962* (Chatto & Windus, 1966)
Robert Shaw, *The Man in the Glass Booth* (Chatto & Windus, 1967)
Patrick Hall, *The Harp That Once* (Heinemann, 1967)
Richard Powell, *Don Quixote, USA* (Hodder & Stoughton, 1966)
Peter de Polnay, *The Centre-Piece* (W.H. Allen, 1966)
Leslie Butler, *The Man Who Crawled Away* (Robert Hale, 1966)

Fiction: Phantasy Life

FRANK HERCULES' CINNAMON-DARK, HANDSOME, AWFULLY male Doctor John Lincoln proceeds to wed beautiful intelligent Barbara Wakeley, a born member of WASP. He then gets her with (she hopes) a Negro child. ('Intelligent' Barbara always wanted a black doll!) Enter dilettante German boyfriend on the side who in one climactic chapter is mutilated to death in front of pregnant Barbara by nasty black types. The chapter before this is devoted to a real live cannibal rite, indeed the cannibal theme is kicked and played with throughout. Much play, too, on food, drink and spice-coloured skin: people are anything from 'champagne' to 'clove' to 'butter-coloured' and whites are 'pink'.

The blurb says *I Want a Black Doll* is not a pretty book. But what else could you call this Peyton Place sugar-coating over, with much make-believe sex and violence, the bitter pill of the American Negro's lot?

If anachronism follows anachronism; too merry usage of late 60s Anglo-Saxon and words like 'affluent', Rosalyn Drexler's Sagan of the 30s, Selma Silver, is still a "gifted singer, writer and pianist" and in spite of her sink condition is precociously irresistible even to her doctor, and don't think Sister and Pappa are immune! On page 158 Selma herself says: "Strange things happen, if they don't happen they're not strange, but whether they happen or not, boy it's something to be ashamed about. I don't know what came over me, but I felt very sexy ... " etc. etc. On previous page long-suffering

Mother banged Selma's skull with a frying pan. This might account for pages 156 to 185 but what about pages 1 to 155? Rosalyn Drexler could be strongly advised to pretend that *I Am the Beautiful Stranger* is a conscious spoof.

Thanks to the long slow dying yet death of Victorian child labour the pains of hell of adolescent phantasy are something new on this side of the Atlantic. Whereas the uninhibited Selma tells all and more that she would want to happen, David Boll's circuitous sensitive Richard gropes on a quieter level through *The Thicket* of a Tyneside suburb out into the Northumberland countryside, where after all his growing-up troubles he takes a symbolical cleansing bathe in Narcissus-like waters: a lyrical finely-wrought most promising first novel!

Andrew Graham is a superb satirist because he has a generous affection, even compassion, for his subject. The *Observer* reviewer of his last book, *The Club*, uses the very word, "embalm". Graham is a kind-hearted if sighing but excellent embalmer. His 'white knights' are summed up by the especial model of "one of nature's church wardens" ... "He's a Boy Scout, if you like. But whichever way you look at it, he's a hell of a good chap. He's not an analytical bastard like you or a crabbed old cynic like me. He's a simple-hearted man with all sorts of illusions ... " In short our make-believe heroes never grow up, even after those of us who made and worshipped them do. In Graham's *The Regiment* as in the Cat and Mouse of Gunter Grass the blame seems to fall more rightly on the worshippers.

After the death of Ian Fleming, Andrew York is your man if you like the edge his hero has of one foot in the grave over his blond-haired black-hearted dolls. President Kennedy, had he lived, would probably have swallowed *The Co-Ordinator* whole—just as after being racked with much complex decision-making he used to dive into his James Bond. But as Selma Silver says, "Strange things happen ... " The monsters in our make-believe world sometimes can shoot into real life via the duller medium of an unhappy Oswald reality ...

Hibernia, May 1967

Frank Hercules, *I Want a Black Doll* (Collins, 1967)
Rosalyn Drexler, *I Am the Beautiful Stranger*
(Weidenfeld & Nicolson, 1967)
David Boll, *The Thicket* (Hodder & Stoughton, 1967)
Andrew Graham, *The Regiment* (Macmillan, 1967)
Andrew York, *The Co-Ordinator* (Hutchinson, 1967)

Ye Olde Bygone Fort

MAURICE LEITCH'S *THE LIBERTY LAD* AND now Jack Wilson's third novel have finally broken the monopoly of the older Ulster novelists who wrote as if Protestants didn't exist, or if they did, it was solely in order to breathe fire down Fenian necks. Nor do Leitch and Wilson exploit any of the violent green and orange hues of a work such as Harbinson's *No Surrender.*

The schizophrenia that is from has nothing to do with politics or religion even. The new generation is burning with its own potency discovered in depths vulnerable to the real. The fits of frustration and impotency, insecurity and inferiority serve only to spur them on, searching and questioning (rudely perhaps, but the very crudity is preferable to those polished off dead conventional novels of the past which accepted every social evil just so long as it was nice and snug *status quo* stuff.)

Written in a large-handed Faulkner, *The Tomorrow Country* centres round an Old Testament Planter Stock family, the Camerons, who loom larger than life as they flounder against the encroaching fake scenery of New Town and suburb. Useless, obsolete as dinosaurs, they are doomed to the jaws of the bulldozer. In a period of learning how to co-exist or camp out in a sunny, open, affluent, if tricky, leisure, their holding on to and defending Ye Olde Bygone Fort is almost touching. Certainly it is quaint. And if the American 'Way of Life' can be detected even in Jack Wilson's very writing who would be more entitled to such a boomeranging influence than the Puritan half Anglo-Saxon Scots Irish who founded the concept of the New World anyway?

Still, poetic justice or no, the Camerons have held the five hundred acres of Sunridge from and against the native "bog Irish" for three centuries now and old Cameron, Hell to his "soule" first, is not going to budge an inch, never mind "industrial development of the area" and it doesn't phase him no matter how many pennies the government are willing to compensate. Sunridge is still the fort and aren't the Camerons like a kind of God-chosen royalty?

Youngest son, Kenneth, gleefully awaits the day though, when father's cancer-eaten body is finally lowered into the ground and money bags or not, Kenneth can free himself from the Big House, the idol to which the human sacrifice of his education was made, the rotten fields and farmyard which brutalised his youth. Kenneth's personal nightmare is that the beasts, and not the humans, are the true Ascendency of Sunridge; after all, they are the only creatures who seem to benefit from the drudgery, and his sly relatives, themselves not unlike the beasts, not unlike the cows which frightened him as a child, never look at Kenneth, never seem even to see him while he is working his guts out after them. Kenneth more than suspects half-sister, Katherine, of dalliance with eldest brother Ray. He feels Katherine has already written to runaway Ray to tell him that with old Cameron dying and the government ready to pay compensation for Sunridge, wouldn't it be well for him to come home and claim Katherine and his birthright no matter if it's ten years since he left home.

Katherine, addicted to the gin bottle, more than often provokes teenaged Kenneth to call her a "bastard" so that she can retaliate by calling him a "virgin". Katherine, in their occasional encounter in hallway or whatever teasingly forces herself on the somewhat priggish adolescent. And so with the return of eldest brother, Ray, and as if almost to aggravate the sons (one of whom, Sebastian, is not even as sly as a beast), old fellow Cameron welcomes the prodigal with wide open arms.

Hibernia, October 1967

Jack Wilson, *The Tomorrow Country* (Frederick Muller, 1967)

New Ulster Poets

DEATH OF A NATURALIST HAS JUST won the Cholmondeley Prize. It is in its third printing and there is an American edition *via* Oxford, Seamus Heaney said, also modestly denying that he was any witless inspiration to the other young Ulster poets. But whether he is aware of it or not, as a lecturer at Queen's, an editor of the 'Festival' poetry pamphlets and head of the Philip Hobsbaum-founded poetry-workshop, The Group, his influence has been both potent and happy.

Seamus is one of the new Ulster poets born in the last war who like his Glengormley contemporary, Conleth Ellis, in his 'This Ripening Time', "... have known no sirens or blitz .../no train to the country with cardboard box/no mangling of family, razing home, shattering identity/(Only the air raid shelter to play in in the factory field—and the tea-chest empty in the coalhouse)".

And yet theirs is not Traherene's 'A World Without Objects is a Sensible Emptiness', the theme against which Richard Wilbur wrote, "Lamp-shine blurred in the stream of beasts, the spirit's right-Oasis.../"—for Seamus and his fellows even 'The Barn' is a wonder world of things to exult in: "Bright objects" are always forming in the dark: "A scythe's edge, a clean spade, a pitch-fork's prong" ...

Gregory Prize Winner, Michael Longley, told me, "No, I'm not coming out in book form. No, I haven't entered for the AE (I'll wait until I have a book). No, I haven't tried Dolmen: I wouldn't publish in Dublin if you paid me." Once a Dublin poet visiting Belfast put it to Longley that surely he didn't consider himself an Irish poet when he didn't write in the Irish tradition, to which Michael replied: "Then perhaps I'll help to expand your idea of what an Irish poet is." This is the uncompromisingly urbane mood of Longley. He feels that he is lucky to have been born at all. Writing of his father, "Between the corpses and the coup canteens/You swooned away, watching your future spill/.../To shrapnel shards that sliced your testicle/ That instant I, your most unlikely son/In No-Man's Land was surely left for dead".

Together with his friend, Derek Mahon, Longley voices the mood of the times, rather than the place. In his 'The Centaurs' he writes, "Into the water our youth is spilled./We make on the causeway our last stands./ Because of the bridge we did not build/ Our whole army fights for balance."

Emerging from hospitalisation after an accident, sanity itself is the prize Stewart Parker fought for and won. He is now "loving the broken lives" and, "Health is my ambition". While fellow Ulster poet and ballad-singer, James Simmons' African experiences have convinced him that we are all brothers in the "same bed", each poet of this generation seems to understand the other. In Studio 3 of the Belfast BBC I watched with awe as Parker skilfully interviewed Simmons about his new Bodley Head collection: "Folk singers were for academics only, and always in the past, the Irish peasant, the Negro slave," Jimmy complained, hitting out at the "terrible failure of the rarified world of poetry itself! I wanted to reach the lads who drank in my father's hotel, the fellahs my sisters courted. I wanted to reach them by a resurgence of popular culture, a middle-class ballad form for the despised middle class."

Derek Mahon in our Glengormley suburb of Belfast is more sensible to the defects of middle-class coldness: "... the very sticks/and stones that once broke bones will not now harm/A generation of such sense and charm" and still realises a built-in immunity which makes himself uncomfortable with guilt: "One part of my mind must learn to know his place./The things that happen in the kitchen houses./And echoing back-streets of this desperate city/Should engage more than my transient interest/ Exact more interest than my casual pity."

Affable, bearded Derek, also a Gregory Prizewinner who received an American Borestone Mountain Prize in 1963, has just returned from the States and, good omen that it is, intends to stay in Belfast. The Oxford University Press are bringing out his first collection in book form shortly.

All these poets had been brought into immediate print by their contemporary, Michael Emmerson, founder of the 'Festival' pamphlets. His enterprise and imagination, already an institution in Belfast, have set the target of professionalism on a high level of style. Some of this miracle-maker's magic has also rubbed off on poet-aspiring Michael Mitchell, founder and editor of the *Northern Review*, and certainly for another poetry-lover in his twenties, Harry Chambers, the magic has been really effective. Harry told me that although he was in between jobs, he alone was the "typist-errandboy-business manager-buyer of cow-gum-salesman" (and editor in his spare time) of the first two well-filled issues of *Phoenix*.

Seamus Heaney writes in his 'The Diviner': " ... nervous, but professionally/Unfussed ... "

Long may he and his generation retain the 'nervous' part for they are even perilously professional. Good luck to their elbows!

Hibernia, November 1967

Isolation in Contemporary Ireland
The AE Winners

AS A LIVING MEMORIAL TO AE (this is his centenary) a £100 prize is given every five years for the best literary, creative or scholarly work by an Irish writer under 35. The Advisory Committee acting for the Bank of Ireland trustees consists of an occupant of the Chair of English Literature in Trinity, the same Chair in UCD, a person nominated by the President of the Royal Dublin Society, one by the President of the Royal Irish Academy and one by the President of the Irish Academy of Letters.

In 1939, out of 24 entries, Patrick Kavanagh was given the first AE. His collected poems came out two years ago, his collection of prose this year. He has denounced his early work including *The Great Hunger*, confessed that he's not sure that he's a poet at all but that he is sure that he's a failure, that Ireland is not a place to write poetry in, that the Irish couldn't be a poet's fellow countryman even if they wanted to and that his ambition in life was not to hate but to be gay and happy.

In 1945, out of 23 entries, Valentin Iremonger (present day ambassador to Sweden) was given the AE, "in recognition of his unpublished poems entitled *Reservations* as having the greatest merit and promise among the entries received". The collection was eventually published in 1950. It might have been written by a non-Irish poet and there was an almost unveiled sexual tone: " ... the unsatisfied dog howling upon the lawn,/Breaking the night's maidenhead." In a post-war world dawning with radio-activity

Iremonger voiced his weariness of irrelevant Irish politics and practically told one of the old-time greats of the Irish Renaissance that it was time that he shut up.

In 1950, out of 22 entries, Richard Murphy was given the AE. Writing of his own christening in the February issue of this year's *Hibernia*, he hit out: "Harmonium pedals squeak and fart./I'm three weeks old./It's a garrison world:/The good are born into the Irish gentry./... Two clergy christen me: I'm saved from Rome./The deaf one has not heard my name./He thinks I'm a girl./The other bellows: 'It's a boy, you fool!'"

Murphy's alienation was stretched to the extent that he was left out of the last *Oxford Book of Irish Verse*.

In 1955, out of 24 entries, the prize was withheld.

In 1957, out of 23 entries, I was given the AE "in recognition of his published and unpublished works submitted and in particular for his collection of poems *Woe to the Boy*". There was much heartburning in Dublin over the decision. Not only was I a Belfast poet, but I had spent over half of my existence in the United States, etc., etc.

In 1962, out of 16 entries, John McGahern was given the AE "based on the committee's estimate of some chapters from an unpublished novel submitted in manuscript form." This novel, *The Barracks*, published in 1963, was followed two years later with *The Dark*. Whereas Kavanagh touched on masturbation and I used it as the theme of *Woe to the Boy*, McGahern brought the aberration out into the open as symptomatic of a deeper wrong. The telling hypocritical antics which followed are widely enough known to speak for themselves.

In a recent interview Sean O Faolain gave to John Boyd of the Northern Ireland BBC, O Faolain said: "The contemporary writer asks why is he alienated? What is wrong with a society which alienates its writers?"

There are 18 entries this year for the AE. The Advisory Committee consists of Professor J.K. Walton, Professor Roger McHugh, Professor J.J. O'Meara, Mr. Patrick Lynch, and Mr. Arlard Ussher.

Good luck to the new winner. He or she is going to need it!

Hibernia, December 1967

New Novels

JAMES BURN WITNESSES THE FIVE-MINUTE-long slaughtering of a pig, and the spectacle of gypsies forcing a donkey on a mare in order to beget a mule. Then there was this snake slowly devouring a living mouse hindquarters first. The little fellow goes on washing its face. The only sign of panic is the panting heart. One more gulp and the mouse jumps in vain for life inside the snake's throat. James has more than opted out of the rat race, he's been squashed, and not all the rich Nancys of Mickey Phillips' black comedy can put him together again.

Billy Casper, on the other hand, finds solace and thrills in the mystery of how his hawk devours the sparrow head first. In a strictly conformist boys' world the fight for integral survival somehow involves the hawk; rather the hawk teaches the boy that his aggressive passion to physically know is a good part of his nature which he must follow to a fine science. How Barry Hines' North Country classic.

But men or boys do not live by cruelty alone. Donald Horne's *The Education of Young Donald* is as tough and generous as the average Australian but it is devoid of malice and wrath. Virtue is a fault in literature and our worst men write the best books. Donald Horne sometimes purrs with satisfaction in his scarcely fictionalised journal of a time when Sydney University bubbled over with such names as James McAuley, A.D. Hope and John Anderson.

Not a purr of satisfaction can be found in the whole of Chrys Paul Fletcher's *Cry for a Shadow*, the first novel of a teenaged poetry-writing beatnik. The search for a dream world helped along by Asiatic concepts of nihilism and drugs and much prattle anyway about sex is as futile and despair-filling as it is true.

The other side of the coin is New York student, Jeff Baker's "Unfulfilled by what I felt to be a life of passive learning and immaterial ideals, I wanted to make my ideals real through action, to learn from rich experience to do something constructive." And so this teenager for one teamed up for a year with Dr. Carl van Aswegen, the one-man medical service, flying doctor.

John Ball, himself a pilot, works his *Rescue Mission* round the decision to constructively act. The hurricane threatens as men fight against all odds somehow to prevail like the hero in legend.

But, generally speaking, we suspect our heroes, or is it because the blackguard is more faithfully portrayed in literature? In *You're So Lucky Darling*, good drab simple soul Fiona, ultimately disillusioned by naughty Jean, doesn't win our sympathy.

Betty King's *The Lord Jasper*, her third historical novel, has the black face of history on it, but her method (and this is not a bad thing) has the blessing of making the book general family reading.

Piteously unpious E.S. Turner's *Hemlock Lane* uses the powers that be of communication (from newspaper to TV) as shooting ducks when the police, raiding a lovers' lane, send the 'incautious' into panic, arousing in others the greed to exploit creatures fool enough to be caught.

Hibernia, February 1968

Mickey Phillips, *Pick Up Sticks* (Michael Joseph, 1968)
Barry Hines, *A Kestrel for a Knave* (Michael Joseph, 1968)
Donald Horne, *The Education of Young Donald* (Angus & Robertson, 1967)
Chrys Paul Fletcher, *Cry for a Shadow* (Arthur Barker Ltd, 1967)
Jeff Baker, *African Flying Doctor* (W.H. Allen, 1968)
John Ball, *Rescue Mission* (Michael Joseph, 1968)
Jane Chichester, *You're So Lucky Darling* (Michael Joseph. 1968)
Betty King, *The Lord Jasper* (Herbert Jenkins, 1967)
E.S. Turner, *Hemlock Lane* (Michael Joseph, 1967)

More Than Wilfred

MOST POETS STAY HOOKED ON WRITING poetry until they hit on some overwhelming subject matter or myth which drives them beyond the confines of their own characteristic day-to-day existences. For Wilfred Owen, a Keatsian youth scarcely out of his teens, tugging away like the Volga boatman at the iambic pentameter, haunted some by his primitive Welsh ancestry, and tempted by, yet seldom giving in to, the half-dissonant, assonance and vowel rhymes, but never the syllabic stresses of ancient Celtic prosody, the First World War became the demon which so possessed and obsessed his (plump for the kill) vulnerable nature, that it was almost a kind of child-rape.

And two or three years later, his subsequent being mowed down by machine-gun fire at the Sambre Canal only served to dramatise a brief, tragic, but enduring, literary metamorphosis. He had been scarcely writing verse at all when he was snuffed out at 25. Like Rimbaud's early homosexual brush with soldiers in the barracks, Owen's first experiences were shocking and violent and account for much of his hatred for war. Hardly a matinée-idol type like Rupert Brooke, he straightforwardly sided with Siegfried Sassoon's aggressive pacifism, though in actual practice his soldiering was of the highest order, heroic even: he was awarded the Military Cross ...

Preparing a first volume before his death, he wrote of his poems: "These elegies are to this generation in no sense consolatory," adding "They may be to the next." To our generation who were yet to experience another and worse orgy of inhumanity, the horrors of Owen's day fade somewhat in the light which burned from the concentration camp ovens and in the radioactive light which claimed so many more victims than our young poet could have dreamt of. But his words remain as pertinent to us as when he wrote them fifty years ago: "All a poet can do today is warn. That is why true poets must be truthful."

Harold Owen, the poet's devoted brother, author in his own right of the autobiographical trilogy, *Journey From Obscurity*, has collaborated with John Bell of the Oxford University Press in editing these letters*, most of which were written by Wilfred to an intelligent, receptive mother. From the poignantly misspelled first attempts of the five-year-old on up to a few days before the end, each letter is interesting and aware, and testifies to that Wilfred Owen whom John Wain described as "One of those men who live most intensely when they give themselves unreservedly to some exterior object."

But in one of his last letters to his mother Owen signed it: "Wilfred and more than Wilfred." This collection of his letters, standing by itself, seems to ignore that there was a "more than Wilfred", at least this howsoever sincerely or lovingly put together mass of detail somehow eludes the point that Owen's war experiences, howsoever deeply assimilated by Owen himself, were bound to have sometimes eluded him: his senses simply numbed. Like all persons in extreme experience, he developed, if only for a short time, a merciful insensibility: "I shall feel again as soon as I dare but now I must not. I don't take the cigarette out of my mouth when I write 'deceased' over their letters", or the paragraph before that: "Catalogue? Photograph? Can you photograph the crimson-hot iron as it cools from the smelting? That is what Jones' blood looked like, and felt like. My senses are charred."

Hibernia, February 1968

* *Wilfred Owen: Collected Letters*, edited by Harold Owen
and John Bell (Oxford University Press, 1967)

Seamus Heaney

THE ERIC GREGORY TRUST AWARD, 1966, the Cholmondeley Award for Poets, 1967, and now the Somerset Maugham Award, 1968 (not to mention that *Death of a Naturalist* is selling away in the bookshops, soaring beyond its 2,000th copy!) "Are you superstitious about your successes, Seamus?"

"Yes. I feel I'll have to pay for them."

"Much in keeping with our Irish-Manichaean form of Catholicism," I grunted. (I was thinking of Edward Lucie-Smith's article in *The Times*: "The Japanese seem the first to explore the notion that the aesthetic sensation can be enjoyed and analysed for its own sake, and not in connection with some other idea— religion, for instance.").

Seamus is not unlike an Oriental: slit eyes in an impassive, mask-like face or, to quote his 'Ancestral Photograph' of a grand-uncle: "[his] look has two parts scorn, two parts dead pan". Our six-year-old, Brigid, watching Seamus emerge from his red Volkswagen, compared him to Barbara Euphan Todd's Worzel Gummidge, the turnip-headed scarecrow with the nest of robins in his pocket; not that Heaney looks like a turnip, but he certainly has a nest of robins in his pocket.

Whereas a poet like John Clare, as Eavan Boland points out in a review of Clare's work, did not have the strength of mind to adhere exclusively to his own images, Seamus goes to the other extreme, so little does he indulge in abstractions or metaphysics at

67

all. His critics use words like 'glib', 'slick', 'clever', 'neat', 'pat', 'final'. Hmmm ... yes, maybe once in a while; but to understand Seamus (and it isn't made easy if you know him as a person) you've got to accept him first and foremost as a child: a strange loneliness for one so externally gregarious (the face always put on his vulnerability). He rightly begrudges time spent too long away from his poems: "No, I wouldn't like to teach in a US university; you'd always be studying the other poet's work; everything would finally channel into the other person's poetry, even your own perceptions."

Benedict Kiely first spotted Michael McLaverty's influence on John McGahern's *The Barracks* and John Hewitt caught McLaverty's "prismatic vision" in Heaney. "What about that, Seamus?"

"Well, yes, but more of a cross-pollination than a siring."

"Are you worried about your second book?"

"No. I'm just letting it happen. It's only that people will be expecting another *Death of a Naturalist* and the innocence of all that is gone."

The new book is called *Door Into The Dark*. In his poem 'The Forge', published two years ago in the *TLS*, he wrote: "All I know is a door into the dark./Outside, old axles and iron hoops rusting. Inside, the hammered anvil's short-pitched ring..." or 'In Gallarus Oratory', published in the *Irish Times*: "... This place—it's like going into a turfstack./A core of stale dark walled up with stone/A yard thick. When you're in it alone/ you might have dropped, a reduced creature/To the heart of the globe ... ?" Or in 'Boy Driving His Father to Confession' he is surprised to find his father: "lost like me". In 'The Outlaw', also published in *Phoenix*, he seems to answer his critics who grind their teeth at his hitting bull's eye: "Just the unfussy ease of a good tradesman".

Picasso, thinking of genius, sighed, "One is always alone." And there is a Birth-Mystery from ancient Ireland: "A child who died and did not die." Is it not the very definition of a poet? It is certainly a key or clue to the phenomenon of Seamus Heaney.

Hibernia, May 1968

New Magazines

TWO NEW LITTLE MAGAZINES HAVE APPEARED in Belfast bookshops within a week of each other, each of them outspoken and saying things 'needed to be said', or at least saying 'what we think'. The setting is as contemporary as worldwide student unrest, the rise of an active humanism within Catholic and Communist countries, the sense of values being reset on personal, emotive and existentialist freedom, as opposed to political or religious laying down of the law. And with politics and religion humanising themselves, the ecumenical movements and the worldwide detestation of war. "If," writes James Simmons, "religion has any future, it is not in ecumenical councils but in the lives of individuals transformed by it." Or again: "Gandhi, whom Winston Churchill referred to as 'this little naked fakir', is the man of the moment, and Churchill seems to have been dead a hundred years."

The humanist movement in Ireland (see 'The Non-Believers', *Hibernia*, December 1967, and 'The Irish Humanists', the *Irish Times*, 11th May, 1968) is only quite recently counting among its numbers many ex-Christians, persons who find their co-religionists ineffectual, unable to cope with the human ills which beset their brother man, whatever be his race, colour, creed, etc.

James Simmons defines the *Honest Ulsterman* as a magazine of 'revolution'. In a letter to me in April, he wrote, "Yet I don't want to bring the people out into the streets protesting. The real theatre of protest is in our own minds; that is why it is a Literary

Magazine." (He then quotes Yeats' quarrel with others, rhetoric, quarrel with ourselves, poetry.) If I'm reading Jimmy right his belief in literature is that it's a kind of guidebook bible to the human and that this is the use of literature. (In our middle-class puritanical materialistic idealism, use justifies the existence of a thing, a person, or an idea.) Jimmy wants us to "use all the wisdom and experience literature puts at our disposal".

The magazine itself consists of poems by lady-go-lucky Stevie Smith, Æ winner Brendan Kennelly, Ulster regionalist John Hewitt, humanist Derek Mahon, W. Price Turner, Peter Lewis, witty Gavin Ewart and Simmons' poetry prize-winning nephew, Michael Stephens, who also in a prose article looks at hashish as a substitute for Guinness. A plea also from John D. Stewart for we Catholics and Protestants of Ulster to consent to be once again human (though Simmons is one up more human than Stewart. When Stewart wrote of King William as a homosexual dwarf, James footnoted: "of course a homosexual dwarf could still be a nice person who did good things".) Congratulations Jimmy!—and what a good idea to enclose an arresting two-page drawing by Colin Middleton!

And congratulations to Mick McAleese for his *square times*, a current affairs monthly with its two strikingly darkish poems by Seamus Heaney, Sean Brelin's searching review of Thomas Kinsella collections, Cathal O'Shannon on my fellow New Yorker, Donald S. Connery's 'Sweet Talk Manhattan Style' peek at the naked Irish. Some of the articles are not signed, such as 'Ireland's Priests Talk about Leadership'. But signed, as if in blood, is the stormy Ralph Bossence in a vile mood over the Mater Hospital and our "scandalously rich" Catholic schools: "Not please with my good atheist taxes. The Government does not subsidise Humanist activities and I see no reason why it should sponsor highly dubious religious beliefs."

A second issue of the *Honest Ulsterman* (which, like the current issue of the *Dublin Magazine* with Francis Harvey's Dallas, has an 'Elegy for J.F.K.' by Simmons, quite by coincidence in view of the present tragedy) is going its own sincere well-earthed way with a pull-out drawing, this time by Carolyn Mulholland and good work by Brian McAuley, Jonathan Brown, Tony Harrison, Derek

Montgomery, Stanley Cromie, James Greer and J.A. McBryde among the new names.

The second issue of *square times* includes a review by a Scotsman on Scottish Nationalism, 'After the Revolution' (with Eddie McAteer as PM and Capt. O'Neill as Leader of the Opposition!), John Monroe about his father, the United European Party, Padraic Fiacc poetry, Sean Breslin on the paperback issue of *Thy Tears Might Cease*, an Orange recipe for the Season and a well-known folk singer on Orange songs and Sam O'Sullivan attacks again, this time that 'institution', the MacPeake Family! ... so nothing, no one is sacred and all for sixpence!

Hibernia, June 1968

New Books

THE CLASSIC FRENCH SITUATION WAS ALWAYS to bundle 'dad' off somewhere into the shadows: prison, death, a suicide, desertion, anything so that formidable Mother (as indestructible as any hyper-thyroid lady out of Racine) can fend with growing male child, and if Mamma doesn't know her own psychic strength, well then all to the better! Mother manages to help son over most hurdles: son confesses earliest mutual masturbations; mother warns him that there is no need to invest in suffering, that there is plenty of misery in store. And later on Mother makes allowances for mistresses just so long as everything is carried out so-so. And almost as bad as Mamma is son's hero, Horace, who, by implanting sterile ideals of perfectionism, stifles son's literary ventures rendering him egg-bound for two decades.

A writer less preoccupied with his subject than M. Borel would have stopped here or there in the first one hundred and twenty pages in order to evoke the tragic inevitability of, say, the later on mother-wounded marriage. Alas genius is prolific and there are grumblings in Paris about the last couple of Prix Goncourts being handed out for bulk, Borel deserves his for the feat of survival alone!

In *Consider the Lilies*, Evelyn Waugh's son, Auberon, tells the story of an Anglican priest who finds his atheist wife, given to running a birth-control clinic, not as satisfying as heiress, Danae, whom he not only does to on the side but does to in "the Italian

72

manner". The ethic 'Thou Shalt not kill; but needst not strive officiously to keep alive' comes in handy too when he lets wife Gillian fall to her death. Obsessed with anal sexuality, he breaks down, is given care and finally returns to his existence the blurb piously tells us "as a useful member of society—in hell". A kind of message is beamed at the reader towards the end: "The immense amount of good one does simply by existing ... I do nothing but add to other people's happiness. In my own way, I think I have become rather a saintly person."

Actor Douglas Hayes' *My Father in His Dizzerbell* doesn't make much bones out of life with dad. Dad is a real-life character. Lots of funny stories about him can be told to grandchildren etc. The boy himself, because of happy relationship with Dad is early to try out his own sexual wings and also confidently wants to go on stage and does just that. Plenty of lusty gusto when men were boys and boys were men and apparently that's the way Edwardian women liked it.

Hibernia, June 1968

Jacques Borel, *The Bond* (L'Adoration),
tr. by Norman Denny. (Collins, 1968)
Auberon Waugh, *Consider the Lilies* (Michael Joseph, 1968)
Douglas Hayes, *My Father in His Dizzerbell* (Macmillan, 1968)

New Work

IN HEINRICH BÖLL'S *THE END OF a Mission*, translated by Leila Vennewitz, the situation (you couldn't call it a plot) stems from an hazard objective, a (chance [?] happening), a seemingly spontaneous but ritualistic act like the prisoners bursting into a hymn to the bees in Genet's *La Miracle de la Rose*. Böll's (pretty stock now) father-and-son incorporated set fire in public to a military jeep, chanting the Litany of the Saints, the *ora pro nobis* part beaten out by clinking pipes together in the rhythm of a rumba. The court, presented with these 'facts' divorced from any motivation, consider the criminal act gratuitous.

The character witnesses (eccentrics to a man) etch the irony deeper with human acid, e.g. the old priest, standing on his head to show that he is a man of the world, is conversing about a 'stripper' to soldiers, who, in deference to the cloth, imagine that the priest is talking about stripping cables, until of course he mentions 'call-girls'. And there's an army officer for whom barrackroom duty has become a sexual fetish and a puritan Catholic lady among several others.

Whereas the perspicacious H. Böll has written another masterpiece within the limits of 'thingism' as an aesthetic device, Professor Galbraith's venture into fiction is not as successful. Very witty and amusing, the novel portrays the rapid turnover in Latin governments artificially induced by Washington to the final twist of the US sending a Detroit-educated native son back to rule: Son's first-hand knowledge of the States is such that instead of desired effect the young fellow perversely swings his country miles to the Left.

Galbraith is too much of a heavyweight for near, new, or non-novel writing. His point is made so forcefully that the characters seem watered-down in order to project the message. If *The Triumph* is not a triumph any more than the policy it condemns it is for the same reason: what's this the French say? 'You can triumph only if you are careful not to' and even a Galbraith failure is immensely readable.

Sheila Macleod, singer Paul Jones' wife, uses phantasy in her *The Moving Accident* so straight-facedly alongside of facts that don't blame the reader if he gets a bit woozy. A handy bread or carving knife seems to be always under the pillow. Singer Jason Friend's wife, Una, daydreams that she cuts at least one of her wrists and stabs bed-friend Trevor in the neck. It's this being married to a famous man who belongs to a swooning girl public. (It's not part of said image to be married at all, and Jason's always dead beat when he gets home; Una fantasises him really dead from dreadful car accidents etc.). A psychologically valid portrayal of a dicey loneliness, it is an excellent first novel.

Sam Levenson's *Everything But Money* starts off with boyhood memories of pre-fridge days of ice-man when kids in New York were kids and wore knickers and hewed wagons out of orange crates with old skate wheels, used bin lids to go sleigh-riding and attended the local flea-ridden 'dump' every Saturday to keep up on the Tarzan serial. The second section contrasts middle-class suburbia where all graveyards are, the third as a teacher in same city gives lie to any slum ghetto seeming cosy or jolly where there is an almost comic direct plea for help. In the fourth section written to his own children he begs, "Do not play it cool, get involved." TV raconteur Levenson has written a kind of Bronx bible with enough truth-telling to get himself arrested alongside of Doctor Spock.

Hibernia, September 1968

Heinrich Böll, *The End of a Mission* (Weidenfeld & Nicolson, 1968)
John Kenneth Galbraith, *The Triumph* (Hamish Hamilton, 1968)
Sheila Macleod, *The Moving Accident* (Faber & Faber, 1968)
Sam Levenson, *Everything But Money* (MacDonald, 1968)

Out of the Cradle ...

THE BORESTONE MOUNTAIN PRIZE, 1963, THE Eric Gregory Trust Award, 1965, and now, Derek Mahon's first volume, *Night-Crossing* is this autumn's Choice of the Poetry Book Society—against the strong competition of that very fine myth-making poet, Geoffrey Hill, whose new collection was given the society's (second best) recommendation.

Bearded Derek smiled his 'secret smile' (minus one tooth which he had just had removed). "The worst is yet to come; I'm jittery about the reviews!" When Padraic Colum met Derek a few years ago, the old poet need not have warned, "I like a poem to be quiet," for, of all the younger Ulster poets, Derek Mahon is the quietest.

Recently at a poetry reading we both gave with Conleth Ellis at the St. Malachy College Clubrooms, a member of the audience asked, "Do you find it hard being a poet?" I answered, "Yes," to which Derek, looking at me in surprise, said, "Do you really? I don't." I was thinking of Pasternak's "The more men in the world who are happy, the easier it will be to become a poet." Mahon's generation echoes the ideal into practice: "I am man self-made ... /We have grown up as best we could/ ... know, as I know, I am not alone."—'After Midnight'.

Time, not others, is the bogey in the Mahon poem: "This is an express/ ... passes all the stations." Then there's his painter's feel for light, his two years in sunny America, all the time yearning " ... to be out of the sun—/To have travelled north ... /To my islands of dark ore/Where winter is long/Only a little light/Gets through, and that perfect/"—'Epitaph for Robert Flaherty'.

In the poem dedicated to me he articulates an entire generation's attitude to Ireland: "... the giants/Who tore up sods twelve miles by six/And hurled them out to sea to become islands/Can worry us no more ... / ... No saint or hero, landing at night from the conspiring seas/Brings dangerous tokens to the new era—"(but before reconciling himself, he admits, "And much dies with them... ")—'Glengormley'.

Derek's myths and legends centre round real people: a grandfather: "Nothing escapes him. He escapes us all," or an admired if naughty uncle, "The crookest chief steward in the Head Line." A suicidal film-actress: "We are slowly learning from meteors like her" or 'Van Gogh Among the Miners' who promises to paint light on "Old chairs, faces and old boots/" and set " ... fierce fire to the eyes of sun flowers and fishing boats,/Each one a miner in disguise". He salutes also 'The Forger of Vermeer' as an artist in his own right, and hails wanderers everywhere: "We are all gipsies now—/Pea-pickers, pick pockets/ ... Sleeping like John Clare/With our feet to the Pole Star"—'Gipsies'.

Ever on the move: "My best bet is to go away./Goodbye, good luck to one and all—/And since I have no choice but to go/" 'Legacies' ... Resignation at twenty-six? John Press uses a theme in one of his poems: the three-year-old daughter of James I had the poetic wit to chirp up before she died: "I go. I go. Away I go."

Derek Mahon is born to a gift which experience or university cannot teach. He is a born poet. And, as for his first collection in book form, I quote his own 'Lines From a Preface to a Love Poem': "This is a night-cry/ ... outlasting stone and bronze/The words are aching in their own pursuit./ ... This is the blind with sunlight filtering through ... " His first collection then is a definition of poetry itself.

Hibernia, October 1968

Derek Mahon, *Night-Crossing* (Oxford University Press, 1968)

Blue Fool

JAMES LIDDY, A FAIRLY REGULAR CONTRIBUTOR to *Hibernia*'s book page, is a 34-year-old County Clare man. His first volume of poetry, *In a Blue Smoke*, was published by Dolmen four years ago, establishing him as a Joyce-loving poet in the tradition of a *Green Fool* Patrick Kavanagh. His tribute to Joyce, *Esau, My Kingdom for a Drink*, published in 1962, was also broadcast on the BBC Third Programme.

Some other, if seemingly irrelevant distinctions are that he is the grandson of the Irish emigrant who first established a supermarket in New York, and that he practised for a time as a barrister in Dublin. His famous sojourn in Spain *'por escriber en la arena?'* James Delehanty wanted to know (Liddy was one-time editor of *Arena*) is over and he is now teaching in California. Two years ago he published a self-revealing 'Extract from a Journal of Departure' in *The Holy Door* when he was preparing to exile himself but not in cunning nor with silence. He took himself to task for comparing himself to Joyce only to conclude that arrogance in a writer is manly. Quoting Kinsella's being impelled to write after having read *Dubliners* "fascination with the idea of the artist as a competent judging figure", he asserted (in a technical age) belief in a raw, free, swinging, casual, open way for the poet, should it be in the shadow of the Black Mountain school, etc.

Actually more revealing is his "certain wild prose quickie" on A.E. Housman: "A good poet, his life teaches something more ...

that love is implanted in us by some sacred force, whether emanating from the top of a mountain, a stable, or the sky itself, and that men have no control over it. Its operation does not coincide with the use of the rational faculty. It is therefore, of God."

(The influence of Blake on Irish poets is a study in itself.) And to add to the Irisch-angst a saying of Blake's such as "The tigers of wrath are wiser than the horses of instruction" would be to encourage Liddy's 'quarrel with others', e.g. "...the Paddy Colums/ Come lately.../...why should we meet them or go on platforms with them?/" or in the poem, 'A Protestant Mystic' (AE?) " ... who/To find the God he talked about through his beard/ ... should have left the proofs unread". Or 'Swinburne at Eton': " ... Passively and curiously he languished/For the literary fairy with the face of a male madonna/To seduce him at an Arabian afternoon tea of poets and painters/Who wore fancy dress, poisoning him midnight after midnight/With dreams of angelic children whose nakedness titillated/He hadn't Shelley's decency to pretend life was real."

To my mind Liddy's best work is personal and more a 'quarrel with the self'. Though I've read some of these poems before this, his second collection, I'd like to echo his own words, "I ask for more versions of tenderness, not art." (I'm thinking of Goethe's definition of poetry as "not art, not a science, but a work of genius".) Liddy shows genius in his love and friendship poems and in his persistent sense of destiny.

Hibernia, 18th October 1968

James Liddy, *Blue Mountain* (Dolmen Press, 1968)

Rondo

PADRAIC COLUM IS EVER DEPARTING, EVER returning, like an ancient Celtic myth-being, a Fionnuala or an Oisin, who in return are liable to find their contemporaries long since under the ground, ghosts, memories: "They are all dead. Therefore, how strange that I am still here." The fear of not withstanding the ravages of time takes on a form of constant renewal: Colum writes: "Like some other beings/They're claimant of a day/Whose grant is lodging, prospect, store./Companionship renewed". ('In Saint Stephen's Green'). It is a feat of Colum's that he can successfully construct a bridge to span across the Atlantic abyss of Irish lostness. (Kinsella writes of a "mutilation of the past", a kind of agony of displacement in time. Montague writes of the Irish immigrants in America as "piteous like animals".) The psychic hungering after a world that has withered away in time! And the Kerry poet Kennelly helps us picture the desolation by aptly comparing the famine dead to the Jewish corpses under the Nazis: the half skeleton of a man dies in the act of trying to warm his wife's feet so that in death the wife's feet are nailed to the man's breast bone. (Peadar O Laoghaire's *Mo Sgeal Fein*).

You find in Colum, therefore, lines of unbearable sadness, and his moods sometimes seem maudlin to those Irish who never had to leave hearth and home. Of course, the most magnificent poem in *Images of Departure* is Colum's 'The Book of Kells'. This poem first appeared a decade ago in the *Irish Times*, then later in a 1957

Dolmen edition, *Ten Poems*. Two personal poems, 'After Speaking' of one who died a long time before and 'Expecting' no one are concerned with regret and the understandable self pity of the aged widower: "Regretting this that you have come so often/ To where I crossed, and that so seldom I,/moved from set purposes, made a festival/Of your approach ... "

Is the Celtic poet like Padraic Colum really no longer considered a valid representative of contemporary Irish existence? To Colum, Ireland is a sea of culture like China. He has never ceased to uncover riches from its earth, riches too much under our own noses for us to appreciate. We want the far-fetched truth and thanks to our politicians we are ashamed of being Anglo-Irish, Scots-Irish, Norman and Dane Irish, Irish American or what have you. Kinsella in his 'Continuity of the Tradition' (*Poetry Ireland* 7 and 8) discounts even Yeats' vision of Ireland as an ancient culture in favour of a Joyce's modernity, but is Joyce modern or is he Victorian Music Hall static? Joyce was a failed or spoilt poet and his mirror of the 'Servant Girl' was cracked like the broken soul of the schizophrenic. Yeats was forever unifying and finding new unities, and Colum after him: "A single line describes them and enfolds,/One line, one course when term there is none,/Which in its termlessness is envoying. The going forth and the return one." ('The Book of Kells').

The poems of Michael Longley are so skilfully abstracted, so depersonalised with detachment, that the notion of his being an Irish poet is altogether irrelevant nor is he, as a Roy McFadden, Louis MacNeice or John Hewitt, an Ulster poet even. The basic, most fertile part of his existence is the world of the University. I have only to mention the *Dublin Magazine* and Trinity to conjure Longley's world of appreciating and straining after general excellence. The poems 'In Memoriam', 'The Centaurs', 'A Personal Statement' and 'Epithalamion' are this poet at his best, but you must go beyond the staggering virtuosity having a numbing effect to recognise, warts and all, old Dr. Johnson of horse-play and horse-laugh fame.

Home is Longley's place and 'Home Anywhere' and 'Home' is where the head is: "riding out the brainstorm,/His weather-proof enormous head at home" ('Dr. Johnson on the Hebrides') and "There was no place to go, but his own head" ('Dr. Johnson Dying', the whole volume ending with "Let solitude be named Man Friday./Our folk may muster then, even the dead,/Footprint follow footprint through my head" ('Man Friday'). An impressive first collection to stand beside Heaney, Mahon, Boland and Kennelly's best!

For anyone who has not read the early Brendan Kennelly volumes this Figgis paperback (riverrun) edition is a must well worth buying. An interesting preface in which the poet (with the generosity and eagerness of a Derek Mahon) tells us about his own poetry and then forty-four poems starting off with 'The Gift', in which he tells us that the muse for him came from the most ordinary of sources: "It was a gift that took me unawares. And I accepted it." He accepts the good things in Irish life and hits out against the bad, the "swinish apathy", etc., nor does he try to use poetry as a weapon: "Poetry will never finally solve anything, because it is the voice of new promise, the art of permanent beginning."

His tributes to the late Frank O'Connor and Patrick Kavanagh, the painful 'Night Drive', 'The Tippler', 'The Pig Killer', 'The Teachers', and 'My Dark Fathers' testify to the reality the poet in Kennelly probes in order like a child to discover "Something that will not acknowledge conclusion/Insists that we forever begin" ('Begin').

Hibernia, 21 November 1969

Padraic Colum, *Images of Departure* (Dolmen Press, 1969)
Michal Longley, *No Continuing City* (Gill & Macmillan, 1969)
Brendan Kennelly, *Selected Poems* (Allen Figgis 'riverrun', 1969)

Harvest of Hunger

JUST UP TO BEFORE NIGHT FELL like a guillotine over the pink sandstone penthouse towers of Manhattan in the early 40s, there was a kind of 'ruddy glow'—you could hardly call it a twilight—the great giants of Europe were suddenly in our midst: Madame Sigrid Undset, whose tetralogy, *The Master of Hestviken* could only have been written by a man's mind, Thomas Mann, a living link with Goethe; Bela Bartok, the theme of whose fourth Rumanian Folk Dance I was never done trying to dash off on the piano, etc ... In the big East-Side galleries I stood frozen before my first Picasso of the Blue Period and was equally stricken in the presence of my first Rembrandt. Paris had fallen; I was now living in the capital of Western Civilisation: books, paintings, music and the genius himself! And I was within walking distance of a great poet who rubbed shoulders with Yeats and James Joyce! One of the greats of the Irish Renaissance!

Padraic Colum's books were my first library readings as a boy, and later, as a youth, Macmillan sent him my first volume of poems. I was summoned to his apartment with his (upon meeting face to face) "I curse the very day I entered into the reading of—" And as time went on I came to know from Colum the meticulous code of an ancient culture adhered to almost with vengeance by the fastidious mandarin writer himself!

It's a good quarter of a century since the old poet read me portions of his second novel, *The Flying Swans*, a work then in progress, but eventually published a decade or so later by Crown Publishers (N.Y.). I recall the totally alien quality of the language, the almost Germanic involutions, quiet irony, inversions: the syntax was old Gaelic in idiom, or even Ancient Grecian. There was a grinding heaviness of thought process. I remarked this wonderful slowness for surety in the Irish people I had encountered up and down the East Coast. My father was from the same part of Ireland as Colum and from them both I came to know that the Irish mind had a character of its own which is not only encased in the Gaelic language but from my own studies of Latin and Greek I was reminded that people in Ireland once spoke in Latin and Greek as well.

The characters in *The Flying Swans** seemed folk-formal stiff, austere, devoid of any props, like an unaccompanied Irish or Spanish folk dance. It seemed that even in his prose Colum was asking you to accept your own Irish character, and when you did so, this made you serious, European, universal and consequently capable of understanding the character closer to my own floor stone, the Ulster Planter mind. (Colum had told me then that he was trying to do in *The Flying Swans* what Gogol did in *Dead Souls.*)

I was also at that time taken by the sense of hunger articulated in the novel and of course mirrored in the old Irish people I knew in New York. Something was wrenched from them which rendered them baffled and mute and squashed. I can only now think of that story by Camus where the young idealistic priest in the wilderness of mission territory has his tongue pulled out by savages and of the aftermath of dreadful breakdown, in which he despairs. Longing, lostness, Colum portrays without caricature the simple excruciating death scene of the mother, who, like Joyce's young girl, knows that she is going to die but feels cheated and afraid. A bleak landscape where the priest appears on horseback, a silver-handled riding crop in hand to wave off the begging tinker man and wife, and, of course, it is the *Apache* tinker who in the end bests the 'gentleman priest'!

All in all, and upon re-reading, I can feel little of Gogol's humour in *The Flying Swans*, probably because the gloomy social cult of the small-town peasantry has no time for laughs; where even the jackdaws on the rooftops seem to jeer and mock the once herd-girl mother returning to her absent husband's big house with their son, Ulick. Her social downgrade is never forgiven her nor forgotten. I feel more the chilly influence of Ibsen via Joyce than I do of that hilarious Peter Lorre-like writer, Gogol.

It is Colum's victory that his characters so restricted, some so revolting, nevertheless stealthily emerge from the most hair-raising emptiness or hunger looking and acting like holy pictures. They have suffered but like most of us are not the better for it; hard lives make for hard hearts, and as for Colum's realism, I believe it can stand up to anything his critics, the younger poets, can offer. Compare, for instance, his pig-killing scene in *The Flying Swans* with Brendan Kennelley's 'The Pig Killer' poem. The older poet does not prepare us for the added horror of a queue of half-starved people standing in line to drink the pig's blood.

The Flying Swans is a triumph of style; a work, which, when our present-day sense of aesthetic values levels to sobriety, will take its place high up there where the giants live on and on.

Hibernia, 23 January 1970

* Padraic Colum, *The Flying Swans* (reissue)

Three Holy Blue Flower People

A WEEK OR TWO AFTER 'BLUE FOOl' (my write-up on James Liddy's Dolmen Press book, *Blue Mountain*, the poet, whom I never met (though, indeed, our paths crossed) wrote me from Gorey, Coolgreany, in County Wexford. "Dear Padraic Fiacc, I would like to thank you for your very friendly review in *Hibernia*, and for the title, 'Blue Fool'." (His first Dolmen collection was called *In a Blue Smoke*), and with his "May I present my San Francisco offering to you," he enclosed another, this time American, collection, *Blue House*. (Obviously 'blue' is a key or myth word to Liddy, and has something of the same density that the word 'formidable' has in French, or for that matter 'Sacré Bleu'.)

I wrote and asked could I review *Blue House* for the *Honest Ulsterman* and received a reply from, of all places, Zürich! "I'm in Zürich, going to Trieste tomorrow. In the steps of Joyce. I am thinking of writing a short *Life of Stephen Dedalus* in prose and verse ..." (His tribute to Joyce, *Esau, My Kingdom for a Drink*, was broadcast on the BBC Third Programme and published by Liam Miller's Dolmen in 1962.) "It would be very nice to have an honourable mention of *Blue House* in the *HU*. It would delight Tom Hill who is only 20 and of the Californian Gold Rush Irish." (Liddy teaches in California.) "The book was printed by Graham Mackintosh of the White Rabbit Press in San Francisco, one of America's most famous poetry presses."

Blue House is indeed a beautiful projection in light midnight sky blue and cream and with that kind of American paper that we just don't have in puritanical skinflint Europe any more and probably never shall again. The cover is a blue-misted photograph of the three poets, Jim Chapson, James Liddy, and Thomas Hill. The title page has the three poets standing up this time (having downed a goodly portion of their beer tins). The three are wearing stole-like scarves (blue I bet).

But here we have what James Kirkup called "greenagers" in his *Paper Windows: Poems from Japan* only, of course, our poets are blue-greenagers or young aquamarines. They are devoted, each of them, to ancient Chinese poets, Li Po especially, the William Blake of China and whose friendship for that other ancient poet, Tu Fu, is something of a holy legend or miracle since these profane saints like some ancient Irish monks and nuns, slept together. James Liddy shares Li Po's love for colour and the ancient Irish poet-sages' 'living it up' or sowing their wildest oats before they entered the monastery for good.

Jim Chapson's way of saying "The world is too much with us" is "A lot of people who never got the point follow us around expecting Miracles but are always eating, sleeping or looking for something to curse when the Miracle happens ..." The Miracle is the Way: "I showed my verses to an older poet/who told me a truth I longed to believe/all knowledge is futile and barren/which does not open the love of your friends" and ends with his last poem: "As I walk to my lover's house again/a saxophone player repeats a monotonous scale./Trying to break free is wasted effort/The Way is adherence to ordinary beliefs/And gradual perfection of our common habits."

In a world of clinical naturalism and sentimental realism and science emptied of the human factor these young poets lean to friendships with one another which are suspect and outrageous to materialistic Western white men of action. And even present day China looks back on its ancient holy men and poets as impractical fools. Thomas Hill's guiding star is the 8th-century Chinese poet Po Chu-i, who, like Li Po (only more so) was gifted for making friends with fellow poets. He had a somewhat shadowed, if deep, friendship with Yuan Chen. And indeed Po Chu-i might have written to Yuan Chen the lines Thomas Hill writes to James Liddy:

"You are from the old world/And I am without tradition". For Thomas Hill, just out of his teens, a day of perfection is "A child's rest—meadow, wonder, rain ... My eyes remember water/A small window ..."

The section devoted to Liddy himself is given over almost entirely to friendship poetry, and, should he crayon-colour the moon ... guess what colour? His homage to Ezra Pound is just the opposite of Paul Potts' famous rhetorical question poem. Liddy's Pound is asked, "How could they hope to keep you/Locked in a Western cell/And how could your way not be of virtue?" And James, being Irish, can bite too: "Voice of the San Francisco poetess .../Heavy in commitment to something/not her death or being near death/And hairsuit young faghaters/waiting with their manuscripts ... "

Liddy and Chapson have a poem on the resentment of the workers in the village towards the poets' setting up house merely to dream and write poetry. Thousands of years later the same thing is happening. And now with automation, the worker will ironically turn to the poet to learn how to live without manual therapy and to,in the words of another poet, learn how to love one another. Or die.

Honest Ulsterman, No 10

Blue House (Nine Beasts Press)

Living Proof

BRIAN COFFEY'S GENERATION—C. DAY LEWIS, Kavanagh, Beckett, Conor Cruise O'Brien, Hewitt, MacNeice, Devlin, Stuart, Milne, Spender, Auden, Sartre, and a host of others— was born at the beginning of this century. They had in common a tradition of rocking the status-quo boat and, indeed, many still do. But their lives spanned two world wars, the Irish, Russian, Chinese, South American revolutions, the Irish and Spanish Civil Wars, Vietnam, the rise of Africa, the rise of the American Negro and our own Ulster Catholic ... so that when Prof. Coffey writes "there is no heaven on earth" in his poem, the phrase glows with defeat and irony.

D.J. Enright's "You need defeat's sour/fuel for poetry,/Its motive power/is powerless" could set the tone and mood of these poems which span four decades. The longish sequences have a remarkable evenness. There's a kind of plainchant organic rhythm. Fragments seem to culminate into climactic lines, the words of which seem to burn truth through the page: "Bitter the cruel times/the lying rulers". It is the disillusionment of the humanist: "In us we saw the human business ended." And not even the socialist ideal is left burning for "... now it's welfare/clean white tiles/skilled aseptic hands/we do a legal job from scrape to disposal/saved from bastards." And in keeping with his disabused contemporaries, he's had to live away from Ireland, and observes his own children in America: "They know nothing of Ireland/they grow American."

Michael Smith is to be congratulated for this book*, but why could he not have included Prof. Coffey's two 'Eleisons'? They would have fitted in the page or two at the end.

If the heavy darkness of time had crushed the grass yellow under the stone for Prof. Coffey, it is no less telling that for the younger poet in his early thirties, Conleth Ellis**, his depressive moods are quite similar, e.g. both poets have references to their own birthdays as if to prove to themselves that they exist, that they survive.

Teaching in Belfast, he cannot blinker himself to the despair of his young students: "Eyes that cannot trust tomorrow" or "They said, 'Teach the child who/Learned in the womb to hate to love'." He really wants to teach these girls and youths to "hold dearest what we cannot learn" or he visualises a sordid heartbreaking pattern of existence for the young girl who, after she turns fifteen will leave school for the factory, an early marriage, and then the dark streets of black Belfast. He is angry with the hurt she unwittingly brings him: "Slum child why must you/Bring me your poems?"

Our restricted and repressive Ulster society certainly depressed Conleth Ellis and he often asked, "Is it in me, this pain, or in this town or both?"

I can't help but perceive that his return to the south of Ireland has lifted the stone that was crushing him, for *Under the Stone* is a good generous flux of a poetry collection. One or two weedy phrases could have done with cutting and one poem, 'Passion', is blighted with the Hopkinsesque bug, but the general quality of the poems is high and there's an almost Kevin Faller eeriness in the intuitive flash which makes its own melodies and technics. There is certainly a visible development from his earlier collection, *This Ripening Time*, some of whose verses hadn't as yet gelled. And now there is enough density of matter to father a whole body of work? *Under the Stone* should establish Conleth Ellis as a recognised Irish poet well on the way to becoming a major one.

Irish Press, 22 April, 1972

* Brian Coffey, *Selected Poems* (New Writers' Press, 1971)
** Conleth Ellis, *Under the Stone* (Gill & Macmillan, 1971)

The North's Younger Poets

FOUR OR FIVE YEARS AGO A group of Flower People invaded, of all places, Belfast! It was about eleven a.m. and the streets were deserted. For the want of people about, these US Hippies hugged the tree trunks in Botanic Park: "But, man, where are the people? This is Ireland, man: where are the poets?"

Six-footer Derryman schoolmaster, Tom McLaughlin, holds an answer in his poem, 'The Men are at Work': "Straight rows of slate and chimney pot/... A terraced street/A red-brick toyland where a child forgot/ To put in people ... " And in another poem, "O self-indulgent boredom!" he bemusingly lyricises: "Our lives at this place could go on forever!"

Tom's friend, Fermanagh man, Frank Ormbsy, also teaches. He and Tom took over editorship from James Simmons to continue to run *the Honest Ulsterman*. Frank handed me his *Ripe for Company*, a generous booklet of twenty-seven poems. He doesn't intend to publish in real book form, he declared, until he is thirty. His poems on friend, brother or chance acquaintance (when he travels from Belfast back into the country), confess to an unusual susceptibility: "I'd nurse a secret awe for one/Who'd sell me for a crooked sixpence/You'd touch me for a loan and I'd agree". Or for a brother who, years ago, took a different parting on the road after Eleven Plus: "I note your hands are twice the size of mine." Or, the perception, that no matter how obsessively one tries to, you can't really ever go back: " ... not sorry at partings, people left in a hurry". Or, of his own father: "I have no photographs to make you new."

Tom Matthew's poem in this month's *Honest Ulsterman* captures the restlessness of the young Ulster poet, enthralled and pleased by the Muse: "She tells me answers I have no questions for./ I am her pupil, her foolish lad."

The Teddy Boys of Michael Foley's boyhood haunt him with seemingly some unrealisable-as-yet truth: "I merely wonder was it just/My growing up which caused their fall?" Foley may well be the most representative of his generation here in the North, hurling himself into the kill with all the generous masochism of the young man wanting to be: "... a river to my people/Dozing before their televisions./Their children won't return/To such a cozy glowing womb./All they know for sure of living:/It doesn't happen in the living room."

Michael Brophy, one of Seamus Heaney's protégés, (Paul Muldoon, the young Armagh poet, calls Seamus "Our father-figurehead") is a science teacher who can compose a wry dry instant poem which fits well into the large newspaper because of its terseness and topicality, e.g., his 'Guns for the Boys' published some time ago in the *Belfast Telegraph*, has a particular relevance just now. It hits out at guerrilla warfare in general, the kind of war where women, children and youths are mercilessly gunned down in 'cross-fire' or 'by mistake', but are nonetheless dead whatever happened, and murdered ironically by those who set themselves up as their 'defenders': "Then the three men with their guns/Lined up and shot me./'You're easier to protect/When you're dead,' they said."

In a recent new poetry magazine, *Words*, Michael Brophy shares pages of poems with Michael Boyle. Born in the same part of Belfast, they even shared the same desk at school. Today they are young daddies in suburbia, Michael Boyle's Belfast is a 'troubled city', but troubled by lonely and half lost people. Bleak existences are eked out on park benches. Michael is a salesman. He has an eye for that moment of hunger or bondage when, say, Marie was twenty-four, the tears streaking lines in her make-up (her price is thirty bob), suddenly remembers cobblestones from childhood as she paces the streets. Or an old man on Carrick Hill watching the bulldozers "make cobbles, make clay", while he himself waits to die. Or Jerry, a youth, peering at the holes between the night-boat's planks, on a 'Belfast Sunday', as he emigrates to Preston ...

"A law unto himself," Michael Longley and several older poets, stand side by side with the younger men. Longley, e.g. through the voice of the Swedish poet, Lars Forssell, hits out against "military solutions", re-affirming faith in the open vulnerability of the poet as opposed to the closed shop dehumanisation of the Military Machine: "The bloodstains on my mind/In my ears the bombs ... The death throes and the screams/ ... the hell that I remember/ Captain Steel has never seen."

This is perhaps the most orthodox answer to those bird-brains who insist that the poet should be more actively committed to his own particular political orgy of blood-letting. Goethe said a long time ago that poets are not war-like by nature. If anything, they fight against death or being dead: e.g. James Simmons' "Imaginative reconstruction shed/Some light upon a vanquished way of life/But I can't live like them and they are dead."

Our dark native city itself becomes the focus of resentment. The older poet, Norman Dugdale, writes: (in his 'Night Ferry' as it edges at daylight into Belfast): "Wall slogans run like wet mascara/Down gable ends. The terraces/Wear jilted looks, deserted/In the morning swollen-eyed ... " Or, in another poem: "City of gull-flecked gantries/Raised by steam and iron from mud ... /God-ranting, canting, pious without pity ... "

Seamus Heaney's 'From Cave Hill' also knocks our Home Town with " ... the City smokes/Up through the dead damp./Roofing the lough and tower flats:/A smouldering hill-ringed pit/Placid and shrunk on itself/ Like a compost heap."

Derek Mahon, whose new collection, *Lives*, via Oxford University Press, has certainly tried to come to grips: "The things that happen in the kitchen houses/And echoing back streets of this desperate city/Should engage more than my transient interest/Exact more interest than my casual pity ... " Yet, what in the end, distinguishes these young poets, together with others such as Brendan Hamill, Joan Newmann, Michael Stevens, Ciaran Carson, Tom McGurk, Dennis Kelly, Brian McAuley and several more, from, say, the Rodgers, MacNeice generation or the Hewitt or McFadden one even?

Derek Mahon, some time ago, rat-tat-tatted off on my typewriter a poem he called 'Homecoming'. It answers "We cannot start/At this late date/With a pure heart/Or having seen/The picture plain/ Be ever in/-ocent again."

Ulster's latest Gregory award winner (the youngest yet—in his early twenties) Paul Muldoon, who together with fellow Ulster poet, William Peskett, has had some work already published by Faber and Faber, and will have his first hardback collection brought out by them next year, also is troubled by the constant violence of our present Ulster situation. He refuses to let it cramp his style: "Words, like 'bullets' or 'bombs' aren't real words." He was breathing smoke over our milk-coffees when I realised that these young poets in their twenties really do have integrity, and Muldoon, the youngest poet in Derek Mahon's *Sphere Book of Modern Irish Poetry*, in his poem on Belfast, sets the mood for hope or peace (but we don't know, and neither does he, if it all isn't just one more euphoric mirage!); certainly he won't be stopped from writing by it: "From the higher ground I look over the city/To know last night's whitewash/Is being given the lie by this morning's rain./That cemetery under the mountain/Is again appearing as a field of seagulls."

Hibernia, 20 October, 1972

Violence and the Ulster Poet

MICHAEL BROPHY IS SPREADEAGLED AGAINST THE boot of his car. A manuscript is snatched from his jacket pocket. Upon scrutinising it, the searching Para shrieks: "Hi men, we've got a fucking little poet here!" After having corralled 73 poets for the Blackstaff Press anthology, *The Wearing of the Black*, I can sympathise both with the Para's shock and Michael's bitter humiliation. Can poetry and violence mix at all?

Michael Longley fights me about including a poem of his on the assassination of his grocer and friend last year. I attempt to rearrange the stanzas. "No, I like it even less after your rearrangement." I persist with Michael until I uncover that the approximation fails in his own eyes because of his emotional involvement. He was fond of the late Jim Gibson and the poem couldn't capture the impact of the horror and the grief Longley experienced at the murder. Herein lies something of the personal and aesthetic drama of the present-day Ulster poet's dilemma.

Being interviewed earlier this year by the then student Gerald Dawe, our conversation was shattered by a flurry of gunfire. Gerald became frightened: "They see the anger and the bitterness in your poetry, but they don't see the terror." The late Padraic Fallon was scandalised at a letter I wrote to the *Irish Times* in which I said the kids of Belfast and Derry were writing better poems than we were. But kids do capture the violent moment more poetically:

The place where a kid says, my coat's a bomb.
—Gerald Dawe, 'Black Cat'

A child did say this in the Abercorn Restaurant after the explosion.

Younger poets who rotate to older poets such as Hewitt, McFadden and myself know that we understand, say, the despair of a Brendan Hamill when he wrote on the Ballymurphy wall the words Seamus Heaney used in his 'Whatever You Say, Say Nothing': "Is there a life before death?"

Riding downtown with Meta Hepburn, I feel the lost backstreet kids of Belfast haunting her like her own 'Ghosts':

Their eyes glitter from the splintered glass,
their bones rattle in shuttered windows,
their flesh cries from the pulp
of the bookstall bombed last week.

The agony is not a clear-cut matter of black-and-white moral opprobrium, it is human: only a poet can convey the tragic:

All in confusion of the ditch,
Guilt, innocence alike ...

Even the 'great man', the ruler:

... blew
His brains out at the afterdate—
God knows from what despair or grief—
Earned his ironic epitaph:
The patriot died execrate.
—Norman Dugdale, 'New Year's Eve, 1969'

The people themselves carry what Robert Greacen calls "the public and the personal wound"; the young Protestant, Gerald Dawe, runs into St. Mary's chapel: built with the hand of eighty-five pounds from the Protestant Belfast Volunteers, a sense of history overwhelming him, a Protestant sense of always being blamed for Ireland's wrongs. He bursts into tears before the votive candles in a chapel where a soldier died from a crackshot at point-blank range and then heads out " ...to the street/world with wonder/waddling/where tears jerked/for this I was born." ('Heritages')

Ciaran Carson, putting himself into the place of an internee, addresses History itself: "When you made my hands, you shaped/Them with barbed wire." ('The Maze')

In my own case, the contusion of being born a "child of hatred" becomes cancerous, and the middle-aged man is now malignant, corrupt:

> 'Can you put yourself into the mind
> Of the man who kills?'
> 'No.' I lie to the priest. 'I can't,'
> *But I can*, I'm polluted
> With the poison of violence, born and bred into it:
> I'm dying of those dark looks I get from boy
> Soldiers from slits in 'pigs', and I try to rub
> The hatred from my eyes but it's deeper than 'looks':
> The Black is in my lungs now, and in my poems.
>
> —'Glass Grass'

The Black Hole, which used to frighten Seamus Heaney as a boy in Derry when the Constable used to call, was a place in the Barracks where a semi-militarised police brought their prisoners. It metamorphoses in my own torture-poem into the dense black holes of the universe. The victim, who is being beaten by the military, sees colours of black he never believed existed.

The contemporary poet is confessional; he is involved:

> The pool of blood in the doorway,
> The incandescent blaze of hate...
> ... I, who have gone away
> To safe and easy exile,
> Cannot quite write them off
> As simply ignorant thugs.
> I, too, am involved in their crimes.
>
> —Robert Greacen, 'As a Child in Derry'

> Is it in me, this pain,
> or is it this place or both?
>
> —Conleth Ellis, 'Belfast, 1964'

> this black death fever
> in the back street
> plague of mine is everyone's
>
> —Dennis Kelly, 'Rubicon'

The violence is almost a kind of release:

the weeping that several decades had repressed
the (CS) gas induced
releases a violence generations old.

—Michael Friel, 'No Truck'

but it is essentially an invasion of the poet's psyche:

Then, in the night, banging bin lids and shouts
along William Street; crack of bullets,
quick battles, and a friend rushed bleeding
into your room.

—Terence Maxwell, 'Report of the Tribunal'

Something irrevocable happens. From the day

we see clouds, but no matter,
Squad-cars police the nurseries ...

to some dreadful concrete details:

a girl's six-inch breasts, levelled
like pistols because of her stomach
which is full of blood.

—Hugh Maxton, 'Two Psalms From Derry'

or

the tears wept fall as stones upon the soldiers
or the soldiers themselves:
Hoarding a massive technology for killing
troops tread the tripwired chequerboard: visored, wary,
aliens from a different planet.

—Andrew Waterman, 'Derry Images'

The bitter universe masochism of the entrenched Catholic, the

half of us, as in a wooden horse,
were cabin'd and confined like wily Greeks,
besieged within the siege, whispering morse.

—Seamus Heaney, 'Whatever You Say, Say Nothing'

They said 'dance little man'
So I danced

And I smiled as they smiled
And enjoyed the ordeal.

—Michael Brophy, 'Dance Little Man'

He matches how terrible it is also to be a Protestant in Ulster. Michael's Protestant friends are forced to emigrate.

There was 'No Intimidation'
Just men—hung back
When you left the yard
'Bullets can spread'
They told you 'in a joke';
Romantic Ireland's
Dead and gone
And there's more than O'Leary in the grave.

—Michael Brophy, 'For Tom and Ann Leaving'

Seamus Deane has something of an answer, but, for the Ulster poet's tragic anguish in his 'The Fable':

This is my point in writing, writing
Not the admiration of fighting
But the desire to be no fewer
Than both pursued and pursuer.
Whatever image you lob
Someone comes on still holding
A gun. He has to be got,
That unfinished youth who fired the shot.
I write to finish the job.

Hibernia, 6 December, 1974

Introduction to
The Wearing of the Black

THIS ANTHOLOGY, WHICH HAS BEEN PREPARED at a certain time—1974—in a certain place—Northern Ireland—does not pretend to offer any final statement on such general questions as how deeply contemporary violence can enter a poet's inner being, or how far it should be allowed to do so by the poet himself. Rather it merely poses the question by presenting poets touched by, or involved in, the situation here, and suggests how they have tried to come to terms with it in their poetry. Together with over sixty poets from Northern Ireland, I have included in this collection about ten or so from Britain, the United States and the Republic. In the main this has been because of their Ulster involvements and connections, but also in one or two cases simply because they have been moved to write about the present-day violence. Of this group of poets, I could have included many more.

The structure of the anthology is symphonic in form: the first movement serves as a prologue and contains poems which set the scene, starting off with the prehistoric days of the Bog People, and moving on to modern times, darkened with the fear that gripped the province during the Second World War and ending on a note of sudden panic after the 1969 upheaval came to a head.

The second movement centres on Derry and the smouldering fears which ultimately exploded into hatred and killing.

The third movement is the climactic section: the terror and horror of Belfast. Here the poetry is pervaded by the endless bombings, the sectarian bullets, the torture, murders, beatings and maimings.

The fourth movement contains poems dealing with the bitterness stemming from the results of violence: intimidation, frustration, the mass exodus of so many from the province, and the depression of those left behind.

I am aware that, in compiling this anthology, I might be accused of a cynical exploitation of what is, it is hoped, a transient situation. It is self-evident, however, that the violence, division and hatred that, in their present acute phase, disfigure the face of Ireland, have roots that run deeper and spread wider than the events of the past six years. Whether or not any of the poems in this anthology have the mark of greatness is for a future generation of readers to judge. But there is a time to keep silence and a time to speak; at the very least there is nothing in this anthology that did not cry out to be said, and that is surely more than enough to justify its existence.

The Wearing of the Black (Blackstaff Press,1974)

Fiacc Answers Back

Fiacc will do what
Fiacc will dare.
—Irish Song

I'VE BEEN LATELY ACCUSED OF CARRYING on a vigorous guerrilla campaign against the earnest Honest Ulster Establishment of pee-the-bed Pyjama Poets. I plead guilty. I'm hostile to what they stand for, even if I have to remind myself:

Poised with pesticide guns
and a pocketful of condoms,
a cosseted war-baby generation of
dandelion killers are
also human beings

—The Burning Garden

I know three Faber poets personally and they have in common an 'odour of sanctity'. Talking to any one of them is always like talking to a holy picture. They answer back like old-time students for the priesthood and the wee-est one of them all talks down his nose to you like a Bishop. Why is this? The answer is because getting published by Faber is canonisation in one's own lifetime. It means 'Who's like me since Leather Arse died?'

Well, what's wrong with a little puffed-up play-acting triumphalism anyway? Everything's wrong with it. Poetry and religion ought not to be kept locked away in a watertight compartment by the cosy select few. Poetry and religion belong to the people, not to some whiter than white clique, some monopoly or other, baptising themselves as the elite, pushing towards the maximum regimentation of the arts and religion because their frightened greed demands a bank-like military security. They lock themselves up in craftily wrought, but sterile, facades of versifications, like hiding in some well-furnished pub lounge. It's the life inside the shell that matters, not the bolly shell! The essence of great poetry is not the uniform it .wears but the psyche or soul that emanates from within it: recently Michael Smith translated Antonio Machado in the *Irish Times*:

> The poetic element was not the word in its phonetic value, nor its colour, nor the line, nor the complex of sensations but a deep stirring of the spirit ...

The bane of our century is the rise of the machine. This is no threat to the rural or non-urban Irish poet, who has not yet confronted such a menace, and in this way is naturally naïve. We only have two or three cities on this island but we are already feeling the violence of one or two of them. This violence does not touch, let alone rape, the rural poet's psyche, particularly if such a poet is insulated in some university shelter belt or other, or is ensconced in some cultural oasis such as the Arts Councils or the BBC etc.

The younger men, the new generation like myself, have not been able to escape the violence. They are hostile, as I am hostile, to those who ignore the facts of our experience or look upon them as something dirty to be kept at arm's length or brushed under the carpet with a sweep of the hand: 'a bother, a nuisance, gangsters, petty feuds! Worse things are happening in Chile, Portugal, or Calcutta. Look at all the car accidents! Nobody writes poems about them!'

The younger men and myself are questioning the validity of art for art's sake, the priority that art is more important than nature, that the artist is a superior being, that poetry is an art at all in the sense that it is a fine science that can be taught in schools. With the clinical automation of sex and its overall mechanical manipulation, there will naturally co-occur an attempt to regiment poetry, to make it conform to some doctrinaire or pre-conceived set ideas. Poetry has a right to wander where it will, even down the back street of a Belfast in shambles.

The moralistic stance in poetry is something more adverse to its nature than compulsive passions of bitterness or hysteria. What is called hysteria is nothing more than raising one's voice in the present-day sickroom of our depressing society.

James Simmons' arrogant stupidity is a form of communication. My bitterness, aggression, shrillness, bombast are also forms of communication. Literature isn't created by good or respectable persons who never put a foot wrong, never speak a word out of turn, never flop or goof.

The bad odour surrounding *The Wearing of the Black* is the bad odour of blood and it stinks of a society that has hopelessly degraded itself and consequently degraded those of use who have to exist in it. *The Wearing of the Black* is a mass of unpalatable truths that I have used or misused poetry to confront. This is the American dimension in me because the tradition on these two islands has never been to face up to evil within our own bounds. I am personally, at the moment, forced to face up to the violence in my own being and I'm not on my own in this. The younger men are confronting the violence within themselves and within their own society. In Simmons' words:

> Study that beggar ...
> He doesn't snigger at the facts of hell ...

Indeed, some of us not only don't snigger, we've been reduced to howling like dogs. In a strictly conformist boys' world, boys don't cry, especially schoolboys. But men have wept 'without restraint' before Gerald Dawe and I were born. If a Frank Ormsby or a James Simmons have yet to howl like dogs then let them be consoled in knowing that their tears, when they do come, will be what distinguishes the man from the boy, and they will find out, all the same, that it's not such an amusing state to be in. No masochistic pleasure can be gained from actual grief or real suffering, and unless the onlooker is a sadist or a psychopath, no pleasure can be gained from watching another suffer in this manner.

Frank Ormsby tells me that by (to him) my exploiting, (to me) confronting the current violence in my writing my 'reputation' has soared from 'relative obscurity'. Can my 'reputation' bring Gerry (Locke) McLaughlin back from the dead? Can this 'reputation' reunite me with my wife and child whom I've lost every bit as much as if I'd lost them in a war because of this pig of a place? For some of us, 'reputation', the promise of an 'immortality on paper', is only another added, if excruciating, irony.

And yet the same kind of shallow brain-ball thinking occurs in Conor Cruise O'Brien recently testifying that the poet, like the politican, is creating his work "because of his yearning for immortality, because he will not die". What ankle-sock depth! Poets die all right and some of them, like myself, within their own lifetime. What lives on is the work, not the worker. Are a few fragments of memory, a 'name' around which a myth can be invented, 'immortality'?

Poetry is a human endeavour and as I was reduced to reminding Eavan Boland on RTE at the beginning of this year: poets are people too. And they are people who know more than most that there are things that are more important than poetry, or as Graham Greene put it somewhere, that there is 'too much poetry' and maybe that's the trouble. At the end of Goethe's life, he hungered out loud, not for more poetry but for more light, that is, more truth. Which brings me to the word *honest*. Compared to truth, honesty is a secondhand virtue, a boy's trait. The boy is honest; the man is truthful. Recently, an old dear was suffering a bad case of dysentery and the home-help's wee boy of four came to pay his respects to the old lady. Upon entering the room, he announced, "I smell shit."

Advancing to the bedspread he pointed to a smoothing-iron burn: "There it is there!" And there are many examples of where honesty is honesty but it isn't the truth.

My wish for the *HU* on its 50th edition is that it stop hiding behind the word *Honest* and grow up. A first pre-requisite would be for its founder, 'Simple Simmons', to get off its back and give the 'little blighter' and all the rest of us a well-needed break from the goo that he so merrily ejects.

Honest Ulsterman, No. 50, Winter 1975

The Birth of a Black Anthology

WHEN I WAS A TEENER IN Second World War New York and had first heard snatches of Shostakovich's Seventh Syphony, the 'Leningrad', I was stirred to the core of my adolescent being and thought, ah, this is my very mood! Later in the 50s I met some Soviet students over from Moscow who knew the man himself and they told me that Shostakovich, far from being fierce, was a gentle, almost feminine, person. Last year, while I was in the process of gathering *The Wearing of the Black* together, the young American poet Terence Maxwell, staying at our house, would leave the symphony with me while he commuted by day to his teaching job in Derry ...

When the troubles first started here in the North, I began to undergo a kind of personality change which puzzled doctors, relatives and friends. I was suddenly hurtled into a nightmare world of drugs and mental hospitals. I had abruptly stopped reviewing for *Hibernia* and the editor, John Mulcahy, kept sending me notes: 'Where are you?', 'Are you living or dead?', 'Are you manning the barricades?' My very poetry was undergoing a radical change: back into the more experimental iconoclastic, anti-social mode I had first started writing in. But I was born into violence and brought up in a violent New York and I hated violence, and now, apparently, I was to die in it. (The sainted, if not noticeably intelligent medical profession had declared my depression chronic, endogenous and I would 'deteriorate rapidly'.) The wife had been invalided for two years and our little girl became frightened of going to the school just opposite the police barracks which was manned by British solidiers.

Yet even as late as 1972 I wrote, in an article on Ulster poets in *Hibernia*, that I agreed with the stance that poets shouldn't be asked to write about violence and I continued myself to sweep it under the carpet. It isn't a black and white situation, I kept telling myself and I don't want even to seem to take sides. But, bit by bit, it was inevitable that I'd become involved. My poetry was beginning to take on an angry tone and like the child in Rimbaud I could no longer stifle the four-letter words. Anxiety, guilt and an embittering fear of emasculation overwhelmed me. They were throwing petrol bombs through the windows of Catholic houses. What would I do with my wife invalided in the top room? I had to buy Brigid's First Holy Communion dress in the Lower Falls. I was caught in a skirmish and met the relatives of an altar boy who was shot dead. A bomb went off at the bottom of our street and shook the house. One explosion began to follow another and Brigid would waken screaming. Like so many others, our little world was beginning to fall apart. Catholics were being forced out of their houses in the district down the hill and Newtownabbey was declared UDA territory … (But I mustn't despair, just keep taking your anti-depressant pills!)

The wife, no longer able to cope, finally fled to the south with Brigid. I was left, emerging from drugs and forced to face the ultimate crunch of darkening reality. Sections of the story still cannot be told but I was caught up more and more in bombings and shootings and I tried, somewhat witlessly, to do volunteer work where I became an obvious target, threatened and fingered and simply had to get out or be killed. Far from being 'The Man Most Touched' as James Simmons sneeringly dubbed me in a recent *Honest Ulsterman* edition, I was more like Seamus Deane's (in his 'The Last Impact') "loneliest man/In the crowd" whose activism consisted of "You act because there is nothing you own./You live between the throwing/And the thing thrown." Rather than a militant roaming the streets of Belfast in a state of righteous anger, as one American reviewer put me down as, I wandered the haunts of my childhood in the Lower Falls and in the Markets in a state of suicidal despair.

My poetry began to take on a life of its own. Like Eliot's romanticism it was always miles ahead of wherever reality was dragging me. Desmond Egan asked for my new collection of poems on the troubles which Dolmen had turned down. Before I had to lift my head he published 300 copies in a garage and they were sold out within the year. I consented to read from it in the Peacock etc, but things became much darker in real life and when I turned to poetry at all now it was to question why I was in this hell and why did it seem so eternal?

After *Odour of Blood* was published my house began to fill with young teachers, priests, lawyers, artists and young poets. I had struck a note which convinced them I was a man of the people, involved, committed, and, above all, anti-establishment. A dreadful generation gap existed between these young men in their twenties (Simmons dubbed them the 'Hostile Generation')—and their elders. I understood them and they me. I was an outsider to my own generation and considered a distruptive force. With no doctrinaire politics (my passion was never political) I tried to warn and fob off these young fellows. Yes, I was writing out of a spirit of vengeance (but vengeance on what or whom?) "Don't invent me. I'm a Dostoyevsky man. I'll only move over and become something else!"

The Ballymurphy poet, Brendan Hamill, came to stay for a bit. He was doing a thesis on Ulster poets and the violence. We decided to edit an anthology together. I phoned Jim Gracey at Blackstaff whom I had met in a recent bomb-scare. But Blackstaff wanted the guts of the anthology within a short time and Brendan had to finish his studies at Coleraine University so I took up the project alone.

The older poets contributed without question and shared excitement and interest in it with the younger poets. The middle or more established poets, with one or two exceptions, gave me a hard time. They were afraid I was going to use them merely to write a political book. I found myself growing more and more on the side of the younger men. We had everything in common. But reality was to relentlessly scatter us: Brendan Hamill holed up in Derry finding it hard to get a teaching post, Gerry Dawe down in Galway,

Terry Maxwell back to the States, Michael Brophy going to England, Dennis Kelly to the continent and Gerry Locke McLaughlin assassinated two months ago with his brothers and my own life threatened so that I too now have to get out of the country.

The Wearing of the Black is our 'Leningrad' then. It was compiled in dark months of bitter black despair and it ended in Gerry's tragic murder. Still, from its shaping and making and final publication, I had come to learn hope from a new generation of Ulster poets concerned and committed to finding some solution to the long-standing tragedy which occasioned and perhaps even flawed the anthology—as indeed the 'Leningrad' was considered flawed and crude by some critics of its time and like the 'Leningrad', *The Wearing of the Black* was sentenced to oblivion. Yet I can say in my heart of hearts I have done what I have set out to do in this work. I have experimented and explored and have found certain healthy truths and solutions, the major one of which is social communication. I declare therefore that poetry is not only a form of social communication but the most human form that there is. In this sense and in this anthology the Ulster poet has socially contributed to his own community and perhaps at its darkest hour.

29 May 1975

Threshold No 28, 1975

Against Death
A goodbye to Norman Dugdale

IN COMPANY OF JOHN HEATH STUBBS and John Minihan (Beckett's photographer), I attended a memorial service for John Wain in Oxford. Wain had stipulated a surprise for us: in the middle of sympathetic chit-chat and endless cups of tea in marched an unashamed brass brand—the noise was naked. The band played a loud almost drag jazz seeming to horse laugh at the pretentious sobriety with which we humans react to the only surety in life, death.

In our last lunch meet I joked with Norman about the Oxford service.

Norman and I enjoyed an almost impossibly quiet friendship for twenty years. We periodically met for lunch and conversation. In a way we were fighting each our own illness. In our last meeting, not long before he died, he looked almost as terrible as I felt. He seemed to be hanging over the chair like an overcoat—so frightening we both were that the waitress was not going to serve us. To her we looked like a pair of drunks.

I joked with him: "Norman, which one of us is going to go first?"

"You Joe, you Joe!" he laughed.

I thought of my religious training in New York, where when a monk died we celebrated his death by drinking cider made from the church's ample apple trees.

Our first lunch-meeting in the 70s (a bad time in Belfast) was marred by his diabetic attack and my shot nerves. We learned in a vivid way how ill we both were and the limitations that illness imposed on us.

I thought of Padraic Colum's words to me in New York: "Accept your own limitations. Limitations are good for a poet." The Europeans understand this. In our own backyard we have only to think of the great work that was achieved by our own Stewart Parker.

Lagan Press is to be saluted for its *Collected Roy McFadden*, Robert Greacen's, which won the last *Irish Times* award, and now Norman's *Collected*.

Yes, it is sad that Norman didn't live to see the publication—the work of a lifetime—but the sadness turns into a marvel of open communal width and depth that finally testifies to another major poet who lived and worked among us, making poor beat-up Belfast a proud place to live.

Je vous salue, Norman.

Fortnight, April 1997

This piece was written to coincide with the publication of *Norman Dugdale: Collected Poems* (Lagan Press, 1997). Norman Dugdale died in 1995 during the preparation of the book.

OUR LITTLE BOAT IS TOO SMALL ...
AUTOBIOGRAPHICAL WRITINGS

Hell's Kitchen
An Autobiographical Fragment

The following is the text of a programme written and presented by Padraic Fiacc on BBC Radio Ulster. It was first broadcast on 1st June 1980, and was produced by Paul Muldoon.

[*Music: from* Antonin Dvorak's Symphony No. 5 in E minor, *op 95: and the 'Going Home' largo movement, with sound of tugs on the Hudson River*]

1959: The wife and I are in an office of the UN building in New York, looking, like miles down, at the graphic East River, the shuddering grave of call-girl and gunman. Kids, naked, used to dive from rotten dock-wood piers into the filthy grey water. My wife Nancy's criminologist girlfriend from Austria brings her gold plaits up around her head into a neat, attractive braid. I banter with her, "No, you can't make me talk. I won't talk." But she really is doing the talking. How, the other night, a young Puerto Rican had invaded their apartment and how her mother managed to talk him out of rape.

I was hurled back to 1929. New York hadn't changed very much in three decades. Money, sex (and/or violence) and politics, the trinity of its one god: Materialism. How I yearned to climb up the gangplank of our French luxury liner, the *Liberté*, and plough as quickly as we could back over the Atlantic into a (corrupt-as-it-had-ever-been) Europe! Yes, the last time I saw New York was twenty years ago in 1959, and first time I saw New York was thirty years before that in 1929.

To a child of five, the city loomed over like gold fangs, the flittering, grinning mornings, the silver penthouses, the yellow-chequered taxi-cabs, the long, widening avenues, the endless, blood-drying sun, a light that dogged your heels and made you feel naked to some half-blind god ...

[*Music: Huge chorus of 'Should Auld Acquaintance Be Forgot'*]

I said goodbye to New York, goodbye forever forever, at least seven times in thirty years. Dog to heel, I returned ever, but only when I was dragged back. The last time I saw her was because a relative had committed suicide. I live in hope that I'll never see her again. But how can you escape New York? This great vulva, this great port of entry enters you ...

> Roller-skating on the tar,
> Hitching a ride on a passing truck,
> Shooting marbles in the gutter,
>
> When they were building the cream
> Iceberg skyscraper on
> 96th Street, we
> Sailed paper boats in the red
>
> Wet cement down a long, wide
> Curb sidewalk to the drain
> By the bank facing Holy Name.
>
> The red clay smelled of sewers and
> The dead unborn foetus ...

We had a kind of childhood, or in my own case, boyhood or youth, but this was of such a complex, inexplicable nature. Materialism pushed nature itself out the door so that it came in windows, from the fire escape in the guise of a sex-fiend. Like a limp child with an earache from teething, exhausted with the heat, we hung over the fire escapes on 98th Street. At night we slept in the baseball pitches of Central Park, and still there was no air. The sand beneath our bodies was like cement dust. They were always building, building, always drilling ...

Can I forget you ever, Hudson River,
Tar and oil stained, your pollution
Shining like a ringworm that is a rainbow?

The smell of baking bread on 101st Street. I'm seven years old buying onion rolls for mother. A young girl is exposing herself at the window. I never saw the sun shine for so long. The El Dorado Twin Towers glinting in the far-off blue heat that anything green becomes in such a red humid morning haze:

How raw you are today, early years
Ingrowing, growing in through
The fracture between
The body and the mind.

I don't rightly know what the wound is
New York, you, me, us?

Some wounds don't heal
And when they don't heal, they start
To weep. They weep a kind of pus ...

[*Music: Agnus Dei from Gabriel Fauré's Requiem*]

My formative years were spent in Hell's Kitchen, the then black heart of the worst part of New York, and now my existence from that time stands out in front of me and I always want to pull a knife ...

Serving on the altar, a mass for the dead, I noticed, before the coffin was closed, the undertaker had to put make-up on the blonde model gangster's girl who died of cancer without knowing it. (The make-up was the mystery of style, the needful fictionalisation, the need in order to communicate ...) I overheard that her gangster friend tried to bribe the nuns in the hospital to mercy-kill her.

Trust comes from this city like a lash and far too early:

With Mae West or Tarzan playing in the 'Rose',
With Sylvia Sidney crying out men,
Men, only wanted the one thing

There was this dark too sunny day
Smelling of Fan-Fan Chewing Gum
When sex seemed the only trouble then ...

In this office in the UN building far above the city, twenty years on, I remember ... No, it's almost thirty years now ...

Nineteen thirty-one,
New York City over on
The West Side, the glittering Hudson River,
Top hats, summer dresses,

A childhood of sweetheart faces
In summer hats like glass plates,
The sun, shining through
Transparent green streets
With pink satin roses, the pink

Sandstone penthouses like wedding
Cakes in German Town, yes

Clean as gone to Heaven,
We were such empty children then
Later the tired faces
Bored with waiting in lines for butter
Flooded back like sea at night...

The only escape seemed the sea, the stars.

As a boy, I had Rimbaud's capacities to transform, say, the reservoir in Central Park into the raging Atlantic, but with Buck Rogers, The Benson Boys, The Lone Ranger, Flash Gordon, and Jack Armstrong, the All-American Boy, all on the radio; we might have been fated to sit in a circle and show each other our pussy willows and teapots until the West of Ireland janitor's wife screamed that there was a "school of sodomy" going on among the five-year-olds down in the basement. "Oute, out! Oute to hell. Yer early awt it!"

The white rot in the back yard where the tree died. There was this kid called Adam who stuck his penknife into the bark and flayed the wood. He and we grew up to midnight muggings. We stone-crazed city kids were bursting into birth through stone like trees or anything green. Half-buried we were in the furnace of a West Side summer, while under the pavement, the subway womb panted far from the "fiddler broadcasting seed".

Will the wound ever close
On the boy of ten
Far out in
The drowning man
Has a deep-
Rooted bad dream

Trudging to the tin
Shed for surplus
Blankets and Cod
Liver Oil knows

Mother will
Never come home
From the Box Factory

And father, back turned
Head in knees
Dead too, is still
Hanging on the Dole.

The Irish emigrant men who ran the city's transport were present-day Saint Brendans whilst they ferried you across the Styx into Hell. There were so many lost persons, like the taxi driver's wife on the top floor dying of a 'tumour'. There was something limp about her like a bad-boned child. She sneaked down the stairs one night and wasn't heard of again.

[*Music: Fauré's Pavane*]

The taxi driver had to go on living. What hunger in that seething mass "like long blue tulips against the caged-in sea"... Bernadette, who became a governess on the East Side but who, alas and alack, boiled the nappies in a kosher pot. Claude, who disappeared. I tried to find you one day but your Spanish father was crazed, was talking to the canary. You were neither black nor white but both, and that was too much for the Americanos.

[*Fade out of Fauré's Pavane*]

Dad fulfilled the American Dream and rose from a Belfast bartender to someone who owned his own grocery stores, one in

Harlem and one on Amsterdam Avenue. The blacks paid their bills, but not the Irish, and so, no sooner did he soar to the peaks than he was cut down. He lost all. We were plunged into a pit of poverty. Mother, carrying her last child, had to work in a factory near 14th Street. Blanche, our maid, had to go elsewhere. One day mother and I were called over to German Town. The cop wouldn't let me go in to see. Mother came out white-faced. "I'm glad they didn't let you go in there." Blanche committed suicide in a toilet. Mother and I wept bitterly last night:

> Drowning, I look back on summer.
> I don't know where to look for shame.
> I look back into bits.

I had become, early on, one of the Night Riders, fending off the sex-fiends on the way to school in the subway. I studied their persons in the subway:

> Vandal-broken glass faces
> Mirror the unguarded bank
> Of us money-marketed are
> Not human sacrifices any more
> To Wall Street's he-whore
> God, but dovetailing, dissolve
>
> Into a tinned tight sardine
> 'Togetherness', our dead
> Silent waiting, train-hooted,
> Shunting, not half-shrieked for ...

Mother was beginning to die. I watched one night the wind rip the gardenia corsage from her coat and scatter it down the dark street. Even in her withering sway she gave off a fragrance ...

> A stray gardenia corsage
> On the subway entrance's
> Top-step, pin scraps down
> Gum-chewed tasteless air ...

In the cinema, at the newsreels, sitting beside her, frantic with weeping at the bombing of Madrid: the frightened people running everywhich-where had wrenched her back to the Civil War in

Ireland. The strains of 'La Palmona' as she tangoed with the Italian chap on the boat as a young Belfast flapper of the Twenties now wore up to the Forties and another world war. She would lose her sons. She would lose all. Her husband plied the streets frantically for a job. She beat her hands against the wall in labour as I, the firstborn, watched and waited. She cursed New York. She cursed the whole of America. It was the end of the 30s. By the end of the 30s the American Dream had become a nightmare of reality ...

[*Music: Brutal break-in of Shostakovich's Symphony No. 7, third theme of first movement*]

The 40s in America still clung desperately to the policy of neutrality and isolation from the European conflict. But I was lucky to study in one of the high schools in New York in which students fleeing the Nazi oppression were welcomed. They had come to this school in Hell's Kitchen because it taught Latin and the humanities. The school was a somewhat old dilapidated building. One day reporters from a local, notorious tabloid infiltrated as students themselves and took photos of the wall paint peeling. The school was also noted for having an overall majority of blacks. Intimate contact with blacks gave me a sophistication undreamt of. I wrote a play in French verse: *Des Arbres Morts*—I can only remember a few lines now, but sombre enough they were:

Dans la nuit
Je suis petit
Comme l'enfant...

—and another play in Latin. Poetry poured forth, and music, and painting. I sat side by side with a Chinese student who brought words from the great ancients of his country: "all under the sky are the children of God". Here, in one school, in my most formative years, were Africa, Asia, the Middle East, and in-pouring Europeans. It was exciting and scintillating, like the last glimpse of the Hudson river as we climbed the stairs down the basement entrance to report our presence to a general teacher, in our case, a Polish lady.

All the terrible truths about Hell's Kitchen were true, but here was the other side of it, the wonderful wide scope, grass-rooted in the seemingly dead but not dead past. I dramatised Hudson's Green Mansions, drawing a jungle scene with green chalk and a blue ghostly Rima, a kind of South American female Tarzan. What liberation, what first-flush flowering! I cut a mother and child out of plaster of Paris in a cigar box with a wet penknife and another one in soap and painted it in pastel. I wrote a tone poem for the right side of the piano, using only the black keys. My girlfriend, Monique, who was black and white, filled in the bass part when she played it. In those days, if war seemed far away, the Jewish students from Rome, Paris, Berlin and Vienna brought it home to us. Refugees like Rolf Pierre Ferand and Lucien and others were my link with the Salzburg of Mozart, the Paris of Sartre, Gide, Mauriac, Verlaine, Rimbaud, Baudelaire and Racine and even the Germany of Goethe and Thomas Mann, whom I almost met through Padraic Colum. Anybody could step out of a taxi or car and be noticed browsing in an antique shop downtown: Rachmaninov, Garbo ...

One teacher in particular took over the uncouth slum adolescent and transformed him into an incurable aspiring poet. Louis Stark forbade me to read Yeats any longer. Mother and I assimilated our Yeats with Christian Brother wine at night. Dad finally got a job as a subway clerk. I helped him with fractions and maths until he passed his civil service exams.

[*Music: Shostakovich's Seventh*]

This subway became his life. He could drink with men from the same part of Ireland as himself, and, under the sagacious dominance of Mike Quill, the Irish Catholic communist as he was dubbed, the subway workers developed into one of the strongest unions in New York. But if our days of poverty were nearing something of an easement, the new threat was war. It finally broke with Pearl Harbour. The attempt to black out New York was a failure. We all kept our lights on. I watched younger brothers volunteer for the Navy and the youngest one dance on the bed with rage and run away to Philadelphia until he got permission to enlist. I watched fellow students throw their books on the floor and dance on them. Art and studies were thrown out the window

... The great galleries on the East Side filled with the treasures of Paris and Rome. I stood with Louis Stark and gaped with tears at a load of Picasso's Blue Period and Rembrandt's 'Old Woman Cutting Her Nails'.

[*Music: Manuel de Falla's 'Nights in the Gardens of Spain'*]

Music became, in Verlaine's words, "first and foremost". I couldn't get enough of Shostakovich and the central European composers: Dvorak, Janacek, Zoltan Kodaly, the other Russians, and, of course, the Spanish Albeniz, Enrique Granados and Manuel de Falla. But my health broke. At least I could finish my education in the upstate New York seminary, even if I no longer had a calling to the priesthood. There I was to meet the real honest-to-God American after years of Europeans in New York. But the world of the seminary, like the American world of the 50s, was the world of a chicken coop; whatever frightened the chickens was evil and I, of course, was a born frightener of chickens, a kind of witless fox ...

My hatred for America increased to the ratio that I watched my mother wither. One night, with Dad drunk pounding his finger on a treble piano key, I wrenched mother downtown with an invitation card from Padraic Colum to the New York branch of the Irish Academy of Arts and Letters. Padraic was in a bad state. One of his lecturers had failed to show up. Yes, I said, I knew about painting and would stand in. Mother had never seen this part. I blathered on in French as well as English. James Johnson Sweeney had just finished a talk on the late Paul Klee, who died in 1940. I hit Sweeney with the new 'ism' in Paris, *surnaturalisme*, and caused a furore. Padraic went over to Mother:

"Do you know that your son is a genius?"

"Yes."

"Well, make it hard for him. The eagle builds its nest of stones and cut glass."

"I don't know how much harder," she snapped back, "I could make it for him."

I returned to Belfast in 1946. When I raced up the gangplank of the Swedish liner, the *Grispholm*, I knew I'd never see mother again. I took to the other end of the boat and wouldn't wave goodbye to the Statue of Liberty. I had hoped never to return.

What was this dreadful wound New York inflicted on us, or was it simply the twentieth century?

[*Music: Maurice Ravel's 'Pavane for a Dead Infanta'*]

Dad could never face that mother was ill or dying. When she did die I had to return from Belfast to New York in the Fifties. New York had changed. It was now an American city. The President of the United States was a world war general, and in the throes of militaristic paranoia, even he was subject to the witch-hunts that went on at that time. Two sorts of individuals threatened the Military Mind, 'perverts' and 'commies'. The red was under the bed and, in their eyes, probably with another red.

I renounced my American citizenship in Belfast in 1948 and had to emigrate back to our father. I watched him one day as he staggered home from the subway. He had a few on him and because he was singing 'The Red Flag' a cop hit him over the head with his night-stick. I ran across the avenue and rescued him from the cop.

The very meaning of the phrase 'Hell's Kitchen' was eating into my mind. I recalled the day I tried to get a part-time job after school. It was a downtown eating place and I had to stir this immense cauldron in the kitchen. I fainted and almost fell into the cauldron. "Who the hell sent you?" the manager yelled. "The customers almost had you with the soup."

When I raced up the TWA stairs to the plane in 1956, I had hoped never to see New York again, but in 1958 I had to return with the wife, and dying brother. I didn't look back at New York as I raced up after the wife to our French luxury liner. I haven't looked back since. I'm keeping my fingers crossed.

New York Night

Hailing a cab
I black out on tar
Am slapped back awake
By cop time nagging
'Do you know who you are?'

Stupid with justice and admiration
Youth old at Grand Central Station
Light pouring down from steel beams
In this subway still dares dreams?

Bags black porters carry to
A cab set me in mind of you
Bad companions of priggish vanity
Who set me in mind of me...

Will it ever be different?
Horizons fawned at of male and girl
For a tiny tip, a bob twirl
Up, flip down, crown or tails?

Tails when the gamble is spent
From cold Belfast to these hell-gales.
Emerging from this air-conditioned house
Of ill fame, I am this man, that mouse.

But what took the wind out of my sails?

[*Music: Dvorak's New World Symphony. Sound of tugs on the Hudson River*]

Atlantic Crossing
An Autobiographical Fragment

The following is the text of a programme written and presented by Padraic Fiacc on BBC Radio Ulster. It was produced by Paul Muldoon.

[*Music: 'Peter Grimes' 1st Interlude, 'Dawn'—played against scene of sound of roaring car motor, wind whistling round speeding car*]

1981: Zoom, Zoom, Zoom! If there are speed limits in Northern Ireland there are none in West Germany. Carl, the camera-man is at the wheel. Cars bore him because he is a licensed air pilot. We are flying through the two-way lanes of Donegal that should be one-way lanes. I howl, without hope, "Not another scene at Yeats' grave, Carl?"

"No, Joe, the roads to Sligo are flooded."

We seem less than an hour out of Belfast before George, the film producer from Paris, wakens in the front seat and announces in German: "We stop here." Here is somewhere on Bloody Foreland. I smell the Atlantic. I hear the Atlantic crawling up the cliff face and crashing down through the ancient black stones and autumn coloured trees. But I am afraid to look. The other two German film workers, Rolf and Holger, announce, "We don't want you to catch cold, Joe" and summarily pack me back into the Swedish car that is still panting for breath and is still beeping for danger.

I forgot how perfect the Germans are. Obviously they have done their homework on my mad existence. They know precisely where to place you to make you emote. Yesterday under the hovering military helicopter at a young poet friend's grave and yes, I'll howl.

Today, the Atlantic; that ocean which James Joyce, in alluding to us Irish emigrants, dubbed "an abyss of tears". It must be twenty years since I last set eyes on its desolate foaming-at-the-teeth in a north east wind ...

[*Music: Scott's Journey to Antartica. FX: Opening sea and ice-crash sounds*]

Endless pre-jet transoceanic liners, dreaming of home and no home, endless 'slow boats to China'.

[*Music: Berg's Symphony No. 3. Fade up music. Opening bars of the second movement quietly prolonged in background until poem reading ends*]

As children in the Belfast of the 20s we used to hang over the rails of the Queen's Bridge with our grandfather and watch the big boats coming in:

> Here on damp docks when it is smell of rum
> Fogs coming round rotten wood
> Of men in caps cursing I have seen
> The boats for one moment come
> In from far sea as such should
> And not near enough to wharf for lean
> Plank to the side to soar in verve
> But send their tenders in with such reserve
>
> That you'd be foundered here. O sea waves roar.
> The sleet deeps down and in and at the bone and oh
> On the damp docks I stand at the Sky's Door
> Quivering but dispassionate
> Watching the boats come and go
> Until the teeth are taut and set.

"George, this is murder," I yell. "I'm not my own stunt man. This wind'd blow the arse off you. This place isn't called Bloody Foreland for nothing!"

"Joe, it's your own country!"

Rolf already has his earphones on and Holger is running somewhere with the lead. Carl is on hands and knees taking extra-curricular shots and I am ordered by Rolf in stiff English, "Say something please!"

I hear my own voice thunder against the roar of the Atlantic:

Fish of the sea my work is for you.
I made this poem for a thing to do
That it may tickle a salmon throat
That an empty seashell ear
Near its bell-tone note ...

Endless waiting again in preparation for the next scene and I begin to drift back: 1929. Childhood. Mother.

[*Music: Ravel's Sonata in G Major—opening bars prolonged to fade*]

I remember everything from childhood. East Street in the Markets. How I used to run to this or that mill girl, coming home in the rain, hoping she were mother: Daisy Fox who always had a bun with a crystal sugar lump on the top, Kitty McKnight who nursed me, Aunt Mary like someone eternal. But Mother? Mother was always somewhere else, someone else, giving suck to my younger brother, Rory, on the sands of the Holy Woods in Bangor, her long black hair streaming in the bleak wind from the Irish Sea. She would come in at night and shower you with kisses, but you could tell by her perfume that she was going out and about 'away down the town'. I only really met Mother on the boat. We were always going to America, us kids, to meet our 'Daddy Ben', as if for the first time, and we were told not to say we'd wash our 'hawns' any more, but wash our 'hens'. And we musn't say 'Och-aye' any more, only 'OK, OK, OK.'

How we grew to hate his America before we even landed there. We were going on the Big Boat, the *Antonia* come in from Liverpool. We would never see Gran'Da again or the cobbles of East Street. America seemed a kind of death to us and the boat was our coffin.

[*Music: Shostakovich's 9th Symphony—opening bars of the 4th Movement*]

Mother had three boyfriends on the *Antonia*: the Italian who taught her to tango, the English chap who argued with her about the Irish Civil War and a huge Russian Orthodox priest who always made her look like a sparrow. These fellows plied us kids with endless sweets, toys, balloons and enamel-painted rubber balls in a blatant effort to buy their way through to Mother.

I was often dumped on the Russian who was called Alexander and who had a long beard that frightened everybody. He and I constantly played Soldiers on the second-class deck. Persons sipping their morning ox-tea on the deck chairs laughed at us.

[*Puckish music from Kodaly's Hary Hanos*]

One morning I dug my heels in. "If you don't want to play Soldiers, Josef, what do you want to play?"

"Dominoes in the Dining Room."

"Because your Mama is dancing in the Dining Room? Maybe, when we go to America, no more dancing."

[*Music: Dark opening bars of Ravel's Heure Espanol*]

The Russian had a flattering way of telling you grown-up truths as if you too were a grown-up.

[*Jazz music from Ravel's Sonata in G Major*]

The *Antonia* was a small Cunard liner plying the very waters that the *Titanic* a decade or so ago sank in. It was the end of the 20s and people were almost hysterically hot in pursuit of pleasure. Indeed, when we landed in New York, Mother and us kids were still flushed with the games, parties, singing and dancing, and when Dad, who took the wrong train, didn't meet us on landing, we were all ready to get back on the boat again. Our first stop was Canada and it seemed a desolate forbidden place:

Punting into Nova Scotia
Nineteen and Twenty-nine, girl
Mother's delph face *creaks*, cracks ...
(I'm breaking in two myself at five!)

Goodnight all from the beginning.
Goodbye 'cobblestones' but
A back street womb wall won't
Let me climb out over it.

We stare at the brick Hal
-ifax sky. A yellow wolf cold
Sits on the leaden Atlantic,
A new world horizon ... Old

Morning you are the night of life:
The Russian Orthodox priest who
Has a beard, is the Bogeyman
Will put me in his bag

Is 'America' the Bury Hole he'll
Put us in IF WE CRY?
On the tiny (it stops tangoing)
'transoceanic motor-ship'

Creaks, I cling hard tight, hard onto
A Belfast flapper's strong
Wrist bone. Her stiff new
Red leather rain-coat *creaks* ...

[*Music: Respighi's Pines of Rome—Pines Near A Catacomb*]

1946: Fifteen or so years later: the Holland Tunnel to New Jersey subway train from Manhattan. My American brother, Peter, is helping me with my bags of books as we speed under the Hudson River. My Irish brothers and father donated their pay-packets to ship me back to Ireland. They don't say goodbye. Mother is ill, we shake hands on the slum apartment's brown-stone stoop. She uses words from a war song of the time: "We'll meet again." We both know she's lying.

I'm happy to board the Swedish boat, the *Grispholm*. It is the first boat back to Europe after the war. The crew are 'angels of mercy', the captain is a 'saint'. During the Second World War they ferried refugees from the Occupation into neutral countries.

The North Atlantic is still dangerously mined waters so that the ship has to veer south and will take nine days to reach Ireland.

[*Music: Debussy's La Mer; Play of the Waves*]

The more we veer south the more incredible the mood of the Atlantic: a warm winter wind, then mild, quiet for a change, water frothing deep silent ink greens and blues and unbelievable pockets of coral and gold. As dark falls the old man from the West of Ireland and myself stroll the deck casually. He is puffing away at his clay pipe, belittling his own son whom he is convinced will have taken over the whole of his 'fa-rr-im' in Connemara. He answers his own question, "Why are you frowning?" with "It's them old books and papers you have. They are worrying your brain. It would be a good idea if you lifted the whole parcel of them and pitched them into the sea."

All at once the waters turn up a pink and orange foam. A huge north moon breaks from ebony clouds and rises more upwards. The old man shouts with delight, "Tan yall-iach ere et in air."

"What is that you said in Irish?" I asked.

"I was saying that the moon is in the air."

The *Grispholm* is made up of French and Irish passengers both of whom, like the Swedish crew, retain their own identity. Who but the French would refuse to attend deck drill? Who but the Irish would fail to realise how heavily mined the waters are? We are returning home to our separate identities. But is identity a dream?

Five years later: 1952: Another boat, the *Georgic.*

[*Music: Shostakovich's Symphony No 5—4th Movement; Opening and ending played quietly against voice*]

Identity? I throw my Identity Card into the Atlantic. I'm tired of restrictions and the endless hangovers from the austerities and deprivations of war. Our stateroom is in the hold of the ship. For the first time I taste the grim heroism of the poor Irish emigrant children, and children of the children of the Famine: always travelling steerage. The *Georgic* is a battleship reconverted into a liner. English engineers in our cabin recall stories of the boat when in action. I'm turned off war and won't listen. I want to forget everything now. I'm tired of Ireland's Wrong, tired of the suffering of my own people, the Irish. [*Music of tin whistle playing The Coolin*]

But am I Irish? Is Belfast Ireland? I don't know. Mother's dead and I am emigrating back to our father.

Seawave wings cat-claw
the glare of gale-swept dawn
Light-house drawn
Crash and stiffen

Feet-up from wing-torn
Clench their feet
In infant frown
In picture of Sea Man

Who up and down
Sea mountain moans
The thole of dreaming clay ...

Poor boy, burning with envy
And hatred, God help me, I
Do not, must not know
The way, I must forget.

Five years in a post-war Belfast smouldering in bombed-out ruins, fuel shortages, clothes and food rationed and now work. I hated the *Georgic* and stayed in the stateroom with the English engineers. I felt I could never say goodbye to an Ireland I never said hello to.

[*Music: Sibelius' Lemminkainen's Homeward Journey*]

Beckett calls a poem a prayer. I prayed desperately in my poems to beat the hangover of an almost inner poverty:

"Moon pulls at wool of the tide
Light to the shore side ...
I have stars in my skull."

I lied and lied again:

Home ever a new one when
Sinking into sand
Stormy changes are lightsome ...

1956: TWA
[*Roar of plane motor, pre-jet air-liner*]

Four more lost years, this time in the slums of upper west-side

Manhattan, hack typing jobs in the Garment district and Wall Street. Suddenly a streak of good luck. I'm going to return to Ireland again. I'm marrying the Princess Nancy. Nancy? Nancy has her own problems. For a starter am I not the Mole in the bedtime horror story for children: the Mole who brings the Princess to live in the Bury Hole he is born in? And home? Is Ireland 'home'?

Flying east to air, I know
Tomorrow, all this blown
Up nest of paper flower
Letters will be only
A toy of the wind, so

Not in tune with time
And deaf as the blind can hear
The drowning beast behind
The iron bar
sink
Back down in
To an island, wild
And icon-black, I do
Not believe even
Ireland is home.

[*Music of tin whistle playing Irish Emigrant Song*]

Hardly anybody on the plane. The co-pilot taking a breather from the cockpit controls, sits with me: "Are you afraid of the plane? Is this your first plane trip?" Hurtling in this huge box over a cloud-shrouded night Atlantic, what a traitor and scab I feel not to have taken the boat back.

[*Music of tin whistle playing 'Johnny, I Hardly Knew Ye'*]

What is this depth of separation from dream into reality? Mind-doctors conclude that only a child of one month can endure the depression of being delivered out of the womb. Our generation, almost as old as this century has been voided from a womb-culture into a bomb-culture: 20th century schizophrenia in which the individual is not split in two, but, torn asunder, exploded and disintegrated into fragments:

Airpockety man
Joe the Eskimo
Student in Moscow
Heart-feared of the plane.

Heavy fog over the Shannon and the pilot is forced to circle for
what seems like hours and then:

Flying back down
To edges of day

Root-wandering with
Fever, we

Reach outside the womb.

How black it is
Against the ice

Without stars
Without tears ...

A long stretch
Of after this

Our sad shelters
Hungering by the shore!

I wish my troubles were
This zooming like a hare

On past out
Of the rat

In the burrow thought

Is a rotten sailor when
It comes down to

A spoonful of love
Would do

Splinters of children

[*Music: Sleepers Awake (Wachet Auf) Piano or Orchestra Version*]

1958: Another death in the family wrenches us back to America, this time a suicide. Nancy and I board the French boat, the *Flandre*, at 10pm in Southampton.

I had to have contretemps with a person in uniform in an effort to get Nancy a vase for her flowers. All night long she's lonely for Ireland, for our little cul-de-sac in Glengormley, the street of cherry trees, the gardens. We wake up seasick and both miss breakfast. The priestlike old steward brings fruit and orders 'no liquids' in French.

The French are in rotten form and refuse to speak English. I feel sorry for the old steward when Nancy turns on him in her fluent French.

This is a dangerous voyage. The sea is very rough. Thursday we're both still seasick but the deck drill is somehow invigorating. The old steward insists (in French of course) that we get up and walk about, that it's going to be a rough passage, that it's a small boat. Something about Paris having trouble with the franc because of the Algerian situation, and right enough, a perfectly dreadful night follows. The North Atlantic, like us humans, seems to wait for nightfall before it behaves at its very worst.

[*Antarctic by Vaughan Williams, ice and sea crash noises*]

We are in the very eye of the Autumn hurricane. The French Captain is obliged to turn off the engine of the boat.

"Is this the way it always is at sea?" Nancy asks.

"Yes, yes," I lie. "Yes, Nancy, it is."

By some miracle lies work: she collapses into sleep whilst I lie awake and sweat and pray.

Friday morning we crawl to deck like two living corpses. Everybody and everything on board is in a state of jitters. In the afternoon the Soviet film *Where Swans Pass* is interrupted by the deck-drill horn going off by mistake. In the middle of it all I write a poem entitled 'Storm At Sea'. At this time the idea that I could ever lose Nancy is beyond comprehension.

"Next time," Nancy orders as we pack for landing—"Next time, we take the plane!"

Several months later I talk her into taking the boat, but "a bigger boat this time and if you want to travel French, there is the

Liberté." In a weak moment she agrees. So in 1959, glad to get out of a perfectly breathless New York we board the *Liberté.* Lunch at noon, some pink gins and the film *Mon Oncle.* We're smoking too many *Trends.* Too many flowers give us hayfever and there is too much red champagne. Nancy becomes moody and exhausted. At night we make love rather too desperately in an effort to unwind.

Next day we miss breakfast again and the Basque steward brings toast and coffee. A sign or two that we are jadedly sick of boats; that we avoid deck drills, hide in the deck chair and chew at each other.

"It's deeper than the French dinner wine," Nancy bites back. "You lied to me on the *Flandre.* I hate the Atlantic ocean. I'm afraid of it now."

"We're going home to Glengormley and it won't be long." I try to lure her back into calm.

[*Music: The Blue Hills of Antrim*]

Nancy is ill and tired after another perfectly dreadful night of rolling. The Atlantic is very rough. "You lied to me," she shines. "You said it was a question of the size of the boat!" The Basque steward encouraged us to bed in the cabin early, and yes, that we should opt out of the Captain-giving Gala Night.

The whole labour of going on existing after another night of storm seems to centre on tipping the steward, the shoe man, the deck-chair stewards and the waiters. Tuesday we land in Plymouth about seven in the morning. England never looked more green, more Irish. Have we finally escaped the yellow grass of America, the yellow trees and the yellow-faced children?

[*Music: Gustav Holst's St. Paul's Suite*]

It's half a century later now and I'm an old man:

The longing eyes of the heart are blind it seems
Darkness here, there are strange things which keep
A mist on beauty that the soul would seek.
The oceans heave between us and our dreams.

[*Mood music from Vaughan Williams' 5th Symphony*]

George prises open the door of the car. "Come on, Joe, you agreed to read your poem 'Storm at Sea'."

1981 again.

George awakens me from dark thoughts:

"Joe, we do some more takes of the same scene. Do you have to wear your glasses? Do you have to read your poems from the book? Try to keep the book out of sight. Come on Joe, one more, 'Storm at Sea'."

"I'm cold George, I'm old now—and this arsehole of a place!"

"Joe, it's our own country!"

The Place, a cliff edge on the North Atlantic, the Time, listening to George's Countdown. Then I out-roar the Atlantic's roar and yell out the poem 'Storm at Sea'.

Storm at Sea

Twice this threatening morning
A stranger stood
In your eyes murderously
Deflecting
Each one half from the other.

Would that home could be reached
(Howsoever far!)
That the great clot of wind
Sore with black cloud
Could be leeched
Dry of black blood!

Behind us the fierce glower of dark water.
Before us jigging deckwood.

The mountain wave
Lifts a slanting black wall
Darkening our little boat.

Our little boat is too small.

The Belfast Fifties

DECADES INTERLAP ONE INTO THE OTHER. After the Second World War ended, rationing, conscription and a host of other hardships went on up to the fifties. The fifties were born in a kind of natal depression, if born at all; it was more like a false labour. We all felt we needed a rest because we were too tired to even unwind. Even an intellectual lull was in order.

Certainly everything began to change and people trapped by events were on the move again. W.R. Rodgers like Louis MacNeice before him was somehow sucked into the London BBC. John Hewitt was literally sent to Coventry. Robert Greacen set up home in London, seldom returning to Belfast, but as a compulsive letter writer he might never have left us, and with my mother dying in New York City I had to return to America for a couple of years.

John Boyd had the good luck to stay in the Belfast BBC where his contribution to Irish and local culture was immense. Roy McFadden and Michael McLaverty remained in Belfast, also in their own well-needed posts. Roy McFadden didn't print much in the fifties. He was like a bad boy holding his breath for badness.

With the return home of the American Military, who, let's face it, jazzed up the dull Belfast scene quite a bit, of all trades, the book trade noticeably diminished. But why? Roy McFadden explained to me that people during the war years read more books, soldiers included, on trains and boats or in any form of travel, out of the boredom of existentially waiting and even for a form of escapism.

The Ulster Literary Establishment at that time consisted of John Hewitt, Roy McFadden, Robert Greacen, John Boyd and Michael McLaverty. There were others of course, e.g. W.R. Rodgers's second published poetry collection, *Europa and the Bull*, came out in 1952, a surprise from Bertie as we called him and Joseph Tomelty's novel, *The Apprentice*, autobiographical in the half fictional style of, say, our present-day Sam McAughtry and as full of bittersweet fun and sharp fettle, appeared. His plays, short stories and radio serial, *The McCooeys*, were a wild uplift and a sane and healthy mirror to us mad Fenians and Prods living together and laughing at ourselves and our own so serious taboos. St John Ervine gave us more plays: *My Brother Tom* (1952) and *Esperanza* (1957) followed by *The Cards of the Gambler* (1953), *Honey Seems Bitter* (1954) and *There Was an Ancient House* (1955). John Montague (alias 'Jack the Taig') made his debut with a first book of poems appearing in Dublin in 1958: *Poisoned Lands*. It was well named. Benedict Kiely went into full spate with *Call for a Miracle* (1950).

Also published in the fifties was Sam Hanna Bell's classic masterpiece *December Bride*, brought out in 1951. Janet McNeill's novels were being worked on starting off as radio plays first, and John Irvine's verse translations of the French poet, Rosand, were already backed up by the French embassy in London. Roy McFadden's chilling 'Elegy for the Dead of the *Princess Victoria*' came out in 1953. And you can be sure the fabulous and elusive Harbinson (to me the Marcel Proust of Belfast) was already engaged in his own *Remembrance of Things Past*, the first volume of which was published in 1960. The prolific novelist Belfast man Brian Moore was also plotting his own impressive array of novels with his first and great success, *The Lonely Passion of Judith Hearne* (1955). To my mind that is his greatest work which will always testify to the depression found here in the North of Ireland at that time.

In the Cork-based *Poetry Ireland*, edited by David Marcus, John Hewitt was made guest editor for an Ulster edition. To my surprise he wrote that he found my poems 'disconcerting' because of my use of archaic Gaelic words such as 'wind of the shee', 'leifer' and even possible neologisms like 'chaunt-rann' etc. Still an adolescent in my early twenties I fobbed Hewitt off (whom I nicknamed 'Johnny Hoot') when I wasn't calling him a pompous, bumptious eerie-wig. It was just a nice start for the nasty tune I was in in the fififties and very suitable to my abandoning the Anglo-Irish idiom Padraic Colum got me hooked on in the beginning, a style Edna Longley likened to a kind of brogue. But I took perverse pleasure in any form of criticism. After all what did I really achieve?   I was less than three years in Ireland when Patrick Kavanagh took a swipe at me in one of the Sundays. I certainly had no collection published. Actually less than ten poems published in one or two Irish periodicals and one in what Kavanagh called 'that little box in the *Irish Times*'. Five of these appeared in a New York anthology, *New Irish Poems*, which came out in 1948, an anthology by the way that Sam Beckett had sent his poems to only to have them rejected as 'not Irish enough'.

Another recollection. Michael McLaverty dragged me to a PEN meeting ostensibly to introduce me to Hewitt. It was, if I can recall rightly, in memoriam of the death of Forrest Reid. Larne-born poet, George Buchanan, seemed to be in the act of reading the appreciation. The PEN meeting was being held in the then Union Hotel in the back of City Hall. The hotel was bivouaced by American troops during the war years. At that time I worked as Night Porter in the dump. When the old day porter came over to serve us (tea, what else?) he nearly had a stroke when he found that he was serving myself. Before we were all drenched or scalded I had to rise from the chair to hold his hands together to steady cup and saucer.

Before we entered this 'Establishment', a personage was pacing up and down the very steps it was my duty as Night Porter to wash and water along with the two huge plants.

"Who," I asked McLaverty, "is that odd looking bird?"

"Och Padraic, that's Roy McFadden, one of Ireland's greatest younger poets."

"What's wrong with 'im that he's pacing up and down 'em steps like that?"

"Och Padraic, he might be having girlfriend trouble … "

Next time I was jostled into meeting the great John Hewitt. I hated him at first sight. Full fed he was posing as the Lion of Judah between two huge palm plants. There was something about his wee blond pencil mustache ...

McLaverty tried to introduce us: "This is Padraic Fiacc, John"; to which the reply was an actual grunt. It was only that Michael is always a person of great breeding ... but it was on the tip of my tongue to say, "You can expect nothing from a pig but a grunt."

May Morton, who may or may not have witnessed this scene, came over to me and said all the wrong things such as , 'someday when you yourself come out in hardback you can join the PEN'. I tugged at McLaverty's sleeve, "Michael, would you mind if I run? Me old auntie in the Markets is expecting me to do her a message."

"Not at all, Padraic. I understand."

In the late fifties, when John became editor of Mary O'Malley's *Threshold*, Hewitt wrote from Coventry asking for some of my poems. I sent him a rather longish one in homage to Padraic Colum which to my delight he immediately published. After that we became the best of friends and when he returned to Belfast I often visited his home in Stockman's Lane where his wife, Roberta (we called her Ruby) made me these beautiful meals. I dedicated 'Jackdaw' to Hewitt because of his love for the Glens of Antrim and later on he in return dedicated his most favourite poem 'The Scar' to me. Not that our relationship became a bowl of cherries. There were some stormy in between times. Just before he died we both attended a reading by the Scottish Gallic poet, Sorley McLean. Sorley and I toured Ireland together back in the seventies and we also read together in Canada. We had a way of our own together. He would joke and heckle me if he was in the audience and I would do the same to him when he was on stage. But in tied-up-in-knots Belfast where Poetry Readings are like being in church I was escorted to the door by none other than Lord Longley. Hewitt was so angry with me his last words to me before he died were, "You need a good kick in the arse and I'm the boy to do it."

I wasn't introduced to Roy McFadden until the seventies in Michael McLaverty's home where I was also introduced to Seamus Heaney. Apart from the same age group I found that I had a lot in common with Roy. What the fifties did for him was to help him consolidate his whole body of work up to that time and helped him to finally determine that he wasn't an Irish or Regional poet but a

Twentieth-Century Belfast man. Like myself he resents the academics who corner poetry into the university sausage machines. When *Rann*, which he edited, folded he took a rest and went through a 50s lull.

And just when everybody got tired and started to peter out, guess who came along and jazzed up the scene? I returned from New York in 1956 and at the end of that year my wife Nancy said that she read about the AE Prize in the *Irish Times* and why didn't I enter for it?

"Nancy dear, this is Ireland but Belfast isn't in Ireland; it's somewhere in New England. And I was brought up and educated in New York."

"Yes, but you were born in Ireland; you're Irish. You're just making blocks. What have you got to lose?"

She got round me and didn't I win it! The heartburning in Dublin was terrific.

The other shock of the fifties was the birth of a certain young poet called Paul Balloon, I mean wee Paul Muldoon.

Gown Literary Supplement, Autumn/Winter 1989

Lives of a Student
New York in the 40s

ROLF-PIERRE AND YOU ARE STROLLING up from West Side 59th Street under the darkness of the elms (then once Columbus Avenue) to Columbus Circle. He covers up his ears with small fur-gloved hands.

"What's wrong Rolf-Pierre?"

"That odious schreiking over the microphones, the very way it was when the Germans entered Paris."

"Poor dear Rolf-Pierre! You're in neutral America now. The war will end soon. There will come a day when your beloved Paris will be free again."

(You squirm and whine as you overhear your own silken Manhattan voice).

We quicken our steps to get away from the mad orators, mouthing and snorting about Communism or Fascism or whatever other 'ism' gets up their noses or cocks or asses.

"In my part of Ireland," you declare, "the trouble is always about religion but here in America it's always politics—politics: the American religion."

(Your voice seems to reach a new high pitch to the ratio that you begin to argue with this blond French Jewish student refugee).

We both try to get off the World War bit, harkening back to our usual conversation—arts and letters.

The aesthetic argument comes to a head when we reach the Natural History Museum.

"So you haven't started a journal yet?" (He tries not to use a scolding tone.)

You reply: "I would only put into a journal what I should be putting into a poem; poetry clothes the nakedly personal thing; poetry is a fig leaf. When I write prose it seems to be the same thing as exposing yourself in public."

"No, no, I don't mean that kind of journal. Indeed keep the personal for your poetry. A journal of books that you have read— when you read them where and how they contributed to your own work—your own painting and paintings you have seen, music you have heard, places you have travelled to, the influences of other artists, and so on ..."

As we stroll from the Uptown 80s into the 90s (another muffled-tone scolding!).

"Here we are again, passing Padraic Colum's apartment house and you refuse to take your hands and go forth to meet the old fellow!"

"Louis Stark warned me about going near Colum at all. He said, 'Older poets are often jealous of younger ones ...' (My voice is almost soprano now!)

"How you block your own self!" (Rolf-Pierre is really angry!) "Do the thing. It is always better to do the thing and then it is done. For the poet or artist the *fait accompli* is a must. Do the thing in stealth, even out of spite or sexual antics. Let it be for whatever bad or good reason. But do it. Act. Act."

"OK, Rolf-Pierre, I'll make a compromise with you. I'll start a journal this very night, the kind of journal you suggested but as for Padraic Colum I'm sure he and I will eventually meet in a casual, natural way—one thing at a time."

***

April 15, 1941
Turned seventeen today. Not even one collection published! I destroy more than I write!

***

April 16, 1941

News pouring in, that last night, Belfast was bombed by the Germans. Mother and I felled and worried about aunt Mary and grandfather. They say that there are a thousand dead. Mother crying so hard at night. I can't comfort her in no single way.

***

Letter from an American Soldier I meet in the Russian Uniate Church on Mulberry Street. He is naming his tank Brian after my poem on King Brian. He writes that he thinks my poetry is 'tantalising'. How did he get the letter to me if he is at the battle ground?

***

Mother read my verse play, 'The Poet and The Urn', on the Dublin Rising—it was more on the following Civil War than the actual rising.

"Your father and I don't like it. It doesn't suit you—it's not you. And it certainly isn't the story as it was in our day. You've put the whole thing down as an absolute failure simply because of the Civil War." (One more masterpiece I have to destroy!)

Rolf-Pierre at me again: "Your interest in painting and music is commendable and doubtlessly informs and enriches your poetry as indeed your attempt at drama and the novel—but you are essentially a poet."

"But not even a good poet," I wail. The head of the English Department gives me the prize for 'The Swan of Lough Areema' (the lough which disappears) which is quite a feat (in chaunt royal no less).

Her words are backhanded: "It's too long and it's not you. You are at your best in your short pieces." (Why doesn't she go the whole hog and add "which we are all capable.")

Spent the summer holidays setting 'The Poet and The Urn' to music (for piano right hand of course—changed the title to 'The Black Stranger'—used only Irish themes in C or D sharp or B flat).

But what really perturbed my experimentation—the music teacher was horrified at my misuse of chords (right enough my chords are definitely not my forte). In one not very valiant attempt at playing it on his own piano, he hurls the whole opus at my head and right in front of the whole class!

Well, is this to be one more failure? Must I abandon and destroy 'The Black Stranger'? Together with other plays written in that hateful language, English. It's not a lucky language. If I vow to write only in French or Latin ...

I promised Rolf-Pierre not to put anything personal in these notes but one of my younger brothers seizes a pencil sketch of a male nude (sideways and showing all that belongs to him) and shows it to mother. I can always count on mother's greatness to shine through her bitter sadness like a star through dark clay.

Sensing my absolute and utter shame she turned on my younger brother: "You should learn to mind your own rotten business."

All the same I sense that mother is worried about my recurrent interest in sex. Looking at the ink sketch I made of Saint Theresa of Avila with the prominent breasts I gave her—she bursts out, "What do you know about a woman's body?"

Her stateroom from the 20s English girl friend B speaks up. "Annie, he's a genius."

Well maybe I'm not an angel, I'm not God!

Managed to finish the Latin play about Nero, *Taciturnitas*. Our Jewish Latin Professor Maidman was fascinated by it, "Where did you get such a beautiful soul?" And then something I didn't catch about something Thomas Mann said about, "that darling of the Gods—Goethe".

Can't get half of what he's saying to me because of that black girl we call Bubbles.

Even as Mr. Maidman and I are talking she goes up to the blackboard where his name, Maidman, is written. She erases the 'i' in his name so that it spells 'madman'. Mr. Maidman is furious beyond words. Not content with this, Bubbles, who sits directly behind me, snips at my hair with her manicure scissors.

"Bubbles," I squeal, "that really hurts!" She is already a blonde black girl. But she wants to dye her hair, "the same colour as yours, sugar!"

We couldn't get through Caesar's wars—for which I was indebted to her. She really hates Mr. Maidman. He had to order her out of the class again. She is called Bubbles because of the ghastly noises she can make with blowing bubble gum.

"Get out of my class. I do not allow persons chewing gum in my class."

She takes the long way round going out of the classroom. We are all petrified with tension and fear. And just when you'd think, "This is it," she takes the long way back round again to pick up a book in her desk.

When she gets to the door she slams it with such ferocity it nearly falls off its hinge. Mr. Maidman orders: "Bring her back!" Bubbles comes back and goes to her seat.

Mr. Maidman rises very slowly to announce, "It is I who is leaving this classroom!"

***

Founded the 'Literary Workshop'.

Horror to hear that Angel, the black girl who played in your *Midnight on the Causeway* killed herself because she was pregnant.

Lucien from Vienna and the Italian girl, Julia, who played Rima in your attempt at Hudson's *Green Mansion*, are going very strong together. Monique to fill in the bass and chord parts for my tone poem 'A Ship at Sea' (from 'The Black Stranger') vows she will play it at the general assembly for graduation. An act of what Rolf-Pierre would call 'Aesthetic Vengeance'.

Actually, she confessed that she was motivated out of love!

***

How I Love Mother and How I Love Dad but I must get away. I can't cope with or bear their unhappiness any longer. What a tragic pity they had to leave Ireland at all! Mother still hates America but not as much as she used to. She hates what Hitler is doing to the Jewish people. She hates American soldiers using fireguns on the Japs. Hiding in caves. She is beginning to hate life itself.

We are hanging out of the front-room windows on pillows. We face Broadway. The cars and buses, bumper to bumper, are streaming downtown to Time Square.

"So many cars," I groan.

"It's only the world passing by," she sighs.

She loves life so much (perhaps too much). I suffer when she complains of existence: "A person would be better off dead."

***

Night: 3 or 4 o'clock in the morning.

For one round hour I indulge myself in a bout of pure hatred. The blood count is at its lowest! Is this the dark of the night of the soul or just bad health. But really it does affect the mind for the worse, then about five or so the air changes and the blood count rises. I feel quite good and start to pray for each and every victim of my former hatred—it is good to be hated by me—not that coals should be heaped on the heads—no really, I really love each one of them but it has to be past five o'clock. Roll on five o'clock always.

Am I a homosexual? I don't care what I am. I'm just a poet. Nothing more nothing less.

Wrote a poem called 'The Boy and The Geese' in the Roxy Movie House in the in-between chorus girl number—the trailer (coming attractions):

Is there anything
more beautiful in us
than our eyes—especially
in love or in longing?
Yes, our courage
and humility

(Ah, I'm still a religious maniac).

Fortnight Educational Trust supplement,
Padraic Fiacc: Poet of the Pagan City (1999)

It's Me, Joe
from an unpublished autobiography

1948: ANTONIN ARTAUD DIES IN PARIS. There goes the Paris of
my daydreams—Sartre, Mauriac, Gide, Camus, Joyce's friend
Beckett and Hemingway (Nobel prize winners all).

Did Artaud's wild dreams contribute anything? Like Colette, a
tug of war whether he'd be allowed burial in consecrated ground—
was his drug-taking suicide or self-murder?

Another Nobel prize winner, the Norwegian Sigrid Undset, called
Paris the 'Mother of Ideas'. Surely Artaud fits into such a Paris ...

The words of Portugal's great poet, Fernando Pessoa: "Next to
real life the fictions of art and letters pale".

***

Two years back in Ireland and with my Irish passport that says
Belfast, Eire, I'm targeted as the biggest nut of the day. Aunt
Mary drags me down to the dole people—and if she can only
keep her mouth shut. "This gentleman is under three flags!" The
dole clerk freezes. "I know that, I know that, but what is he—
Irish, British or American?" It dawns on me that even I don't
know. The cops won't give me a permanent ID card. Somehow I
frighten them but not as much as they frighten me. Long black
coats and even longer faces.

I have to take the night boat over to 'Ink Land' to relatives in

Romford, Essex, where I get a job in a Ford factory in an effort to procure a permanent ID card—which, thanks be—I finally do.

***

New Irish Poets 1948 published in New York, me the youngest in the collection.

***

Get a job in the Union Hotel as night porter. Roy McFadden there over some PEN meeting.

Watched him pacing the outside entrance. I ask Michael McLaverty, "What's wrong with him?"

"Probably girlfriend trouble," says Michael.

***

Really, really pleased with *New Irish Poets*. The Americans have the know-how to make a good book—and the money.

***

In Galway Seán Lucy's wife uses a long (1920ish) cigarette holder and invariably dumps the ashes on my balding pate. "Stop that at once," I squeal—but all to no avail.

***

Maurice Harmon, the then literary editor of *Hernia* (I mean *Hibernia*) and me at our wits' end trying to find John McGahern in Belfast—all in vain.

McGahern falls in our Glengormley door with flowers and sweets for Nancy and our daughter, Brigid.

He's been persecuted for his last novel, *The Dark*, and thrown out of his school as a teacher. The outcry was 'Wouldn't touch him with a bargepole'.

(Child abuse and incest have always been with us. We in the twentieth century are not the first to discover it.)

***

Sorley McLean from the Isle of Skye and me from Hellfast, Ulcer selected by the British Council to represent British culture abroad.

Meet in Toronto. Sorley a really sweet guy. When we read together we heckle each other to take the church-like silence out of poetry readings.

Back in Ireland *Poetry Ireland* has the two of us tour wee southern towns—landing up in Cork University—where, horror of horrors—I introduce Sorley as Shirley McClean.

To get even on me in the Dublin train to Belfast and the two of us broke—I find enough to get us two miniature whiskies.

Sorley, telling me a joke, swings his burly arms about knocking over one of the whiskies—"Curse you, Sorley, and your rotten bombastic ways. My apologies to the red-haired raving raven!"

I take out tissues to wipe the train table.

"No, No,"—Sorley has the last word—"this stuff is gold. You don't wipe it up with a tissue." He takes out a brand new Irish-linen handkerchief—always an ace up his sleeve. We share what is left of the whiskies.

***

A chat with Anthony Cronin in an *Aosdana* meeting—'I love your Titanic' etc ...

"Tony, what's wrong with Francis (Stuart)—he looks so depressed ... I better go over and cheer him up ... "

"Hello Francis, you look down in the dumps, anything wrong?"

Francis (replying in his German accent), "No, no, I was just sinking."

***

The last I saw of Van Morrison, at the Galway Arts Festival where I launched *Ruined Pages*—he seemed tired and diminished somewhat beneath that boisterous veneer—the vulnerability of an aspiring poet but his lyrics are his own poetry ...

***

To read with Richard Murphy and James Liddy at Galway

University. Richard and James, lifelong enemies, vying with each other who will read the most. Richard read his whole collection (Bird-calls and all). I've loved James Liddy for years but in reading he was out to best Richard. The organiser tapped me on the head, "I strongly advise you to read tomorrow." I agreed.

***

Summoned down to Dublin again to receive the *Poetry Ireland* prize. John F. Deane awarded me £500 plus a bronze by John Behan. The bronze was a masterpiece of the poet with poet's wreath and out of his mouth birds flying—all mounted on Connemara marble.

Kevin Faller was to read his poems at it—but such is his waning health he had a fellow read them for him. When he died I missed a lovely person and a good friend.

John Behan got me onto the Belfast train.

***

Called over to poet/photographer John and Sonia Minihan's house in London. John's pride in knowing Van Morrison. "Van Morrison is coming up to meet you tonight!"

"Oh John," I lied, "I'm just off the plane—I'm suffering jet lag."

"Padraic, you don't suffer jet lag crossing the Irish Sea. The Irish Sea's only a river now. Don't you like Van?"

Making Sonia laugh when warning John, "I like him but not too much of him."

When Van arrived I was struck by his resemblance to me. He mightn't be of the same religion but we were of the same race, Celtic probably.

Endless nights out with John and Van and Van footing the bill …

In an effort to contribute something I give Van my old copy of Evelyn Underhill's Mysticism classic (my bible), writing on it 'Cherish this book. It's a lifetime!'

***

When Blackstaff first started Rowel Friers and I gave them a book boost each.

Rowel and I invariably met at the same traffic crossing discussing our common illness, depression, that it is an actual illness, etc ...

***

When I finished editing *The Wearing of the Black* in 1974 John Hewitt and Michael Longley descended on me on behalf of the Arts Council.

Before their entrance Jim Gracey begged, "Joe (My 'real' name is Joseph Patrick O'Connor), don't fight them—they're funding the book."

Jim is a sweet guy but I didn't heed him and braced myself to put on my boxing gloves.

Michael was the first to bellow out, "Joe, I was never more embarrassed in my life! The editor putting at least ten of his own poems into one or two of others."

Hewitt put his two cents in, "There are too many poems in it—and there's one poem I think shouldn't be in it." (I forget which one). But Longley disagreed, "No, that should be left in!" (So they didn't both always agree!) I was really going to have a fight on my hands.

Longley who from the beginning could read me. (It was uncanny!) "Joe," he came straight to the point, "what will it be? Scotch or Irish?"

"Irish," I lied, not to let the flag down but I really preferred Scotch. After a glass of booze I mellowed somewhat—"You know I'm not afraid of you two British lions but I really appreciate anything or anybody who will help to make the book better!"

***

Graham Reid and me summoned to a debate in Trinity against Medbh McGuckian's 'that we shouldn't write about the troubles'. The usual sherry or two to give me Dutch courage. Montague and Brendan Kennelly don't show up—they are, or were, to flank Medbh ...

I whisper to Graham—"I may be old-fashioned but two men against one woman!"

"She's not a woman," says Graham.

"But if she's not a woman what is she?"

"She's a woman's lib and if you cherish anything on you ... and think of me too ... tear right into her for a start!"

Medbh can be disarming (to look at). She was stunning in her evening gown.

"You're nothing (I start off with) but a flower-pot poet—you wrote about your husband as a hairy begonia."

"And you're nothing but a frustrated dramatist!" (Touché, Bullseye).

Graham was right to make me go aggro. The lady gave me a big hug and kiss as the debate ended.

**

Staying with John Minihan in his London flat, he was summoned to go to the BBC to photograph Liam Neeson in a TV play about Liam giving his screen wife AIDS. I waited down the road a bit with John and Sonia's wee daughter.

Liam's co-actor went home to get a better dress than what the dear old Beeb could offer. Liam saw me and said to John, "Has Joe any of his books with him?"

"Yes, *Missa Terribilis.*"

"Would he give me a copy?"

"Go over and ask him. I'm sure he will."

This towering guy came over and I thought he has what the French call presence—he didn't have to act. He just has to be there.

"Glad to meet you. God, you even look like a Christian Brother, Joe. Don't you remember me? I lived a few doors down from you in Cromwell Road. You were the poet we used to watch every morning walking to the off-licence in India Street. 'How many black eyes has he got today? He must have two, he's wearing his shades.'"

I signed good luck to Liam in the *Missa Terribilis.*

**

To the ratio that the troubles worked their way up to Glengormley, I was trying to fend off an oncoming breakdown. I put too much emphasis on being published (for Nancy's sake).

Liam Miller had accepted my *By the Black Stream* in 1967 but didn't publish it until 1969.

I was diagnosed as an endogenous depressive which was of course only a symptom of schizophrenia internally and externally. I finally broke into bouts of crying and fits of sullen staring into space.

***

Every time one of us 'poets' went to the loo—we'd all criticise him.

'He really thinks he is a poet!' etc.

When Jimmy Simmons went I kept saying, "He's awful long in there—what is he doing?"

"He's writing a sonnet to his thing!"

Derek escaped early. Seamus begged him to stay.

"I've got to meet a girlfriend."

"Bring her back here!" says Seamus but Derek had his head screwed on.

When I was ready to go I felt my blood draining and I'd go white—a warning that I was going to wail.

Michael Longley took me by the hand as if I were a schoolboy in one of his classes. He marched me over to Seamus. "Well, my fat friend, say you are sorry to Joe."

Not a blink, bleep or blurp from 'Tweeds'.

As they all departed, Jimmy Simmons and I were left at a table of what seemed a feast of half glasses of whiskey.

When I was in the loo I asked Jimmy: "What did Seamus say about my poems?"

"He said he didn't understand them and therefore he didn't like them."

By now I was wailing like a banshee. These two old girls came in and I told them to take the whiskies. They thought that Jimmy was the cause of my squealing and yelling and were going to hammer him.

"No, no, he's a friend, a very good friend."

I thought that would make him get me to the Glengormley bus and it did.

***

Liam Miller invites me to lunch to introduce me to John Montague in Dublin. In Liam's office, Thomas Kinsella sitting at the typewriter looking as if he is putting the beef on. Walking to the eating house can't help but notice how everybody talks to and salutes Liam. The place is empty but for a priest and boy student. Montague shares New York experiences—Padraic Colum, the fact that both our fathers worked in the New York subways and the earlier life experiences of the pains of hell of dispossession. John in pissy mood, glaring at the priest until I tried to make a joke: "Montague, if you write anything, write a confession." The priest and Liam himself burst into laughter when they looked at John's poker face.

***

Derek Mahon drags me downtown via the Glengormley bus to the Crown pub to meet Michael Longley who's looking like a red-faced blooming English happy-go-lucky fellow. He had a dry wit and could be devastatingly humorous.

Next day a letter from Maurice Harmon—could he come up to Belfast for me to introduce him to Seamus Heaney?

Derek Mahon pops up to my house—that John Montague was to be in Lavery's pub (The Gin Palace). Would I come down with him to introduce him to Montague?

Everybody seemed to have had their first collections published and were exchanging them, Longley accepting Simmons'—"Thank you, James, though it's not my kind of poetry."

Seamus was there presiding over all of us, dressed in so much tweed, with his feet up on the table; he was almost a caricature of himself. I first met Seamus in Michael McLaverty's house where he yelled from another room, "Do you know, Joe, that my first collection is being published by Faber and I've had some poems published in the *New Statesman*?" (On a previous occasion Roy McFadden and me in Michael McLaverty's house, embarrassed that we have the same make of crocodile-leather shoes.)

Michael had had his last novel *The Brightening Day* just published and I had two poems in the *Irish Times*—one 'Letter from Michael McLaverty' and the other 'Luck'. Seamus and an academic friend don't like the air letter one but liked 'Luck'.

To get back to the 'Gin Palace', I had already confided in Derek Mahon and Brian Keenan that my marriage was breaking up.

Michael Emerson, who helped to create the Belfast Festival, said Seamus is bringing out festival booklets—"send some of your poems to him", which I did but no answer, no reply.

There were quite a few of us there that night, a Guinness heir with a German girlfriend, and, of course, we were all drinking—Quidnunc of the *Irish Times* etc.

I caught Seamus off-guard, "Seamus, now that you are in your cups tell me why you haven't returned my poems if you're not going to use them."

"Joe," he said, "Why don't you opt for a posthumous reputation."

Fortnight

material edited by Rudie Goldsmith

It was I who left You
Critical Responses and Encounters

The Bleeding Bough

TERENCE BROWN

ROY MCFADDEN'S FIRST BOOK *SWORDS AND Ploughshares* closed with a poem entitled 'The Girl'. In this the poet, for the first and last time in his work, uncomplicatedly evoked a simple Gaelic past, imagined as it might have been before the arrival of the conquering invader. It is a glimpse of that idealised version of Irish life that for Samuel Ferguson, for the writers of the literary revival, and for some contemporary Ulster poets is a Golden Age, a romantic pastoral myth by which modern social experience is measured and rejected.

> She walked this way a thousand years ago,
> The loose veil of hair dark in the lane's shy shadows,
> The water chuckling with each quiet footfall
> The Gaelic liquid-smooth in throat,
>   like deep winds flowing,
> Before the foreigner, when sea and sky
> Were safe, and broadchested brutality strode naked
> Lusting blood without hypocrisy.

McFadden's is a poem Ferguson would have found impressive, as might indeed McFadden's poetic contemporary, Padraic Fiacc, if he could overlook the violence of those final lines. Fiacc is a poet highly responsive to the vision of the Gaelic past. But he, unlike Ferguson, saw violence early and has never written, as Ferguson did, poems in its celebration. For Fiacc is a tough-minded, sensitive poet of painfully bleak awarenesses. And in Fiacc's writing the loss of the Gaelic purity is not allowed to sentimentalise republican militarism or to glamorise violence.

Padraic Fiacc was born in 1924, as Belfast was enduring one of those periodic acute inflammations of its chronically painful wound, which erupted especially in the Catholic ghettos:

> Between the year of the slump and the sell out, I
> The third child, am the first born alive ...
>
> My father is a Free Stater 'Cavan Buck'.
> My mother is a Belfast factory worker. Both
>
> Carry guns, and the grandmother with a gun
> In her apron, making the Military wipe
>
> Their boots before they rape the house.
>
> —'Son of a Gun'

His family emigrated to New York, where he grew up and where he was educated. But this was only a partial escape from one ghetto to another where:

> Monklike cops in fours patrol
> My morningside dark night of
>
> The iceberg-tip 'child soul'
>
> —'A Still Floating Child'

and an RUC swagger-stick metamorphoses to the 'night-stick' of a vicious law enforcement officer. The ghetto is one pole of Fiacc's consciousness:

> In the communal shower after the drowning
> We felt like Jews in Nazi Germany:
>
> The water, flagellating down, took on
> Something of the hostility in that
> dooms
>
> -day for all who are born ...
>
> —'The Other Man's Wound'

At the other pole in Fiacc's apprehension of the world is a sense of the lost Gaelic world of Ireland's rural past. Fiacc's first published volume takes its title from lines by James Joyce in *Poems Pennyeach*:

> I bleed by the black stream
> For my torn bough

and the pain of that wound, of the tearing apart of the Gaelic civilisation, is raw on the nerves through each of his published books.

> I was brought up in a rampart
> On top of a slieve where the heart
> Had its wine fill of beauty once.
>
> —'The Stolen Fifer'

Some of the poems in *By the Black Stream* are clearly modelled on Gaelic poetic practice. They suggest translations for poetry in that language. Bright, clear visual detail creates a haiku-like impressionism in poems such as 'After the Storm':

> Wrecked white lupins
> To sods crack the young
> Red boughs still
> With gold buds ...
>
> The pink ash
> Of a fire-dead
> Cornflower sky
> Has no wing left
> To ring us a tune

Nature and landscape are viewed in such poems as if history was of no significance. They are poems of naïve, lyrical observation— sharp perceptions of a natural stasis (in which motion is repeating patterns) that history has not yet dared disturb:

> I am the chaunt-rann of a Singer
> Who has sung to heart at night
> How the rust-loch's hazel waters
> Mirror the stars all right.
>
> —'The Poet'

Into this self-contained world of enamelled miniatures, paradigm of an innocent now-invaded cultural reality, images of pain and ugliness obtrude. Images of city, industrialism and agonising loss suggest a contrasting order of being:

> Entries patent leather with sleet
> Mirror gas and neon light ...
> A boy with a husky voice picks a fight
> And kicks a tin down home in pain
>
> To tram rattle a ship horn
> In a fog from where fevers come
> In at an East Wind's
> Icy burst of black rain.

—'Haemorrhage'

The formal aspects of Fiacc's work are appropriate to this vision of a simple, whole world broken into by pain and suffering. His poems are mostly in a free verse, clearly influenced metrically by American experiments. Metrical unsophistication (in the sense that his poems abandon centuries of literary practice and ignore classical canons) allows, in his simpler pieces, haiku-like images to exist in uncluttered, clear poetic contexts. These define a fundamental simplicity of vision. Syntactical reorganisation of language, disturbing customary relationships (rendered more easily possible by a verse which needs obey no complex stanzaic or prosodic requirements), can then be employed to suggest pain, tension, psychic disruption and disorder as the vision of Gaelic simplicity encounters the contemporary experience of fragmentation and, in the poet's second volume, *Odour of Blood* (1973), the violence and emotional horror of urban guerrilla warfare in Belfast. 'Vengeance' is a poem of rhythmic simplicity from which a central image emerges with hard clarity and where the complex syntax of the second sentence suggests difficult emotion that has disrupted what at the poem's opening was a simple perception:

> I am a child of the poor.
>
> For me there will have to be

Tinfoil: the pink light
-ning pale aquamarine
Morning sea-splashed

Soil dream against

The grave night gale.

In *Odour of Blood* the poet employs this aesthetic strategy to confront the contemporary Ulster crisis in Belfast in a sequence of poems. The vision of lost Gaelic purity in this collection is tested against brutally explicit images of sectarian warfare and guerrilla activity. The initial perceptions, as in his first book, are often simple, the images horrifically clear, but a convoluted syntax suggests a pained response on the poet's part. Fiacc encourages his readers to seek a relationship between his earlier volume, with its sense of a culture broken, and this book, since he includes three poems from *By the Black Stream* in the more recent sequence. The title-poem of the earlier volume, for instance, recurs re-entitled 'Haemorrhage' and with the Joycean couplet which prefaced the earlier book now serving as an epigraph to the poem. Fiacc's implication is that the blood now flows by the Black Stream from the broken bough of a lost culture. The poems in the book are stark compilations of brutal image and pulsations of bitter, raw emotion released in staccato rhythms, blunt, colloquial diction and taut, occasionally complex syntax. The imagery is uncompromisingly urban, mediating without evasion the life of a sectarian ghetto:

A grey cloud of pollution from Power
Chimneys, mill house, laundries, cars.

The drunk ones take to the square
From eating off soiled linen with

Cigarette ash in the cauliflower
...
Drunk on flat stout and watered gin
'Come on on ahead!' sons shout, 'in!'

Steering our fathers home to bed.

—'Our Fathers'

In the midst of these images of depressed urban working-class domesticity, Fiacc inserts his images of "the flowering fire of blood", occasionally presenting us with an equivalent to the lyric simplicity of his first book in image-sequences of unrelieved horror:

And guns under the harbour wharf
And bullets in the docker's tea tin
And gelignite in the tool shed
And grenades in the scullery larder
And weedkiller and sugar
And acid in the french letter

And sodium chlorate and nitrates
In the suburban garage
In the boot of the car

And guns in the oven grill
And guns in the spinster's shift

—'The British Connection'

The list becomes a nightmare litany of terror.

Superficially, *Odour of Blood* seems a break with Fiacc's earlier work. The nostalgic pastoral mode is forsaken for city realism, for the grisly trauma of violent conflict. Yet the two volumes share a fundamental similarity in that each embodies a static vision of loss and disruption. In the first book the unchanging present is a Gaelic world broken. It is from an apprehension of this social and psychic reality that the poetry springs. Analogously in the second volume, the urban catastrophe, in which human possibilities are savaged by conflict and anguish, is a permanent condition of being, from which the poet apparently cannot escape:

I go on nightmaring

Dead father running. There is a bull
In the field.

—'Son of a Gun'

Most of the poems in *Odour of Blood* are cast in the present tense. The effect of this repeated syntactical deployment is to suggest an almost timeless present. Many of the poems reach no conclusion, but terminate in mid-sentence and mid-breath. 'Fire Light', in an extreme instance, terminates:

> It never really were
> Or never will be
>
> Only always is ...

The poem itself is part of an unchanging present and reaches no conclusions, moves through no logical journey to any kind of resolution; nor does the poem embody an emotional teleology. Rather, it halts arbitrarily where it might well have continued to pile image upon image of the unchanging psychic and social misery of the ghetto. When some poems reach more stark points of break-off, they do so with an imagery that quite deliberately denies their readers any emotional withdrawal from the grim experience the poems embody, in the customary aesthetic satisfaction of perceiving a poem's ordering powers. Fiacc's poems move to points no reader could wish to reach, as they almost callously shatter any misplaced expectation of poetic resolution. This is particularly noticeable in some of his final lines:

> Cancer of the intestines.
>
>   —'The Poet and the Night'
>
> Splinters of children.
>
>   —'Circling to Land'
>
> Screams to 'Get Out!'
>
>   —'Icon'
>
>   burnt
> To death as witches!
>
>   —'Victory on Ship Street'

The implications of this sense of life are worth considering. It represents, I would argue, an essential simplification of the processes of history. Indeed, for all the violent explosiveness of the imagery in *Odour of Blood*, the book is almost without any suggestion of process. A conviction of the inescapable present is its most basic historical awareness. This is certainly understandable in work written in the heat of response to a dreadful present, but in so simplifying, as I see it, the complexity of history from a tension between being and becoming to static being, Fiacc in fact displays in an extreme form what is a recurrent predilection for Irish poets' persistent tendency to mould the details of historical flux, within which permanencies can be discerned only partially, and with difficulty, into the permanent *statsis* of myth. In the poetry of Samuel Ferguson, we saw the Irish past mythologised to express a number of broad notions about the permanencies of Irish identity. The writers of the revival exploited these in the service of national resurgence, while (as we shall see) more recent poets such as John Montague and Seamus Heaney apprehend Irish history as a saga expressing central and unchanging truths about Irish reality.

In *By the Black Stream*, landscape is mythologised into a symbol of Gaelic civilisation broken. In *Odour of Blood*, Fiacc rejects the simple historical myth which underlies the earlier volume, but substitutes for it a more complex sense of historical permanence, of an existential present that cannot be changed but can only be endured. In that book the city at its moment of torment serves almost as myth of civilisation itself bleeding unendingly to death. The sensibility determining both volumes is in fact one responsive, as are those of so many Irish poets, to the ordering efficiencies of myth and to its intimations of permanency. To be Irish in *By the Black Stream* is to know a permanent condition of loss; in *Odour of Blood* it is to know unending psychic pain. The one is a vision of poignancy sensitively presented, the other of anguish confronted directly with moral and aesthetic courage.

Northern Voices: Poets from Ulster
(Gill & Macmillan, 1975)

Introduction to
The Selected Padraic Fiacc

TERENCE BROWN

THIS SELECTION OF PADRAIC FIACC'S POETRY, drawn from his work of thirty years, allows a reader to see his recent disturbing poems, which deal directly and painfully with the violence that has overwhelmed many districts of his native city in the last decade, in a broader context, a context that may provide a clue as to how these later poems should be read.

Padraic Fiacc's early poems on first reading seem apparently simple lyrics in that tradition of Irish verse in English which owes its inspiration to Gaelic poetic practice. Here are poems that remind of translations from the Gaelic, attending to the natural world in bright, finely etched images, evoking the mythological past, the dedication of the scholar, the freedom of the poet, the austere reflections of monk and hermit, all suggestive of a timeless world of Irish antiquity that can still sustain poetic utterance of a conventional kind. Closer inspection reveals however that the work is much less conventional than a first reading would suggest, for these poems, so reminiscent of Gaelic poetic effects, are not simply well-managed imitations of Gaelic verse but lyrics sharply expressive of individual feelings and states of consciousness. There is a closeness to experience and a sense of the immediate apprehension of the particulars present in these poems that make them sensuously and emotionally vital. Both vividness of perception and feeling are present, for example, in the opening of a poem like 'Master Clay':

On top of the mountain, the school,
                              a monastery ...
I take the road up to the bells.
(The bells are a childhood memory!)

Monks are at prayer. Birds at laughter.
Bells peal in still blue air.

I am afraid of the wall of woods though
Afraid of the sea below, the shadow:
(Lest I fall!)

Poems such as the charged love poem 'The Burning Garden' and the hauntingly exquisite 'Two Solitudes' seem, each employing the metaphor of a fire that glazes clay bone hard, moments when consciousness is so intensely absorbed in experience that only the present is truly real.

It is this intense realisation of states of consciousness, of perception and feeling, that characterises Fiacc's early work even at its most conventional. It suggests a poet primarily concerned not with art as the rearrangement of experience into satisfyingly aesthetic forms but a writer concerned in an innocent, almost naïve fashion with the intensities of the moment, intent to express the world as he sees and knows it.

The heightened states of awareness which Fiacc's early poems record sometimes so stimulate the poet that sense impressions, particularly visual sensations, begin to form strange patterns in a kaleidoscopic world of colour effects, as in the transfixed light of 'Patrick Turns the Sod':

Gold as a sun through a wine from pears
In a glass moon in a spring wind
Sheds tears
On redhaired rusted willow.

An unremitting green
Scars of the ground sing
Clouds in torrents, then
A thousand stars
Waken the birds and the children.

Feeling and sensation can be so charged, such a poem

announces, that a discursively logical poetic mode, which might separate perception, thought, and emotion would misrepresent the poet's experience. So from the first Fiacc has been ready to experiment boldly (and not always successfully) with syntactical abbreviations and elisions, with an imaginative shorthand in the interests of truth to the vital movements of consciousness.

It is in Fiacc's later poems that deal in their uncompromisingly stark way with the brutalities and horrors of urban guerrilla warfare and military repression that this ambitious experimentalism, which insists that a poem must risk obscurity or even fragmentation in the interests of truth to experience, can most readily be seen at work. The early poems have instructed us not to expect from Fiacc poems which comment on his world. Rather, we must expect states of mind and feeling rendered in a verse that risks much, but which can achieve moments of powerful immediacy. And read in this way these later poems compel attention. The convoluted syntax, the harsh sequences of jagged images grimly realise bitter and vulnerable emotional states of anger and fear, of outrage, in poems such as 'The Black and The White', 'Credo Credo' and the very powerful 'Glass Grass', whilst the poems as a whole exude the very reek and stench of a violence in the streets which oppresses and damages the psyche.

I am not, however, suggesting that Fiacc should be read simply as a poet who has accepted a crude version of realism or a literalism that values simple reportage too highly. It is true, it must be admitted, that there are poems in the latter half of this volume which are perhaps little more than aggressively realistic accounts of gruesome matter. But these are merely moments when Fiacc fails in his more fundamental poetic endeavour. For Fiacc, it seems to me, is a poet who believes that experience is significant in itself and that the poet's role is to attend to the difficult, often painful, meanings that experience unfolds, meanings which cannot be reduced to statement and comment, but which must be accepted when they proffer themselves. The poet cannot indeed be certain always that the significance he seeks within experience is in fact present. He must record his awarenesses employing such techniques as may be necessary to preserve the uniqueness of the moment as he lives it, hoping that significance will reward an obsessive, sometimes anguished attentiveness. And in the best of the later poems in this collection, such a sense of meanings discerned amidst the squalor and pain, is the fruit of the poet's absorption with raw, unrefined experience. In the best of these poems a sense is present of the moments charged not simply with the intensity of heightened consciousness, which is the dominant impression in the early work, but with a sense of moral significance. Horrible and savage as the events and feelings recorded in these poems may be, there is also an intimation in more than a few of them of stern lessons to be learnt—that suffering is certain and that moral responsibility is inescapable even as the most bestial impulses flourish in the self and in the world. In such poems the moment of perception seems permeated by an undeniable human significance which transcends mere reportage, encouraging compassion:

> No one will help
> The rubber-bullet-collecting kids.
> No one will help the grim
> -faced teenaged British soldiers or young
> Cops, hating the being hated.
>
> We all
> Go down the road now sharp and small
> As razor blades ...
> I pick my steps across
> My backstreet childhood as a soldier would pick
> His steps across a little mine-filled field.

—'The Wrong Ones'

The Selected Padraic Fiacc (Blackstaff Press, 1979)

Darkness Visible
Some Hidden Aspects
of the Poetry of Padraic Fiacc

DAVID GILLIGAN

THE RECENT PUBLICATION OF PADRAIC FIACC'S *Missa Terribilis*[1] once more focuses attention on the work of the controversial Belfast poet and yet, as Gerald Dawe has pointed out in his review of the above collection[2], the work of this centrally important writer exists in a critical vacuum. This critical evasion and apparent hostility have rendered Fiacc a somewhat isolated figure whose work is viewed in an estranged and oblique manner. This new collection, *Missa Terribilis*, is a selective representation of Fiacc's work of the 1970s, which earned him a tempestuous reputation as a poet who consistently confronted the horrors of the Northern Ireland situation and its political implications. This was full-frontal poetry tracing the effects of oppression upon the lives of ordinary people. The new reformulation of his work takes the form of a dark missal which guides us into, and allows a vicarious participation in, the individual and collective trauma of this disturbed period of Irish history.

However, as Gerald Dawe pointed out in the October 1980 review[3] of *The Selected Padraic Fiacc* (Blackstaff Press, 1979), the predominantly stark and anguished imagery of this 'dark' phase in Fiacc's career tend to present a somewhat unbalanced view of his work and do less than justice to its imaginative range. The concentrated intensity of this late phase in Fiacc's verse is in some ways reminiscent of that period of locked intensity in the career of Austin Clarke, when he wrote such poems as 'Tenebrae'. Clarke's poetic mood was more sullen and the oppression he wrote of was of a different order, yet despite these variations they share a similar sensibility and intent, through the recovery of a Gaelic mode which Fiacc had shown an interest in but subsequently abandoned. Fiacc's verse is a stylistic contrast to Clarke's traditional metre in its sparse, cubist and shockingly energised expression of that "house that we must mourn" that Clarke touched upon in his poetry. Yet both poets are poets of political conscience who have responded in their own authentic manner to the particular social oppressions of their time. Such comparisons are a necessary aspect of a more comprehensive review of the Belfast poet's work, which would take account of all its moods and tones and give due consideration to its technical intricacies and, most importantly, locate his work in its social and cultural context—in its relation to Irish literary tradition. This is an attempt at such a review.

***

Fiacc's 'Ulster' is a place apart, an estranged and enclosed society. It is a natural law that within enclosed systems energy atrophies until the system is re-energised from an outside force. Within this inner circle of Ulster is yet another one, insofar as Fiacc presents Belfast as a little world of its own. Of course, other writers in different contexts, such as William Faulkner, Flannery O'Connor and Nadine Gordimer, have also presented microcosmic literary versions of their own social world in a variety of ways. These are not 'other worlds' in the sense of a Tolkien-like fantasy but are linked with social realities. Indeed, in Fiacc's case we are dealing with a poetry of disenchantment. Generally, it may be said that within the span of these fictional and socially real continuities individuals and communities exist in a state of tension and conflict and fear of cultural seduction accompanies real or imagined violence. Contorted ideas inhabit the crania of the besieged and produce an inverted response in the collective psyche of a dispossessed minority, or in the South African case, a majority. There is a common link here, and that is the Huguenot Diaspora which has touched all three areas. It is not surprising to find that pattern of an elect people, a 'new Israel', be it Afrikaaner or Ulster Protestant, engaged in a struggle with the "dark secret being" (to quote Fiacc) of a subjugated native population. This is a potent situation and the possessive dark angel on one side of this struggle usually has a powerful feminine and chthonic aspect to it. For this very reason, the theme of miscegenation figures powerfully in the fiction of William Faulkner and features in Gordimer's short stories, while in Fiacc's verse an equal fear of native seduction is balanced by the contrary concept of an Imperial system which spreads its "male cancer cells" through the infected body-politic of a ravished Ulster. Much of this, as Gerald Dawe has remarked, is "too close to the bone" for the comfort of many critics.

Within the circumscribed parameters of life in Northern Ireland, a poet is brave who gives expression to the varieties of paranoia that underlay the political attitudes of society. Fiacc is not afraid, at the risk of being labelled sectarian, of giving blunt expression to this element in the mentality of the 'extremist', in such a way that it implicates the 'normal' citizen in a silent conspiracy, which is in effect a confederacy of idiocy, moral cowardice and sectarian reaction:

> 'Well, it's like this:
> Fenian gets out of Hell are spawned in
> Filthy Fenian beds by Fenian she-devils[4]

In Fiacc's search for an authentic artistic response to his/our situation, he has taken enormous risks and has been criticised for the grotesque elements in his verse, but this has also been charged against writers like Faulkner and Carson McCullers, who emphasise these distorted aspects of their society. The pertinent question here is the degree to which the writers, be they novelists or poets, inflate the grotesque within their work at the expense of social fact.

In this respect the question of authenticity looms large. In relation to Northern Ireland, over the years there has appeared a flood tide of ephemeral, superficial and commercially parasitical literature which has fed off the Northern troubles. By way of contrast there is also a literature of commitment which has grown organically from within the Northern communities and which has made an authentic, rooted response to the Northern troubles as but one aspect of life there. This type of literature would, I think, be best represented by writers such as Michael McLaverty, John

Hewitt and Padraic Fiacc. The Belfast poet has undoubtedly
responded more intensely than most to the violence in the North
and in his verse there is an emotional grappling with violence and
its effects. But the presentation of violence is never gratuitous
because buried within the totality of his verse are those rare and
precious glimpses of those elements that are precious in human
life, and also, something of the uniqueness of Ulster, and of Belfast
in particular, has been distilled. This is found I think in that
tenuous celebration of life in 'Alive Alive O'[5] where the "altar boy
from a Mass for the dead" discovers anew the Edenic tree of delight
in the midst of urban ruin (third stanza omitted):

> The altar boy from a Mass for the dead
> Romps through the streets of the town
> Lolls on brick-studded grass
> Jumps up, bolts back down
> With wild pup eyes ...
>
> This morning at twist of winter to spring
> Small hands clutched a big brass cross
> Followed the stern brow of the priest
> Encircle the man in the box ...
>
> ...
>
> O now where has he got to
> But climbed an apple tree!

Terence Brown in his *Ireland: A Social and Cultural History*[6]
writes of an oppressive period in Irish history, the 1930s, when
"moments of personal fulfilment" seemed to be "wrested from an
unyielding oppression" and where, given the context of "a
dishevelled, often neurotic and depressed society", the short story
was a register of a self-denigrating social reality. In many ways
Fiacc's poetry occupies a similar niche at present in relation to the
Belfast of the last two decades. In the expressionistic, wry, almost
cartoon-like verse of Fiacc's, Belfast becomes the setting for a
comedy of evil:

> ... the fat-faced politicians
> Grinning on TV at their own witticisms, that all
> I want to do is to lie down and join the other
> Grinners, grinning with horror, the skull ones ...[7]

This is the bitter irony to be found in Joan Littlewood's *Oh What A Lovely War!*, which also has its roots in documentary realities, but there is also the tendency in Fiacc, as there was in Synge, to perceive life antithetically and to accommodate disharmony. Those moments of "cold grace" found in the writing of another Catholic, Flannery O'Connor, who also writes out of a distorted environment, are rare in Fiacc's work. It is as though the environment smothers like a wet blanket any flare-up of life or note of celebration. Concepts ancient and modern are held in common in Fiacc's verse. He shares in continuities and also disrupts them. For one thing Fiacc shares an idea of a blighted landscape—going back to the plantation—with writers like Michael McLaverty and marries this to modern ideas about inner-city urban deprivation. Fiacc's cityscapes reflect an architecture of alienation and atrophy, a scenario painted battleship-grey on stone, as in 'Sanctus' from *Missa Terribilis*:

> Sinking on iron streets, the bin-lid
> -shielded, battleship-grey-faced kids
>
> Shinny up the lamppost, cannot tear
> Themselves away, refuse to come in
>
> From the dying lost day they douse
> With petrol and set the town's holy
>
> Cows on fire ...

Fiacc also participates in a continuity of imagery which is found in O'Faolain and Joyce and can even be discerned as far back as the *Tain Bo Cuailgne*. This is the image of the shroud, natural or otherwise, which falls upon the land, blanketing all in snow and silence. It is the symbol of death in Joyce's 'The Dead' and it is picked up by O'Faolain in his collection of short stories, *A Broken World*, where he writes: "under that white shroud, covering the whole of Ireland, life was lying broken and hardly breathing". It is interesting to see the way this type of image seeps into the consciousness of the Northern poet and is creatively adapted to contemporary life in the 'Black North's' major city:

... A sudden black snow of
Charred newspapers, a lava of lead pencil leaves ...

The chimneypots flower smoke for a teatime now,
And Belfast is a beaten sexless dog, hushed,
Waiting for when or where the next blow
Will fall. Against this black, the white seagulls
Glide in again, like hazy-eyed drunks, star the dark.[8]

Fiacc is writing here of a Saturday night in Belfast tense with the
expectations of violence, yet that ominous hush, that sudden
snow, go back a long way: the army of Ulster waiting, while an
ominous blanket of snow and silence descends upon Ireland in a
section of *The Tain*. They await in anticipation the destroyer
Cúchulainn. There is a continuity of mood here. Not without
reason does Terence Brown make the comment that one
immediately thinks of the words 'Cúchulainn' and 'Ulster' on a
first reading of Fiacc. The northern poet has captured the sense of
resolution and menace to be found in the northern province. Our
consciousness in a reading of Fiacc has to some extent been
primed—every word in his verse is carefully picked with precision
and is loaded with significance, ready to detonate in the
consciousness of the reader. The final stanza of 'The Wrong Ones'
taken from *The Selected Padraic Fiacc* tells us a great deal about
Fiacc's poetic technique:

>   I pick my steps across
> My backstreet childhood as a soldier would pick
> His steps across a little mine-filled field.

In their own context, Fiacc's silences are as ominous as some of
his images. The northern poet's juxtaposition of those ever-present
seagulls against the darkening sky of Belfast is a chilling emblem—
the gulls are usually heralds of death or destruction in his scenario;
they are, in effect, white vultures (another Fiacc inversion), preying
on the "manna from Earth" of human flesh, be it that of terrorist or
victim. Silences work in combination with image in Fiacc's work.
Unlike the aesthetic reticences built into the tradition of Protestant
poets like John Hewitt, the lean armature of Fiacc's verse evokes a
sense of loss. The 'cryptic' nature of Fiacc's verse is in many ways a

self-inflicted distortion reflecting a distorted existence.

This pared-down primal quality may also be found in early Irish nature poetry. In Gaelic verse this quality may be attributed to a sense of restrained exuberance, whereas in the early Irish verse there is a wholeness and freshness of experience which contrasts with the blunt and anguished utterances and silences characteristic of Fiacc's later work dealing with modern urban existence in Ulster. When Fiacc incorporates swear words into his verse, it is not just as a closer approximation to the colloquial realities of the streets (which Fiacc does well) in terms of speech, but an imploring expression of the inadequacy of the word to express certain experiences and situations. Fiacc takes on the paradoxical demand of writing a poetry which deals with the obscene without subverting the poetic enterprise. Fiacc refutes the rhetoric of terrorism. He seems to give up on the verse midway through its progress—many endlines stop abruptly or tail off at a tangent and disintegrate. This is the poetry of alienation which fractures under its own stresses and the pressures of external realities.

One poem is pivotal in this respect: 'Against Oncoming Civil War' from one of Fiacc's earlier collections (*Nights in the Bad Place*, Blackstaff Press, Belfast, 1977). The pattern of much of Fiacc's later work follows his sense of disillusionment and loss at the contrast between a mythical Ireland of the imagination and the reality of modern-day Ulster. The horrors of terrorism and state repression are only some aspects of this disillusionment pervaded by the "odour of blood" which makes "all Doric discipline vain". Fiacc also laments the loss of a whole way of life, a lost culture, and, in the words of Hugh MacDiarmid, "the tragedy of an unevolved people".

Fiacc's poem referred to above illustrates this cultural break and sense of loss. The first four couplets show considerable use of an interplay of assonance and alliteration in a modified Gaelic style:

Salmon silvering grey to die
The summers of the past day

...

The silk cloud's spider-fingering pine
Against the going away to sea sky

The feeling of a sleepy, dreaming advance to death pervades this section until there is a sudden break, a wrenching away, in style and tone, in the following verses:

> Cannot be wrenched back nor hoarded
> But given only as the black ever-
>
> Greens go on living high up over
> The mountain hill wall, high up over
>
> This little mill town, the mornings
> Growing darker than sundown.

There can be no continuity, in Fiacc's view, between the "evergreens" upon the mountainside and the different reality of the "mill town". Fiacc shares something at this point with poets such as Edwin Muir and Hugh MacDiarmid, who have also reflected upon this loss of a more simple natural order and another cultural past in the midst of industrial urban squalor in Glasgow. The sense of the Gaelic past and the mythic perceptions of childhood are handled in a creatively different way to Fiacc—for one thing MacDiarmid has a more positive attitude to the future, derived from his Marxism, while Muir effectively tries to recapture the magic of childhood through the employment of myth. All of this has gone astray in Fiacc's perceptions. Significantly, Fiacc closes his *Missa Terribilis* with 'Ite Missa Est', a plea to go in peace, a flight into Egypt rather than any attempted reconstruction of life in a hopeless situation. Fiacc accentuates the sense of Belfast's distinctiveness through the utilisation of vernacular speech patterns, loaded down as they are with linguistic throwbacks to older forms of English, Lallans and Gaelic. Words as common as fossilised (in Ulster they are both) as 'fornenst' and 'scalded' crop up naturally and frequently in his verse. In his earlier verse, written in a semi-medieval style (showing perhaps the influence of Padraic Colum), he uses archaic words in a very significant and calculating way to load a whole poem with significance. An example of this would be his use of the old English 'liefer', through its root 'lufu' (meaning 'to love'), in the poem 'Deranged', featured in *The Selected Padraic Fiacc*. The Ulster poet is expert at throwing the balance of a poem through the use of a single word in this way.

Language shift is particularly significant in the work of a regional poet like Fiacc. The 'descent' into the vernacular in his later work is a register of Fiacc's changing attitudes and the special characteristics of the place he inhabits come to the surface of his texts. This is achieved through a distillation of language and a shift in sensibility, which is displayed in a selectivity and isolation of certain words.

The peculiar mindset of Ulster is shown in other ways. In a region where, like Scotland, it may be said that even the Catholics are Calvinist, Fiacc senses that some are predestined, being of the un-elect, for an inglorious existence. Fiacc expresses the spiritual 'hangover' of this Calvinistic mood very aptly in 'Our Fathers' from *The Selected Padraic Fiacc*. The spiritual aspect of the oppression which Fiacc has experienced is fused with images drawn from industrialism and features of working-class urban deprivation into "a grey cloud of pollution" that falls like a shroud over every aspect of life. The "cigarette ash in the cauliflower" and the "flat stout and watered gin" are symptomatic of a social life gone sour, stale, dead and bereft of comport or significance:

At this unholy wee hour of
A Calvin Sabbath river-drags the body

-deserted road back to the condemned
Kitchen house in the blind street row

Under a God is a Scotsman in that
He makes use of all even the dead

The theological concerns of Fiacc are difficult to discern at times but the shock of disillusionment runs through it. On a basic human level, however, some of his verse has a universality which goes beyond parochial significance because it deals with socio-anthropological realities such as the 'territorial imperative' and group fear. A poem such as 'Orange Man' from *The Selected Padraic Fiacc* has implications which are easily comprehended as applicable to situations as diverse as South Africa or Israel's West Bank:

Navy blue jackdaw, the brute size
Of a graveyard raven, invades

The territory that the tiny orange
-breasted robin only thinks is all

His own garden, just can't get let
To stay that dead lonely in.

The couplets of this poem, like the species of bird, crowd and chase each other in frenetic activity in an obvious political parable. Within the "all-wombing tomb" of the Ulster back garden, two crazily entangled, landlocked, infantile species crowd and harry each other, locked in infertile conflict and refusing to be born, as Fiacc has said, "into a new reality"[9].

This abnormal situation creates a diseased mentality within those who are caught up in it and this is a common syndrome in a colonialist situation. One aspect of this condition is a black contagious mood which manifests itself in excessively aggressive assertion or in a convoluted and fatalistic defeatism. Contra Chesterton, the wars in Fiacc's vision are as unmerry as the songs. The Belfast poet shows how any repressed minority or colonised group lose their essential identity and also their masculinity or femininity. The men become boys rather than men, emasculated by their political paralysis—this idea has also been explored by Heaney in a rural context in 'Wintering Out'. As Fiacc puts it:

Like water sitting in a lead pipe
Are only us 'boy men' in a club sung.[10]

The blackness of the North in Fiacc's verse becomes a metaphysical condition and a fated aspect of social life but it also seems to have its objective correlative in the topography of Ulster. Many points in the landscape carry the adjective 'black', be it the Blackwater, the Blackstaff or Black Mountain which overshadows West Belfast. The 'Blackness' is as much a part of Fiacc's mindscape as Yeats' grey West-of-Ireland vision. In his explorations of the common mind, Fiacc is a modernist in his view of the irremediable nature of man trapped and conditioned by the past. He has the uncommon ability to pick up those aspects of life that are so obvious and sometimes so obnoxious that they become invisible, repressed or absorbed into the commonplace, as the poem 'Foetus Papyraceous' in the *Missa Terribilis* collection:

... We
Chat about the 'troubles' and/or

The weather, and, like, horse laugh:
'What has murder and torture to do
With us? There is no war.'

Fiacc is expert at exposing these flaws in our perceptions,
engaging in the defamiliarisation process advocated by the Russian
formalists. He breaks away at many points from the received
traditions of Irish literature. Like some other modern poets, he lives
on the frontiers of language and sense, at times cutting away the
euphemisms of hypocrisy, the clichés of servility and status-seeking
with a painfully blunt language, which is sometimes modified with
compassion when dealing with the child 'victims' of the troubles or
is open to the vulnerability of a child as in the poem 'Goodbye to
Brigid/*An Agnus Deï*' from the *Missa Terribilis* collection.

Fiacc is a strange poet in that he combines so many diverse
elements within the total range of his work, among them a sense
of the past and of tradition communicated in a dislocated
modernist style. He oscillates between the presentation of brute
facts and touching, almost sentimental, asides; between a close
involvement with society and absolute disengagement. There is an
autobiographical strain in his poetry in which personally
experienced events register the isolation and oppression of many
aspects of life in a large city. To this are added the peculiar
alienations and oppressions of life in a place like Belfast. In his
poetry raw individual experience tends to replace an abstract
universality, although there are dark hints of something
numinous, something eternal, in the background, as in the poem
'Credo Credo', where a sense of something transcendental lends
support to the secular 'hang-in-there' attitude of an oppressed
people withstanding state repression. Fiacc imaginatively depicts
the predicament of the displaced and dispossessed through an
Imagist technique, with its emphasis on the concrete and its
utilisation of everyday speech.

The idea of a numinous presence in the background can
sometimes be sensed, as through a glass, darkly, in some of Fiacc's
contorted 'religious' verse and this is apparent and pronounced in

the *Missa Terribilis* collection. But there are also moments when a sense of the numinous is encountered in a less obvious way in some of his earlier poems when the poet recalls those moments of a lost sense of beauty and completeness in the life of the individual or of a people who have lost their cultural integrity. One must remember that, as with the writing of the Old Testament prophetic poets, the 'personal' does not necessarily mean individual as in this extract from the poem 'The Stolen Fifer':

> I was brought up in a rampart
> On top of a slieve where the heart
> Had its wine fill of beauty once
> I was brought up in a trance.

Yet there is also a descent from the "slieve", or mountain, down into contemporary realities following this dazzling vision. The vision of a mythical Ireland still dazzles the poet but this vision darkens suddenly. The metaphysical yearning in his later verse is combined with a vague populism. With Padraic Fiacc there is something of a mystique of 'The People' but in his conception they are the eternal losers rather than some great evolutionary force as one finds in the poetry of Carl Sandberg and similar writers. He has also a tendency to create 'Christ' figures who are the equivalent of 'Everyman' in the sense of the collective figure suggested by Hugh MacDiarmid in 'The Innumerable Christ' and other poems. Fiacc has an unfortunate tendency to over-employ this motif at times.

Like many other Irish poets, he addresses himself to the question of identity and in the process is not untouched by received tradition and myth and their influence upon individual and community. One gains the impression that the poet is trying to make some sort of personal declaration of independence in the formulation of the self, rather than the acceptance of a received identity. However, one also gets the sense in Fiacc's verse of a deprivation of soul and social being, the inheritance of the Catholic poor, which is eternally destined to return and pervade the present. His work is tragic in the classic sense because the past always returns.

In his search for authentic life and identity, Padraic Fiacc encounters a constant factor in Irish life, tradition and literature—

the land—through the experience of its antithesis, the city. Fiacc
has prefaced one of his collections with a quotation from Joyce:

> I bleed by the black stream
> For my torn bough

and it is apt that he should do so because there is the same concern
with cultural and social deprivation, individual impoverishment
and spiritual suffocation that one finds in Joyce. Fiacc extends
Joyce's concept of Ireland as an "all-wombing tomb" into new
dimensions amongst the backstreets of Belfast. His nocturnal
mindscapes of that city show at times that glimpse of Hades found
in *Ulysses*. There is also that same sense of macabre humour and
the prolongation of death into an eternal present to be found in
much of Beckett's work. The sense of displacement and loss of
contact with the land found in *Ulysses* is also echoed in Fiacc's
verse. The same horror of death in all its manifestations is also tied
up with remembrance of life found in Beckett. Like Beckett and
Joyce, he is concerned with our present condition as the symptom
of some kind of fall from grace. In this condition darkness pervades
everything and religion itself is an aspect, a condition, of the
darkness. This is symbolised in Fiacc's 'Credo Credo' where the
"Madonna of the People" is a Black Madonna who "hangs in the
depth of our dark secret being". When Fiacc writes of 'The Black'
being absorbed into his being, his poems and the collective life of
'the People', it evokes the graveyard sequences in *Ulysses*:

> Wombed in Sin darkness I was too, made
> not begotten ...

> You find my words dark. Darkness is in
> Our souls, shame-wounded by our sins,
> Cling to us yet more, a woman to
> Her lover clinging ...

> —*Ulysses*, pp.45-61

Although the dark Madonna in Fiacc symbolises a source of
consolation and fertility, it is a bitter consolation. There is an
inferred protest against a theology in which the original crime is to
be born and a more overt protest against having to endure an
inhuman existence which is human in origin and is politically

manufactured. Fiacc too is "made not begotten" and he constantly refers to the "blind back streets" he was "hand-made a madman on" inside a "coffin country", and he is determined in his verse to make this darkness visible.

Given all of this it is not surprising to find a dominant monochrome aspect to Fiacc's verse as he presents us with frank snapshots of Belfast city life. The photographic metaphor is particularly suited to Fiacc's desire to 'show it as it is'. The black stream of a polluted culture is a particularly apt symbol for Fiacc, who, ironically enough is published by Blackstaff Press—the River Blackstaff being the heavily polluted, walled-in subterranean stream which underflows much of industrial west Belfast. Fiacc is now seen as a poet of the city, in many ways a ghetto poet, a literary version of Chagall, whose inverted worldview is that of the hanging torture victim as in 'Internee' in *Missa Terribilis*. Like Beckett he resents the "cursed progenitors" who create this Frankenstein existence in which perpetrators and victims are interchangeable and childhood is "more murdering than murdered"; Pearse's 'Murder-Machine' is inverted like all else in Fiacc's world.

Given the urban orientation of his verse, it might be said that the land is almost symbolised by its own absence. The pine-covered mountain and the flowing river are evocative of the lost Gaelic civilisation in Fiacc's early work and it must be admitted that there is something incongruous about a poet "highly responsive to the vision of a Gaelic past"[10] who deals in a very expressive manner with brutal and uncompromising urban realities. Many of his early poems, especially the 'Monastic' group, are demonstrative of the Gaelic early-medieval style in their use of bright primary colours, trisyllabic rhythms and a fresh, almost naïve, view of nature as a wonder disrupted by the hand of man or contaminated by his very presence, as 'Hoot Mon' from the 1973 *Odour of Blood* collection suggests:

Black horse fly on the white rose, yes
You are more real for being less.

The hard, sharp clarity of vision is carried over into Fiacc's urban poems where there is an abrupt shift from the vibrant colour of his

'Gaelic' styled verse into the more usual monochrome vision of city life (and there is a corresponding descent in language patterns as well). In the early verse certain figurations occur in a deeply emblematic way—as in Austin Clarke's 'Straying Student'. The intrusion of a blackness and corruption into life is linked with certain images such as the worm (a sign of repression), the dust of death, industrial pollution and the gathering storm. A defiled landscape and a torn culture bleeds red in Fiacc's imagination and this stains all his experience and is set against memories of an ideal rural past which is evergreen. The first poem of *The Selected Padraic Fiacc* is 'The Stolen Fifer' where the poet recalls a time of vision when "the heart had its wine fill of beauty"—his early education means that he is "brought up in a trance". This may refer to his period in St. Joseph's Seminary, Calicoon, New York State or there may be a wider range of reference intended involving a collective experience of the Gaelic past. In the final stanza of this poem, it is "the town of the earth", in which he does not believe, that pulls him down. There is a bitter, ironic accommodation to this reduced state and to this disillusionment in the later poem 'Reds/*An Et Sepultus Est*' from *Missa Terribilis* in which he declares:

I am of Ireland of the Black Flag
And/or Hunger Striker Crosses.

I am of Ireland of the Red
Buses, not the Green Buses.

This is a form of political accommodation as well but in a seminal poem like 'The Stolen Fifer' one can discern how Fiacc's imagination enters into an idealistic obsessional condition—suspended, entrapped in a matrix of its own desire. He is "locked in the dun", trapped in an obsessional condition symbolised by the traditional symbol of the fairy mound; he has surrendered his development, and this can be the condition of a whole people:

And I am a boy forever from growing
And I am a man forever from sowing
And no man knows what I be knowing
When wind is on the pine and blowing.[11]

In Irish culture, language may function as a form of delusion, an insulation from reality as Brian Friel possibly suggests in his play *Translations*. It is easy to see that when disillusionment sets in and the 'tyranny of reality' takes over, then another form of compulsive imagination runs its course, hence the "almost compulsive obsession with the present-day Ulster violence" (to quote the blurb on the *Nights in the Bad Place* collection) that is a feature of the later Fiacc. This is the "lyrical reflective talent compelled towards elliptical intensities of insight by the violence of the streets" as Robert Nye puts it in the *Irish Press* review of the above collection in 1977. The 'death of God' school of theology was to a great extent the result of those who had previously been followers of the transcendentalist theologian Karl Barth and Fiacc's verse bears the mark of a disappointed idealist. In Fiacc's own words, from the final stanza of 'The Stolen Fifer':

> I was brought up on top of a slieve
> And cannot live on the earth, for the town
> Of the earth which I do not believe
> In, pulls me down, pulls me down.

Something of the pain that is induced when reading Fiacc's verse is attributable not only to the recorded acts of violence, the litany of dead and maimed, but to another factor—that one is sharing in the emotion engendered by the disintegration of the poet's relationship with a cultural landscape, which, being personified, thus 'suffers' through the process of demythologisation and spiritual colonialism:

> O dolly-Eurydice, my dark Ros
> -aleen dream
>   of bog on bog of bone
> -grounded cloud, Ireland, my dear
> Dragon seed pod ... [12]

The absence of landscape in Fiacc is noticeable, it is invisible, but a memory, while cityscape and seascape predominate, reflecting on the day-to-day reality of Belfast as a northern, industrial seaport. The combination of city and sea has much to do with the peculiar experience and imaginative response of the poet and its dominant mood of insecurity and restlessness (Fiacc's experience of New York may have much to do with this):

A dark field at the bottom of the pavings
Starred with shard upon shard
Of day-eye or sunny pee-the-bed;
Another world behind the dyke
An endless sea behind the brink of brick[13]

In terms of Gaelic tradition, the opening stanza of Fiacc's 'North Man' (from the *Selected*) is very much in the traditional style of dealing with nature as a subject for poetry:

Silent the river red in the snow.
In faltering twilight year after year
A lifting wind falls:
The red sun is down, the swans disappear.

This, to some extent, echoes the ninth-century Irish poem, 'The Coming of Winter':

I have news for you; the stag bells, winter's snows,
Summer has gone.

Wind high and cold, the sun low, short its course,
The sea running high.
Deep red the bracken, its shape is lost; the wild goose
Has raised its accustomed cry.
Cold has seized the birds' wings; season of ice,
    this is my news.[14]

Fiacc's poem is, however, the expression of contemporary experience written in the present tense and after the simplicities of the first stanza the process of disintegration, increasing complexity and the broken rhythmic responses associated with his 'city' poetry begin. This is a recurring pattern in Fiacc's poetry. Broken relationships whether natural, social, cultural or individual and personal are imaged in such lines as:

Along the evening Lagan we
Walking the broken dream under the bent bough

... Creating poetry without words
Building silence like a house

... But how far were your words flung like seed
Over stone.

The Belfast poet does indeed build great silences into his poems. There is a sense of the inadequacy of the word, almost an anti-literary stance, in his urgency to communicate the essential miseries of the poor, suffering and deprived. He is a tough-minded yet sensitive poet and his sense of avocation, in the context of a seminary education, is captured graphically in 'Theme from a Gloss' where nature intrudes in a comically black manner, as in Beckett's work, to enforce the bitter irony of discovering oneself to be a misplaced person who has realised their avocation. In this little cameo, Fiacc, or more correctly, his poetic persona, copies psalms "under wing-flowering oak" until:

> The cuckoo above
> (By the way he can read)
> Shits lime on the page
> Cuckoos with me.

This is a direct parody of an early Irish poem on the same theme and is indicative of a growing disillusionment in Fiacc's consciousness. In his other autobiographical pieces, Fiacc finds himself a real "cuckoo in the nest" in being unable to accept the role assigned to him through a tradition of republican militarism in his own family; instead he opts for the poetic vocation, yet cannot deny this atavistic blood heritage haunts the consciousness, as these extracts from *The Selected Padraic Fiacc* indicate:

> 'Yes/No,' this is my tribe,
> This is my clan. By these pre
> -arranged bones, I live and think,
> By this skull on a stick, I am
>
> Womb-wall-barricaded
> Bulldozed-down man'[15].

> Barman father, sleeping with a gun under
> Your pillow, does the gun help you that much
> I wonder
> For the gun has made you all only the one
> In of sex with me the two sexed son (or three
>
> Or none?) you bequeathed the gun to
> Still cannot make it so. I can

Never become your he-man: shot
Down born as I was, sure, I thought

And thought and thought but blood ran ...[16]

In his 'monastic' poems such as 'Master Clay', Fiacc shows us the purity of life and simplicity of those who live apart, literally and metaphorically at a high altitude, in another world where,

Monks are at prayer. Birds at laughter.
Bells peal in still blue air.[17]

In Fiacc's cosmography, the natural world is an 'upper storey' category, is other-dimensional and at odds, set apart from, the 'manufactured world' below, upon which the dust of death sifts. In some of these early poems, the mechanistic world, the city, eats up grace and nature, the modern urban experience devouring the rural, Gaelic past. Such poems are littered with fused images such as "rust-loch", "copper-nut", "glass grass", "red-haired rusted willow" and "brick studded grass". There is that slow descent from the "black evergreens" of the hillside and the monastery to:

This little mill town, the mornings
Getting darker than sundown

This is one aspect of the darkness that pervades.

***

This analysis seeks to locate Fiacc in Irish literary tradition and to show how much he owes, in part, to its spirit. He is a poet of continuity as well as a poet who expresses his own idiosyncratic discontinuities. Fiacc, of course, is primarily known as a poet of the city and this environmental aspect of his work is an interesting field of exploration in its own right. Again, he is here part of a minor tradition which deals with the city of Belfast in verse and fiction. A tradition that runs from Richard Rowley up to Michael McLaverty and beyond.

Fiacc does illuminate the psychological infrastructures of his society and probes the darkness of the "blind back streets" in which ordinary people live a Kafkaesque existence, caught up in inescapable, infertile and destructive relationships. There is certainly a lack of any future vision in his verse (perhaps what the young poet Damian Gorman alluded to as the "imagination of peace" in the Northern context) and the memory of a golden past is obscured by the shadow of the present. Like John Hewitt, he does confirm some stereotypes of the Ulster character such as a rather dour cast of mind, a caustic wit and an absence of colour and imagination, but there are tentative glimpses of another world to be seen occasionally in his verse. With Fiacc the *aisling* or vision has become a nightmare gone out of control and in his personal mythology the Tir na nOg across the "bitch Atlantic" is a New York "bury hole" that offers no relief:

> From cold Belfast to these hell-gales.
> Emerging from this air-conditioned house
> Of ill fame, I am this man, that mouse.[18]

However, in his awakening to reality, at least to an aspect of reality, he has opened up a dark and tragic little social world to the awareness of the reader. The misfortunes and sufferings of the socially insignificant are written large in his conscience and in his verse. Fiacc's relationship to the past reveals a geography of the heart and a sensibility as complex as that of Goldsmith, which makes him a more complex figure, as Ulster is more complex, than is often assumed by outside observers. As such, Fiacc is a poet who is not as fully comprehended or as appreciated as he should be. There is a substance and depth to Fiacc's work which is unfortunately dismissed as obscurity, but in a proper and comprehensive reading of his work this darkness does indeed become visible.

NOTES

[1] Padraic Fiacc, *Missa Terribilis*, Blackstaff Press, Belfast, 1986.
[2] Gerald Dawe, 'Poetry Review', *The Linen Hall Review*, Vol. 3, No. 3, Autumn 1986.
[3] Gerald Dawe, 'Our Secret Being: The Poetry of Padraic Fiacc', *The Honest Ulsterman*, October 1980.
[4] 'Elegy for a "Fenian Get"', *Missa Terribilis*, p. 40.
[5] 'Alive Alive O' from *The Selected Padraic Fiacc*, Blackstaff Press, Belfast, 1979

[6] Terence Brown, *Ireland: A Social and Cultural History*, Collins, Glasgow, 1981.

[7] Padraic Fiacc, 'Glass Grass', *Missa Terribilis*, Belfast, 1986.

[8] Padraic Fiacc, 'Glass Grass', *Missa Terribilis*, Belfast, 1986.

[9] Padraic Fiacc, 'A Christian Soldier Song' from *Choice*, edited by Egan and Hartnett, Goldsmith Press, The Curragh, 1979.

[10] Terence Brown, *Northern Voices: Poets from Ulster*, p. 141, Gill and Macmillan, Dublin, 1975.

[11] 'The Stolen Fifer', *The Selected Padraic Fiacc*, p. 1, Blackstaff Press, Belfast, 1979.

[12] 'Elegy in "the Holyland"', *The Selected Padriac Fiacc*, p. 35, Blackstaff, Belfast, 1979.

[13] 'East Street', *The Selected Padraic Fiacc*, p. 30, Blackstaff, Belfast, 1979.

[14] ' The Coming of Winter', *A Celtic Miscellany*, Penguin Classics, 1980.

[15] 'Night of the Morning', *The Selected Padriac Fiacc*, p.46, Blackstaff, Belfast, 1979.

[16] 'Son of a Gun', ibid., p. 51, Blackstaff, Belfast, 1979.

[17] 'Master Clay', ibid., p. 10, Blackstaff, Belfast, 1979.

[18] 'The New York Night', *Nights in the Bad Place*, Blackstaff, Belfast, 1977.

Etudes Irlandaises, XII, 2 (1987)

An Interview with Padraic Fiacc

MAÍRTÍN CRAWFORD,
HENRY MCDONALD & JOHN BROWN

When did you start writing? Is there an impulse to begin?
I started to write in New York in the late 30s, the early 40s. I had
an English teacher who was Jewish and communist, who started
me writing because he thought I'd a flair for words. And that's it ...
there was insanity too in the family, of course ... (Laughs) ...

Did your early life in New York influence your life or work?
Socially there were important influences—the violence on the
street, the bad social vibes. There were also writers like Hemingway
and his wonderful style. The French and Spanish writers—writers
like Mauriac influenced me. They gave me to some extent my
pessimism, my bite, my darkness.

*You came back to Northern Ireland, what impact did this have
on you?*
Well, it brought back my childhood again which I'd tried to bury in
the garden. I tried to escape childhood memories but, of course,
they were always there. When I came to Glengormley and Belfast
in 1956 I tried to live in the suburbs and get away from the ghetto
mentality and the troubles. I'd always thought my childhood was
murdered, or rather, 'more murdering than murdered' and there
was an aggression born with me in childhood. Here in the 60s
there was a certain amount of euphoria—O'Neill was meeting
Lemass and all that and Nancy and I wanted and hoped for a happy

Ulster, where we could bring children into the world. We did have a sense of hope at the time.

Was it difficult to establish yourself as a poet? Are you established as a poet?
Well, I'm accepted now. But I did find it hard to begin with, maybe because of my American dimension – coming back from America and not being British – I was Irish and had come from Belfast. In Belfast they would only give me a temporary ID card because my passport had said Belfast, Eire, so I had to go to London to get a permanent passport and renounce my American citizenship.

Do you have any advice, then, for someone starting out?
I don't think I'm in a position to give advice, though I do think if you are a young person writing poetry then you should let it happen. It will happen anyway. I don't think you can force it.

What do you see the role of the poet to be in Ulster or Ireland?
For centuries the Irish poet took part in what happened around him. He was part of current affairs and the very Kings of ancient Ireland were frightened to death of the poets and poets' sharp tongue so they took them in and fed them. The poet always had a certain power in Ireland. He still has a certain power if he wants to wield it. He can still, perhaps, say something which can illuminate the dark corners no-one cares to speak of. He can say what he wants if he's a sharp tongue.

You talk in one poem of being able to comprehend the killer mentality. Care to enlarge on that?
Any poet, I suppose, likes to think of himself as a non-violent person and imagine himself, perhaps, as a kind of saint, but in my particular case there's a keg of dynamite somewhere and there's a terrible aggression I have to fight. There's aggression in my writing though I wouldn't like to think of myself as a callous person. And yet I'll be judged by my work and not by what I think of it. Perhaps the aggression comes from existence itself; it's hard to be born, suffer and die and perhaps it's this along with my own aggression that allows me to understand the killer mentality more than the ordinary person. Although I'm a Catholic and believe in

my religion, there are times when I wish to blaspheme against existence, which I find, for any human being, very dark or tense or unbalanced. We are trying to balance it ...

You're a pessimist then?
Yes, I'm a pessimist.

You talk of Catholicism. Is your Catholicism pessimistic?
Yes! It helps me to see the dark side of life. Of course my Catholicism is not the same kind as, say, Seamus Heaney's: I'm an unorthodox Catholic and my Catholicism is tainted with Calvinism. This is a very Protestant society and the Catholic living in it is bound to be Protestantised up to a point. I do not find it as hard perhaps as Heaney, who talks of this in 'The Other Side', to communicate personally with Protestants, particularly of the fundamentalist sort, like Paisley, because of my individualism. I find it harder with my fellow Catholics, particularly the bourgeois or middle-class Catholics with whom I've no social contact.

Did the 'Troubles' mark a decisive break in your work?
Well, you see, I was married to a sweet, orthodox, Catholic girl from America and I was trying, when I came back, to make a whole little world in Glengormley, in the suburbs. And then the troubles came and my childhood came back, which I'd hoped I'd buried in the garden like a dead cat. External events killed my marriage and I feel resentful about that because I'd tried to make it spell 'mother' or 'the garden'. I swung back to my early work which was critical of the society in which I'd lived – a euphoric, Protestant, white society that had no understanding of minorities that lived beside them. I saw that in New York with blacks and here.

What is your attitude to the men of violence? Can violence be used to protest?
I feel bad for them. I can understand why they are the way they are, but it's not the answer. That's why I feel bad and sad for them because ... they're mad. It rhymes – bad and sad and mad.

If we draw a simple distinction between poetry that is crafted and

poetry that is spontaneous or from immediate inspiration, into which category do most of your poems fall?
I would like to think that my poetry is not a rigged card game. I think it should be a game and there should be some element of play, but if I thought for one moment it was going to be all rigged then I couldn't do anything. There's a certain amount of fun with the inspiration bit and word play – in fact, that's what it's all about – play. Take Mozart, for instance, he didn't work: he played. And Picasso didn't search: he found. But to talk of the way a poem comes is a different thing. Some talk of a process, some about seed and growth as in gardening. I would say seed and growth though there is always something miraculous too, a touch of fortune or luck; it could start off from a few words or a phrase that goes round in your head and then finds its way from seed to growth or to nothing at all. It's like sex too: it grows within. But each poem is a new thing so I mustn't generalise.

Is there a conscious development in your work? Are there any threads you have taken from seed to growth?
Yes. I think it has become darker and more mature with the darkness. This is probably the darkest century with the technological weaponry and the concentration camps into which we put millions of our fellow human beings. The only good thing was the development of communication which allowed us to see what we were doing – which must make for some kind of sanity. This is more than background in my work because, in a sense, I began a womb culture and became part of a bomb culture. It's what the Germans call *Der Bomben Poet*. That's what one German said of me in one of their Sunday supplements. And it's right, I think.

In your early work though, there seems to be more hope. Does your present stance mean that you wouldn't write a lyrical poem like 'The Chaunt Rann of a Singer' now?
No, I couldn't write that again. It was one of my earliest poems, a beautiful and religious poem. I think, perhaps, it's the only really religious poem I've written. At that time I was going away to study to be a priest and life crystallised around the fundamental Christian concept of belief in Christ and a washing of our lives. I change the last line of the poem so that it ends with a union with God or with

death, of which I'm terrified now but in those days I wasn't and thought of it as a great relief.

How do you see Christ now?
As a Catholic I see Him firstly as the Son of God, the ultimate figure, who figures for us all as the children of God. My favourite story about Christ is the Sermon on the Mount—it is beautiful—and making more bread for the people. He tells the people who are suffering in life, "Blessed are they that mourn for they shall be comforted." In our macho and militaristic civilisation this concept is supposed to have no place and men aren't supposed to cry but his whole concept I find beautiful … truthful and beautiful.

In your later poems like 'Victory on Ship Street' the emotion seems more compressed, more painful and violent. Is this a fair comment?
I don't think you can drag out emotions as fierce as these and make long poems out of them. Someone criticising my stuff has said my poems are like explosions. Well at this stage they are. Again the image of the time-bomb in the parked car comes to mind as linking what's happening here with what happens before and in writing a poem. To write a poem well puts you under a lot of pressure. Perhaps that's why Michael Longley has called me the patron saint of the insane.

Is there one poem you regret?
There is one poem I regret. It's 'Intimate Letter'. I regret it because it must embarrass my wife. That is why I regret it.

There is little self-doubt about other poems?
I do believe in my stuff. Where the uncertainty or incertitude comes in is in self-criticism. You may, for instance, spend years perfecting a poem because you don't think it has gelled or because one word or small phrase you have used is wrong. It took me ten years to write 'Alive Alive O' all because one phrase was wrong. It had the problem of the wide language of the English-speaking world, where American English is different from English English or Irish English. In New York when the priest served a requiem mass you called it black mass because the priest wore black, but over

here that's an obscene mass. After ten years, instead of 'black mass', I finally said 'in a mass for the dead'. It took ten years. You see the beauty of getting old: it takes longer but you can wait.

Is there a poem you would like to be remembered for?
'Glass Grass'. It is not only the longest poem I've written but I think it was my most self-critical as a human being. The priest had asked me if I could put myself into the mind of the men who kill and I said 'no' – but, of course I was lying and I said so here. It's my most critical of my natal city, Belfast. It's also my most self-critical as an individual living here because I see myself as contributing to the hatred just as much as anyone and I can't emerge as an angel.

You have mentioned American and other literary influences. Are there any Irish writers you admire?
I admire Beckett a great deal and what Joyce did. I like Beckett who is terribly, terribly serious and very aware of our existence and how terrible it is to be a human being. If there's any comedy in Beckett it comes from tragedy and this is what they are finding out about comedy although the ancient Greeks knew it a long time ago. Socrates always had a joke because his life was tragic.

A final question: what is your favourite drink?
Whiskey ... Whiskey. Where is it? Where are you hiding it?

Gown Literary Supplement, Autumn/Winter 1988

Our Secret Being
The Poetry of Padraic Fiacc

GERALD DAWE

I

PADRAIC FIACC HAS BEEN PUBLISHING FOR almost fifty years. The unmistakable shape and sound of his poems have found a lasting artistic echo in the personal and social traumas of his own life and times. That this poetry radically subverts what we often expect to see and hear in a poem is clear from the outset of Padraic Fiacc's *Ruined Pages: Selected Poems* (1994). The collection is intended to serve as an introduction to Fiacc's work—from the earliest surviving poems of the 40s to those of the present—and also includes 'Hell's Kitchen', Fiacc's account of the autobiographical and cultural sources of his writing.

The poetry of Padraic Fiacc departs from the Gaelic otherworld of myth and folklore before settling in the uncharted territory that is Belfast's violent history. It is a story, told with fantastic realism and melodramatic relish, which anticipates many of the most hotly debated issues of contemporary life and literature.

Fiacc's work is preoccupied with language as a physically despoiled body—the violated page, the exploded word order. There has been much talk of late about the theme of inner exile and the use of dialect as a means of refurbishing the jaded artistic persona and poetic of contemporary literature in English. Here, too, Fiacc's work is central, for no figure of the Poet could be more isolated and more aware of the fact than Fiacc himself, while his poems are obsessed with the actual word ordering and depth-charged nuances of common speech.

Fiacc's ability to use idiomatic phrasing and cliché is a marvellous illustration of one of his poetry's main values. Similarly, the voice that in 'A Slight Hitch' describes the "ghost-faced boy-broadcaster" who breaks down, "(can you imagine, and him/'live' on the TV screen)", is drawn against "the usual cold, acid/and dignified way" of the "NORTHERN IRELAND BRITISH BROADCASTING CORPORATION". This linguistic battle for authenticity, at the very heart of Fiacc's poetry, aligns him with the work of Tony Harrison and other 'Barbarian' poets of today. It is a verbal dexterity also paralleled by the imagery of his poetry, like the opening of 'More Terrorists':

> The prayer book is putting on fat
> With *in memoriam* cards.
>
> The dead steal back
> Like snails on the draining board
>
> Caught after dark
> Out of their shells.

Throughout Fiacc's work, the pervasive sense of childhood (of the poet's own childhood, of his daughter's and, in a bizarre way, of the city's) cuts up against the deadly inheritance of sectarian hatred and violence, "crossing our stunted lives", as he writes in 'Glass Grass'. It is the ordinary lives that are stripped of stability and forced instead to live with fear:

> She said she saw a man's head pass by
> The second-storey window.
>
> 'Och notatall granma
> Or else he'd be an awful long
> John Silver!'
>
> Then the lamp was hurled
> And geranium pot after geranium pot
> Before whoever it was could
> Find her a bed in the asylum from
> Childhood to childhood, in a world
> -womb to womb: to womb removed.

This comes from 'Dark Night of the Mill Hag' and there are other similar portraits, like the Kafkaesque 'Dirty Protest', which asks how life ever became so broken: "Blown up, thrown down born alive."

The intellectual legacy that shadows Fiacc's poetry draws upon a classic Catholic one, turned on its head and spliced with modernism, as Pascal, Mauriac, Baudelaire and Joyce coalesce in Fiacc's troubled imagination. There is, too, a wry, terse, almost despairing humour reminiscent of John Berryman, as in 'Intimate Letter 1973':

> Our Paris part of Belfast has
> Decapitated lamp posts now. Our meeting
> Place, the Book Shop, is a gaping
> Black hole of charred timber.

Fiacc can also blend these poetic skills into a beautiful poignant lyric, such as 'Goodbye to Brigid/*an Agnus Dei*', with its opening evocation of Belfast offering up the unforgettable plea:

> My little girl, my Lamb of God,
> I'd like to set you free from
> Bitch Belfast as we pass the armed
>
> -to-the-back-teeth barracks and
> Descend the road into the school
> Grounds of broken windows from
>
> A spate of car-bombs, but
> Don't forgive me for not.

II

Padraic Fiacc's poetry traces his imagination's troubled and broken course through the impounding claims of Irish history and mythology. Chronologically, *Ruined Pages* charts Fiacc's engagement with both these forces—a process marked by personal idealism, and then disillusionment, which finally breaks down, recoiling from any such 'logic', withdrawing from possibility itself into the "depths of our dark/Secret being" ('Credo Credo').

Up to and including 'First Movement', the poems from Fiacc's first published collection, *By the Black Stream* (Dolmen, 1969), are written with a clear conception of the Irish monastic style.

Sharp, syntactical inversions, bright colours, and sense of the world as a natural wonder against which man is a sort of tragicomic intrusion: these traditional features conceal the stolen joy of the poet in the world.

Yet these innocent perceptions seem to exist in spite of the encroaching strain of the world, of experience threatening to stain the poet's consciousness, and it is here that the jagged thrust of Fiacc's imagery takes over. 'Der Bomben Poet' (1941) strangely anticipates Fiacc's poetic fate in this regard. The more disharmonious nature is seen to be, the more discordant and unpredictable the world, the more the poet tries to cast images in chaotic likeness, as in 'The Ghost':

> Out of bull resentment
> Snores to the moon
> At black nightfall
>
> By my side a skull
> Hunted Dermot down:
>
> In all the land the lack
> Of what was whole ...

Poems like 'Master Clay', 'Lives of a Student', 'Themes from a Gloss' and 'Alive Alive O' are tuned into each other. This complementary process becomes disturbed and disjointed, however, at quite an early point, as in 'First Movement'. Fiacc is obviously aware of the importance of this poem since he has brought it into two collections, marking points of hesitancy and anticipation of change. The poem is also noticeable for its accomplished simplicity and the characteristic contrasting of urban with natural imagery:

> I was born on such a morning
> Smelling of the Bone Yards
>
> The smoking chimneys over the slate roof tops
> The wayward storm birds

But the following passage is particularly relevant here:

> And to the east where morning is, the sea
> And to the west where evening is, the sea

Threatening with danger

And it would always darken suddenly.

That sudden darkening and threatening with danger is the first key perception which Fiacc makes of his disintegrating relationship with the world around him. 'First Movement' demonstrates the characteristic style in which Fiacc's poems circle to the source of danger and threat; stunned by the sudden eruption of buried energies and forces that obliterate danger (which is immanent, an exposure to harm) with the deluge of reality. It is for this uncompromising recognition that Fiacc is best known, as he wryly says in 'Glass Grass':

My fellow poets call my poems 'cryptic, crude, dis
-tasteful, brutal, savage, bitter ... '

The tempestuous reputation that is all too often associated with Fiacc's poetry is deduced from the "brutal, savage, bitter". Yet such a reading is one-sided because it fails to account for the sources of Fiacc's poetry, or to describe the technical skills he brings to his writing.

The general impression given by Fiacc's work is one of entrapment: man is held in a painful stasis, pinned between the past and the future and, in this vision, images drawn from religion and impoverished social conditions coalesce. One of the most powerful physical images of this stasis can be found in 'Internee':

And it does not hurt
To be jeered at

When you are hanging
Upside down,

When hanging upside down hurts more.

As a cumulative condition, it is compounded of a range of imaginative experience. For instance, Fiacc's own experience of Ireland as the conflict between an ideal world and terrible reality is a persistent theme in his poetry. In 'Icon', Ireland is the cause and effect of the individual's entrapment:

Unholy mother Ireland banging
on the wall in labour
...
We were born in her

Screams to 'Get Out!'

But if Ireland is seen as a mother giving birth, in 'Fire Light' the
life given is interpreted with existential despair:

... in this so strange
'So Be It Now' as if

It never really were
Or never will be

Only always is ...

Fiacc constantly stresses an enclosed, trapped world; one where
"We all run away from each other's/Particular hell" ('Intimate
Letter 1973') and the force that superintends the hell has an
absolute stature in 'Our Father':

The evil thing being
That which crushes us ...

Fiacc rarely attempts to overcome the darkness, but in 'The Fall'
he makes the gestures of rebellion:

It's vengeance I want
But vengeance on whom?

It is as if Fiacc refuses to acknowledge this life; our being is
corrupt, and his poetry speaks of the disintegrated ontology we
have inherited with all its vast psychic (as much as social) injustice.
But if Fiacc's work operates on this level in general, the poems deal
with specific and identifiable onrushes of reality: the oppressive
'military machine', the deprived environment of a discarded
working class, or the impact of mythology on everyday life, as in
'Elegy in "the Holy Land"':

-aleen dream
of bog on bog of bone

-grounded cloud, Ireland, my dear

Dragon seed pod ...

Most poignantly, this sense of failure resides in family life, where the contradiction between dream and reality is most acute, as in the imagery of 'Goodbye to Our Father':

I see your bone-naked
Face scrutinising 'Injustices' still!

Never bother! You have a hole to hide

in now ...

If there is no release from the entrapment, if there are no ways out, Fiacc can also see the black humour of being there. He does this through self-dramatisation and by the use of the aggressive understatements of Belfast vernacular speech.

Fiacc's poetry deals with the urban landscape and, in this, he separates himself again from the general drift of Irish poetry. With its bases in rural landscapes—decayed, mythic or desolate—and its metaphoric wells sunk far from "the damp down by the half-dried river/Slimy at night on the mud flats" ('Haemorrhage'), Irish poetry has tended to evade the city as imaginatively hostile or indifferent. In 'The Black and the White', Fiacc strikes the exact note of city life, the hostility is embraced, the empty night-time streets, the loneliness, violence and loss:

Sinking on iron streets, the bin-lid
-shielded, battleship-grey-faced kids

Shinny up the lamp post, cannot tear
Themselves away, refuse to come in

From the dying lost day ...

It is not that city life is a contagion; in 'Our Fathers', it is infected by industrial wastefulness:

A grey cloud of pollution from Power
Chimneys, mill house, laundries, cars.

When this environment is seen to be born of a corrupting past, the violent present spreads through every perception, affecting it with an inevitable meaning that imposes itself, like the remorseless rain, on our consciousness, as in 'The Wrong Ones':

> The howl of the rain beating on the military tin
> Roof is like the tolling of a bell
> Tolling for a childhood more
> Murdering than murdered.
>
> I rise and stalk across the scarred with storm
> -erected daisies, night in the north, grass.

Throughout Fiacc's poetry, and in his past commentaries upon it and upon literature in general, there runs a deep hostility to the paraphernalia of art. Fiacc's Beckettian anti-art abandon caustically overthrows, so to speak, the pretentiousness of art, while cauterising the poet's own unavoidable and reckless bonds with life. Fiacc's sense of himself as a poet is, accordingly, both mocking and tragic.

The often ugly parasitic relationship between literature and its immediate or historical world suffering can, in Fiacc's book, lead to a neutralising of that suffering. Literature seems to stabilise the violence by drawing it into its own circuit of imaginative ordering. In the lived world, the suffering continues to overwhelm. Such contradictions and ambiguities cannot be left out of the picture, because they are part of the imaginative process: to excise them damages and destroys the terrible truthfulness that Fiacc's poetry struggles to articulate, for his poems dramatise the human effects of moral and psychological decay upon the lives of the ordinary people for whom, and of whom, he speaks. Time after time, his poetry points to the erosion of human potential, and the indictment is laid at the door of the political establishment.

No other poet writing in Ireland today has been so forthright and committed in saying the uncomfortable thing. Padraic Fiacc is the first of Belfast's poets to have imaginatively possessed, with such unremitting intensity, not only his own life, but the life of his profoundly troubled city as well. It is an extraordinary and disturbing achievement.

Ruined Pages: The Selected Padraic Fiacc (1994)

Belfast on the Cross

DES WILSON

The prayer book is putting on fat
With *in memoriam* cards,

The dead steal back
Like snails on the draining board

Caught after dark
Out of their shells.

—Padraic Fiacc, 'More Terrorists'

POETS CAN USE WORDS EITHER TO mask reality or to enhance our sight of it.

Poets who haunted our schooldays romanticised the countryside and the life of poor peasants when they could not bear the sight of the reality of their own environment, the city.

Poets and singers who would not ride a horse or sit in a caravan for a world of wealth sang out, 'Oh for the open road and a crust and a bottle of wine.'

Others avoid present reality by agonising over their forebears and their identity, the meaning of their lives and their history. Hewitt wondered at length about who he was and who we are, Heaney ponders the relationships between his forebears and himself, between his implements of livelihood and theirs.

For them the present, with all its hurt, is a problem to be masked in words.

Padraic Fiacc on the other hand reflects the real world we live in: reflects it too well for some who would be glad to have him quietly hide behind a wall of words that shield the respectable from too close a look at unrespectable reality.

> My fellow poets call my poems 'cryptic, crude, dis
> -tasteful, brutal, savage, bitter...' and I remember
> The cobbles, cluttered from broken glass, glittered
> Like hailstones melting in the warm May noon, and yet
> I can put myself into the mind of the man who is cold ...
>
> —'Glass Grass'

You don't simply read his poetry, you feel the scrunch of glass under your feet, the taunts of the street, the smell of the burning and the cries of agony that have gone up almost incessantly from these streets. While other poets weave myths to persuade them and us that they are a mystical creation, pondering on their identity as fulsomely as the romantics pondered on lost loves, which they have probably thrown away, and impending doom which they will doubtless be the first to avoid, Padraic Fiacc writes about reality with a hard edge made harsher by the light of the bonfire, the houseburning and the cruel joke:

> Dandering home from work at mid
> -night, they tripped Him up on a ramp,
> Asked Him if He were a 'Catholic' ...
>
> A wee bit soft in the head He was,
> The last person in the world you'd want
> To hurt:
>   His arms and legs, broken,
> His genitals roasted with a ship
> -yard worker's blow lamp.
>
> —'Christ Goodbye'

There is more of Christ's torture and death in Padraic Fiacc's poetry than there is of His resurrection, but who is suffering is not in any doubt. As long as you did it to one of the least of my brethren you did it to me, is the Jesus message. Padraic Fiacc takes the Jesus saying literally.

No other poet in the country has penetrated so far and so unerringly into the heart of what people have suffered here. With an almost fierce economy of words, precise words with edges of broken glass and steel, he not only invites us to feel, he *makes* us feel the hurt which our own people have suffered and often inflicted on each other.

He does not condemn us for it. He tells it as it is and makes us share the pain. Having got us that far he may hope he will do something real about it. If he were living in, say, Latin America, writing about what he saw there, he would be hailed there not only as a poet of great power but as a hero as well. But prophets are not duly honoured at home.

Often in these poems, he entices us along with rich-meaning, meticulously chosen words until we see and hear and smell the reality of the city which both fascinates and frightens him. Then he delivers the last line of a poem like a hammer blow.

Each street, each word chosen with infinite care and precision, full of internal echoes and assonances, paints a word picture of the city which encroaches on virgin country, dragging along with it a human world which even yet has not found its own life harmony to bring with it as a gift:

A dark field at the bottom of the pavings
Starred with shard upon shard
Of day-eye or sunny pee-the-bed;
Another world behind the dyke
An endless sea behind the brink of brick ...

—'East Street'

But Padraic Fiacc's poetry is not pessimistic. He sees the humour in the real life breaking through all the imposed and unnecessary suffering:

At the Gas and Electric Offices
Black boats with white sails
Float down the stairs ...

—'Enemies'

It would be unfair to poet and reader to quote the rest of this poem. Padraic's humour is sharp and kind and gets a lot of its vigour by placing opposites where opposites should be: opposite each other, without trying to pretend that opposites will really turn out the same if you pray hard enough that they will.

Padraic Fiacc—Joe O'Connor—was born in Belfast, lived for some years in New York, returned to Belfast and has *lived* Belfast—not just lived *in* Belfast—ever since.

One of the most miraculous things about his poetry is that he searingly describes the horror of physical destruction without that condemnation which is the lazy writer's path to honour, but with compassion that never involves self-praise. For any writer in our time and place this is an unusual achievement.

Joe O'Connor's work is not comforting to literary establishments, who acknowledge his brilliance while resenting his realism.

Andersonstown News, 18 June, 1994

Padraic Fiacc
Sketches and Drawings

JAMES MILLAR

JAMES MILLAR IS A BELFAST ARTIST whose work has been widely exhibited throughout Ireland. During a friendship which has lasted well over thirty years, Millar has drawn, sketched and painted the poet dozens, if not hundreds, of times. Essentially private and not meant for public exhibition, all the pieces were untitled and undated but the vast majority date from the 1970s and 80s. Non-systematic and *ad hoc* in approach, the pieces include oils, watercolours and pencil drawings and have adopted various techniques—realism, symbolism, surrealism. We present a brief selection of this vast and unique body of work.

THE POET, PADRAIC FIACC.

Padraic Fiacc

Padraic
Fiacc
P.B.A
29·10·93.

the ARTIST & the Poet
Padraic Fiacc & Martin Wedge

The Artist & the Poet
Martin Wagge
a passing face

Jan-1985.

PADDING BEACH. POOL.

PÁDRAIC RÍACC
Poet

PADRAIC FIACC
Poet

Pádraic Fiacc, Poet   Tom Millar.

A Testimony
to the Human Spirit

GERALD DAWE

IT WAS IN SPRINGTIME IN 1973 that Brendan Hamill, the Belfast poet, introduced me to Padraic Fiacc.

Brendan was, like myself, a student at the fledgling University of Ulster, but he knew just about everybody who was writing in or about the north. Fiacc, he said, was thinking of doing an anthology on the north. I was writing and publishing poems here and there, and so we should meet.

I hadn't actually met many poets up to that time. In fact, I don't think I knew any, so this meeting with Fiacc was very important. He lived in the end house in a row of typical suburban houses on the outskirts of Belfast.

His home had been a stop-over at one time or another for many of Ireland's best-known writers. Fiacc himself had been very close to Padraic Colum. He was a very real link between the lost world of the Revival and the disintegrating world of Belfast.

He also knew the work of Joyce (Fiacc's first book was called *By the Black Stream*, after Joyce's poem, 'Tilly'), Beckett, most of the classics, European writers like Mauriac, Baudelaire and there was that poem of Derek Mahon's, 'Glengormley' (the suburb where he lived), dedicated to Fiacc.

After our first meeting, I made a point, whenever I was in town, of seeing Joe (for he reverted to his real name when the defences went down and he became Joseph O'Connor again). We would sit in the living-room and talk about 'the situation',

215

which was turning from bad to the worst it can be, and also about writing.

His quiet demeanour, spliced with acerbic wit and self-mocking, the domestic chores which he religiously went through (lighting fires, clearing the garden of leaves, making coffee, spotting the return of birds, putting the 'garbage' out) concealed an obsessed artistic temperament that was struggling with the break-up of both his personal and social life.

What was going on in Belfast in 1973 and 1974 makes for grim reading, with nightly assassinations, bombings and this net of fear cast over the city.

When I finished my studies at NUU, driving from Belfast to Coleraine for final exams through the UDA barricades of the Ulster Workers' Strike I took a job in the Fine Arts Department of Belfast's Central Library.

Every week, one or more of us would visit Joe; sometimes there would be gatherings. At one of these I met a very young lad called Gerry McLaughlin who wrote under the name of Gerry Locke.

He was like the rest of us: a Belfast lad who loved literature but couldn't sort out how it could relate to what was going on around him. When Joe's anthology, *The Wearing of the Black*, was published by Blackstaff Press, I had left Belfast and was living in Galway, studying at UCG. My girl and I travelled up on 14th December, 1974 by train—Galway to Dublin, Dublin to Belfast. The party the next day was the last time we were to see Gerry McLaughlin. He was murdered four months later on the 7th April, 1975.

His murder changed everything and it represents a terrible watershed in all our lives.

I turned my back on Belfast and the sickening reality of sectarianism and the rhetoric of political gurus in this state and further afield.

Joe visited us in Galway. He was devastated but slowly his writing led him to a way out, or is it in?

There is no other poet from this country who knows the cost of our history and has suffered as a result. All the faddish talk about inner exile, violence, and post-colonialism and so forth; all the business about the supremacy of our own colloquial voices; the image of the marginalised writer; all these issues we hear and read so much about find in Padraic Fiacc's poetry their first real expression.

A few years ago, an old friend of mine (and Joe's), Aodan MacPoilin, decided we should make a selection of Joe's poetry and include in it introductory, biographical and bibliographical material. *Ruined Pages* is the result. As a bonus, we also included a marvellous programme Joe wrote in 1980 for Paul Muldoon at BBC Northern Ireland called 'Hell's Kitchen'. Padraic Fiacc's poetry is the lasting testament to the human spirit that has kept Belfast from turning to Sarajevo.

Irish News, 28 April 1994

Many More Bright Aprils
Padraic Fiacc at 70

BRENDAN HAMILL

PADRAIC FIACC WAS BORN IN BELFAST in the Lower Falls district in April 1924. After a childhood in East Street in the Markets area, he and his family went to New York city in 1929.

It was the year of the Wall Street Crash and people were jumping out of skyscrapers, With many Irish families, they had left the Civil War period in Ireland for the Great Good Peace, like Steinbeck's Okies moving to California, except in Fiacc's case it was across the Atlantic ocean—what James Joyce called "the abyss of tears".

In New York, it was intended that Padraic should manage the two grocery stores his father owned. But the family lost everything in the depression. "The Irish got everything on tick but the blacks always paid," he told me recently. He attended Harem High School, where he founded the writing workshop which produced the earliest of his plays. His studies were completed in Calicoon, New York, and at Holy Oak, Delaware, where he produced his verse play, *Fire*. During the Second World War he was, like Robert Lowell, a conscientious objector.

Though Belfast has always been an especially neurotic and oblique place, deeply wounded by maladministration and sectarianism, Fiacc decided to return there in 1946. His brother Jimmy carried his cases to the port at Hoboken, New Jersey. The Atlantic was still mined and a Swedish boat, captained by a Portuguese, was the first vessel back to Europe. The ship anchored at Cobh, a nine-day journey, and from Cork to Belfast took one day.

Fiacc lived with an aunt in Eliza Street in the Markets. There were horses everywhere in the Markets at that time and 'the cats played with the rats'. He remembers the dole was £2 per week and the Morning Star Hostel in Dover Street made one sausage for breakfast. In 1948, he travelled to London to get a permanent identity card.

In these early days as a writer, Padraic Colum encouraged Fiacc and he ascribes his perseverance, in a sometimes-discouraging career, to the kindly interest and advice of this poet who, along with Yeats, Joyce and Æ, inspired the Irish literary movement. In August 1956, Fiacc married an American girl, Nancy Wayne of Detroit, Michigan. They had been engaged in New York and decided to marry in Ireland and make their home there. They have one daughter, Brigid. They lived in Glengormley where the village atmosphere and peaceful seclusion provided a delightful backdrop for a life of intense creative activity.

In Belfast, Fiacc was inspired by Michael McLaverty, the renowned novelist and short-story writer, of whose work he made a study for the *Irish Bookman*. He wrote similar studies of Mary and Padraic Colum at the insistence of the poet Austin Clarke. At the same time, his work was also being published in the *Catholic World* in New York, and four of his poems were chosen to appear in the anthology *New Poets* (Devin Adair, 1948)

But it was in J.J. Campbell's *Irish Bookman* that Fiacc made his literary debut and where the presentation, in 1946, of seven of his poems was favourably received by the critics. He was subsequently published in *Poetry Ireland*, the *Irish Times* and *Rann* in Belfast.

His poetry up to then—marked, in the words of the *Irish Times* critic, by "a simplicity of vision"—was greatly influenced by the music of Jean Sibelius. As a tribute to the composer, Fiacc wrote an elegy which he sent to Sibelius' widow, who acknowledged the poem with gratitude from Finland.

During the mid-to-late 40s, Fiacc wrote three collections of poetry. Of these the first, *Innisfail Lost*, is lost. The third, *The River to God*, only partially survives in elements of *By the Black Stream* (Dolmen, 1969). Of the second, *Brendan Odysseus*, the one surviving poem appears in a new selected poems due out this month from Blackstaff Press, under the title *Ruined Pages*, edited by Gerald Dawe and Aodan Mac Poilin.

Fiacc was presented with the Æ Memorial Award in 1957, on the recommendation of the advisory committee considering the various entries, for "the best literary work, either creative or scholarly, by an Irish writer living in Ireland who is under the age of 35". The committee said the award was to be taken "in recognition of his published work submitted for the award and, in particular, for his collection of poems entitled *Woe to the Boy*". The author had submitted one play in verse from his cycle *Men as Gods*, two volumes of poetry (including an incomplete collection called *Haemorrhage*) and excerpts from four novels.

In the mid-60s in Glengormley, he and his wife entertained other writers such as Derek Mahon, Seamus Heaney, John McGahern, the late and much lamented Conleth Ellis and James Simmons. Students of Ulster literature should be familiar by now with the importance of this period. By 1974, Fiacc had published two collections, *By the Black Stream* and *Odour of Blood* and had edited the controversial *The Wearing of the Black* (Blackstaff, 1974).

That 'simplicity of vision' in the earlier poems had been transformed into a vision of evil not so simple. It is from this period that the influence of Baudelaire, Rimbaud and Verlaine begins to make itself felt in his work. Also, the music of Debussy and Shostakovich took root in his creative imagination.

By the Black Stream and *The Wearing of the Black* were more thematically integrated than the critics of the time would allow themselves to note, partly through fear and horror. The poet John Hewitt, however, remained unshaken and observed with typical dignity and reserve: "Padraic Fiacc is not an easy poet. He constructs poems with scrupulous craftsmanship, weighing every syllable. He suppresses the connections of formal narrative and leaves the reader to supply them for himself. Even the way the words lie on the page and the spaces in between are part of their significance." Robert Nye, in the *Irish Press*, wrote that the volumes contained "automatic and moving poems made out of the chaos of immediate history. The impression this poet leaves is of a gentle, lyrical, effective talent compelled towards elliptical intensities of insight by the violence in the streets."

Others have been less visionary and more didactic in their appraisals. But the poet and critic Gerald Dawe and the former hostage Brian Keenan had special insights into and appreciation for his work from the early 70s on. They had more empathy with the fractured streets and knew the volatile passions of Belfast, with its gritty integrity. Each in different ways has given witness to the vicissitudes of the New World Order.

The 70s was a period of great oratorical rabies, promising nothing under the sun. What was being kicked out the front door was returning through the back. There was, too, a way in which the weight of the 'troubles' paralysed the imagination and many citizens upped and left the wounded place, believing it to be intractable or not worth the bother.

But Fiacc was undaunted and irrepressible. With a mixture of absurd good humour and simple tenacity, he lived it year by year and the books grew like dandelions out of the debris. There was *Odour of Blood* (Goldsmith, 1973), *Nights in the Bad Place* (1977), *The Selected Padraic Fiacc* (1979) and *Missa Terribilis* (1986), all from Blackstaff. Awards came from the Arts Council, in 1976 and again in 1980, and a *Poetry Ireland* Award in 1981.

Major anthologies began to pick up his poetry: the *Penguin Book of Irish Verse* (1970), the *Sphere Book of Modern Irish Poetry* (1972), *Ten Irish Poets* (Carcanet, 1976) and *Poetry One* (London Arts Council). There were readings in Irish universities, colleges and schools and the circuit culminated in a tour of Ireland with the Scottish Gaelic poet Sorley McLean in December 1979. In 1982, Fiacc was elected member of the Irish writers' academy, *Aosdana*.

As this tempestuous little poet became, in the eyes of many, 'more probable' as an Ulster poet, the volume of work written about him grew. *Der Bomben Poet*, a film portrait by Georg Stefan Traller, brought Fiacc to a television audience of seven million in Germany. Autobiographical features, 'Hell's Kitchen' and 'Atlantic Crossing', were produced for BBC Northern Ireland by the poet Paul Muldoon, whose musical ability—put to good use in his recent libretto, *Shining Brow*—was evident even then with a superb choice of music.

For our post-modernist times of the instant news flash, the

relation of past to future is re-emerging as the central question. Fiacc represents a staging post between these conditions. Urban, vernacular, lyrical and tough-minded, he has had a long jig. He did not cave in under the weight of often hostile and niggardly criticism. He is, as Hewitt said, 'a different poet' and he ploughs a stony and prickly urban acre.

In Fiacc's poetry, in the tradition of Edvard Munch since the 'troubles' began, is a subtle autobiography. What remains of his work? Fiacc is at work on a new collection, *Dead Trees* (a little borrowed from his own play *Les Arbres Morts*, written in the 40s while at school), and the unpublished 1957 collection, *Woe to the Boy*, is due in a revised form from Lapwing in Belfast. His autobiography will be in four parts, provisionally entitled *Cold Water*. There is reason to believe he has a large body of work.

As well as the new selected poems, there are also celebrations and readings from Fiacc's work planned in London. These will be fitting tributes to a poet whom the Labour MP John Battle called "the brilliant Padraic Fiacc whose controlled capacity to face up to 'the worst' is a testimony to the human spirit".

One can't pronounce upon the future but I hope it is fecund, with many more bright Aprils.

Fortnight 327, April 1994

Failure as Strategy in the Poetry of Padraic Fiacc

FRANCIS HAGAN

FIACC'S WRITING TENDS TO RADICALLY DIVIDE critical opinion. In 1979, James Liddy, writing in Robert Hogan's *Dictionary of Irish Literature*, commented: "Fiacc [is] the first of a European species to appear in Irish writing: a Holocaust child, whose mental cast is formed by the milieu of violence". The same critic suggests that "Fiacc is perhaps the most considerable poet emerging from the Ulster disturbances and is more committed to enduring the terror and the bloodletting than any other Irish writer" (this was the same year that Heaney published *Field Work*). John Hewitt has said of him: "Padraic Fiacc is not an easy poet. He constructs poems with scrupulous craftsmanship, weighing every syllable. He suppresses the connections of formal narrative and leaves the reader to supply them for himself. Even the way the words lie on the page and the spaces in between are part of their significance." Fiacc, characteristically, registers the other extreme. He tells us, in 'Glass Grass', that his fellow poets think his poems "crude, cryptic, distasteful, brutal, savage, bitter". In fact—no small indication of their opinion—Fiacc has had little serious critical attention from his fellow Northern poets. Writing a review of *The Wearing of the Black*, James Simmons says rather lamely of him: "most literary people I know have little time for him". This remark seems to have gone unchallenged, except by Fiacc himself. In his introduction to that anthology, Fiacc explains that he is "posing the question ... how deeply can contemporary violence enter a poet's inner being?" Gesturing towards this remark Simmons indulges himself in a cheap jibe: he entitles his review 'The Man Most Touched'. More typical, I suspect, than a string of pejorative adjectives is this sort of barely acknowledged contempt. In his one genuine critical comment, Simmons writes: "I respond to his sharp insight, although many of his poems tail off into hysteria, are not properly worked out." That was in 1974. Ten years later, by which time Fiacc had published a further two collections, *Nights in the Bad Place* and the *Selected*, Heaney published his pamphlet *Place and Displacement: Recent Poetry of Northern Ireland* without making in it a single reference to Fiacc.

Another decade on, opinions seem no less divided. While Brendan Hamill, in his birthday tribute in *Fortnight*, can point to a loyal following, admirers such as Robert Nye, Gerald Dawe, the Labour MP John Battle and, endorsement indeed, Brian Keenan, it is the conspicuous absence of other names which leads me to believe that most "literary people" still "have little time for him". That, and the fact that after fifty years of writing and publishing there has not yet been, so far as I can gather, a single full-length study of his work. In any case the paucity of response, whether positive or negative, has meant that the moral and aesthetic issues raised by Fiacc's poetic practice have remained largely unexplored.

Frank Ormsby, in his 1979 introduction to *Poets from the North of Ireland*, also locates the failure of Fiacc's poetry in this discrepancy between intention and execution: "What he essays— the reflection of an unbalanced, tortured society—is, generally, more significant than what he achieves." At one level, this is true. A section of the poem 'Tears' (entitled 'Lullaby') reads:

> When the ricocheting bullet bites into
> The young child wanted to walk
> In her mother's high heels to push
> The doll's pram, she
> Gives out a funny little 'oooh!'
>
> And lets the blood spill
> All over her bright new bib ...
>
> No pallbearers are needed.

The young father is able himself to carry
The immaculate white coffin but
Stains it with a dirty-faced boy's
Fist-smudged tears
                              then suddenly cries
Out like a man being tortured by water.

This poem finds its occasion, as do most of Fiacc's, in a violent event. The moment of death is caught, the rhythm dutifully tottering in imitation of the tottering child, and falling with her as she "Gives out a funny little 'oooh!'" The last stanza, in its caesuras, measures a funeral march. Typical of Fiacc is the everyday speech, the banality intact but the rhythmic expectations disappointed. Typical, too, is the ruptured syntax. The everyday speech is bleached of conversational emphasis; it achieves a precarious neutrality of tone, resolving overall into a listless incantation. And, as usual, there is no metaphorical uplift: the child is identified with the Immaculate Conception, and the last line situates the father's experience in baptism, but this affords neither the poet nor the reader anything of what Heaney might term 'transcendence'. From the conventional poetic or critical standpoint, it seems to come nowhere near meeting its dreadful occasion. Indeed it seems, rather, to betray it. The formal gestures emerge as trivial: the vocabulary is facile, the rhythmical dissonance trite, the understatement ostentatious. The thin texture does not so much hint at emotional restraint as at emotional anaemia. The poem deals in externals: the facts, the sounds, the pictures; there is something almost revoltingly coy about this in the second stanza. The poet mentions the father's torment—and notice how both father and child remain nameless, as depersonalised as figures in a newsreel—but he does nothing to lift the idea of 'torture' out of the abstract. Nor does his religious vision contribute anything towards a mitigation of the awfulness. Milton, in his sonnet on the Piedmont massacre, finds his faith triumphant: in an Old Testament voice sonorous with authority, he calls upon God for vengeance; he situates the atrocity within its eternal time frame; he envisions the victims as martyrs, compensated for their suffering by an eternity of bliss; and he manages to make the formal perfection underwrite all. Fiacc's Catholicism, although obviously deeply held, does not seem to have likewise fortified him: he sees Christ in the victim, but always the suffering and never the risen Christ. His poems are not written to console, or to lend dignity, or to celebrate. He is transfixed by human anguish, and by its putative meaning inspired hardly at all. The Lament, as a way of dealing with death, has a long and honourable tradition in Ireland, but that too is a catharsis in which Fiacc will not indulge. The 'Lament for Art O'Leary' invites us at once to mourn and by mourning have done with mourning, to remember and by doing so have done with remembering: it is essentially purgative. Fiacc will not lament because he will not mourn, and he will not mourn because he will not forget. For all that, he is unable to transcend the suffering by displaying it aesthetically, religiously or emotionally; he, like Job, tactlessly continues to insist upon it. He does not attempt to articulate others' suffering for them. In this piece his presence as a poet is, in its ineffectualness, a trespass, an impertinence.

This sort of criticism of Fiacc is grounded on an aesthetic which privileges certain linguistic strategies, in particular a certain type of equation between language and its occasion. The nature of this privileged equation is very nearly articulated by Heaney in the aforementioned pamphlet. He begins by quoting Anthony Storr on Carl Jung: "Jung describes how some of his patients, faced by what appeared to be an insoluble conflict, solved it by 'outgrowing' it, by developing a 'new level of consciousness'." Storr continues: "The attainment of this new level ... includes a certain degree of ... 'detachment' from one's emotions. One certainly does feel the affect and is shaken and tormented by it, yet at the same time is aware of a higher consciousness looking on which prevents one from becoming identical with the affect, a consciousness which regards the affect as an object, and can say 'I know that I suffer'." Heaney clearly draws an analogy between the Northern poets, including himself, and Jung's patients. Poetry is a use of language to 'outgrow' intolerable conflicts. Wordsworth's *Prelude*, for example, becomes for Wordsworth, and for those of us who share his predicament, "diagnostic, therapeutic, and didactic all at once". Poetry "is the resolution at a symbolic level of conflicts within the consciousness of the poet". Speaking of the "coarseness and intolerance" of Northern Irish life, Heaney writes: "It seemed that condition had to be outstripped and it is probably true to say that the idea of poetry was itself the higher ideal to which poets unconsciously had turned in order to survive in the demeaning conditions." Again, he speaks of the poet being "stretched between politics and transcendence", and in an allusion to Keats writes, "The poet ... is often displaced from a single position by his disposition to be affected by all positions, negatively rather than positively capable." Keats, we remember, went on to say "that with a great Poet the sense of beauty overcomes every other consideration, or rather obliterates all consideration". Jung speaks of an 'affect' which he identifies with suffering. This 'affect', according to Heaney, "mean[s] a disturbance, a warp in the emotional glass which is in danger of narrowing the range of the mind's responses to the terms of the disturbance itself, refracting everything through the warp". Poetry is seeing the 'warp' rather than seeing through it. The poet's business is with emotion recollected in tranquillity, a tranquillity wholly or partly facilitated or induced by the play of language itself. Language then, for Heaney, becomes poetry only when it 'outgrows', 'transcends', 'displaces', 'obliterates' its occasion. To this end it employs the devices of poetry, chiefly of simile or metaphor: both, in the same pursuit, yoke the occasion to an image, depriving it of its unassimilable integrity. Poetry is language dominant: it exemplifies, at a semantic, phonetic and graphic level, 'detachment', 'resolution', 'recollection', 'dispassion', 'synthesis', 'distillation'. In poetry it is not the cry itself, neither in the street nor in the heart, to which we are directed, but to the cry as chord in verbal music. Poetry is language triumphant: whatever its occasion, the Midas touch, it transforms it into self-referential song. Language 'fails' to become poetry whenever it 'fails' to honour this equation, and the poet 'fails', as Fiacc has 'failed', whenever he refuses to use language this way.

Most of us, writers and critics, share this prejudice. Through an almost exclusive exposure to literature which exhibits this equation, our sensibilities have been educated into it. In general, the degree to which we find an utterance aesthetically satisfying is dependent upon the extent to which it meets our expectations. And it is not without cause that we prefer our poetry thus, for it works exactly as Heaney describes: for a contemplative instant we can be released by it from an 'affect', positioned outside the 'warp'. But we find consolation only when we are consolable: the inconsolable will not be detached from their grief. They will remain identical with the 'affect', there is no place outside; they are composed of suffering. For the father whose child has just been killed there is no detachment from anguish; it is probable that such suffering will never be recollected in tranquillity. For the mother who has lost her teenage son, even in his own explosion, there is no getting over it, though "some days", she says, "are better than others". Intense grief is languageless. A profound sense of loss is almost always complicated by feelings of lacerating guilt: to know that I suffer is merely to know that I do not suffer enough. Poetry, language, is communication; the quintessence of suffering is isolation. The moan which rises unbidden from the mouth; the continuous, wordless, uninflected moan, signals language's apocalypse. The moan or the stricken silence. Heaney and Wordsworth and Keats and Ormsby know their place: this is not the domain of poetry. That comes afterwards, if at all. And even then, always expressing the inexpressible, it will articulate the detachment more than the affect.

What Fiacc essays is not "the reflection of an unbalanced, tortured society", but rather an encounter between language and suffering, and suffering whose local habitation and name happen to be Northern Ireland. He is our War Poet, and it is to the unassimilable cry he is directing us. It is part of his project to reverse the equation, to reveal language's inadequacy in the face of its awful occasion. It is in their decomposition that his poems resonate with apocalypse. He has to find ways to fail—we are reminded of Beckett—and to fail better each time. These poems are declarations of complicity and guilt: they invite the accusing finger. The irony is that they succeed so often.

Honest Ulsterman, No. 98 (Autumn 1994)

The Troubles He's Seen
Fiacc and Belfast, 1967

BRENDAN HAMILL

BELFAST AGAIN, AND THE BOAT, THE *Ulster Prince*, had been droning deeply for the past fifteen minutes. We felt like people who had socks washed in our eyes. It was seven thirty a.m. on Belfast Lough. The hills were a creamy patchwork of snow jigsaws between the television masts. The little house with the trees on the Hatchet Field was lightly dusted with snow, too. The boat gave a violent spasm and docked with a blank bump against the wharf. It was November 1967. A few stiff morning faces broke in verticals and horizontals when they saw their loved ones on the dockside.

Off the middle Falls Road at that time was a broad stony lane which led to the Whiterock Road housing estate—by and large, a decent, settled working-class red-brick housing estate built in the late 1920s. The broad lane was known as the Giant's Foot. It was about three hundred metres long and was so named because it resulted in a long curving instep. About halfway up, two old penknifed telegraph poles held sickly yellow lights. They flickered rather than burned. At right angles to the Giant's Foot was a long dark road with a large gate at the end, which led to Our Lady's Hospice—a hospital for old people, run by nuns. It was forbidden and screened by large thickets of laurel and tall Scots pines. The Giant's Foot was imaginatively named, but nobody ever knew by whom. No plate ever endorsed its name.

Girls were afraid to walk that way at night because it was wild

with tall nettles, and a bump in the slushy pebble-dashed wall
was supposed to have been a nun's head. That's all we ever
knew. Also, because of the depression of the 1950s and official
neglect, a smattering of localised crime was evident.
Unemployment was chronic and the railings turned year after
year to rusted husks.

Big box-like suitcases were packed in sad silences for England,
America and Canada. The squat boats made their way to
Liverpool with their cargoes of human grief. They went away in
the frosts and rains over the glassy seas. Those people remained
alive only in conversations in dark little fortresses with small
glittering fires, and soon faded from memory. An occasional
photograph arrived postmarked Sydney, California or London.
Few had telephones then.

It was November 1967, and brown and yellow leaves were
everywhere and skirling in wind gusts now and again. They packed
against the old granite walls and railings—slippery underfoot, but
sweet-smelling.

After some years in London, I thought Belfast was a quiet city—
full of sullen repressed raw energy and clotted with hard men who
asked you with fierce eyes, 'Who the fuck do you think you're
lukin' at?'—to which the reply was a derisory 'Not much', and
then you ran for dear life.

Big melancholy constables passed by in preternatural silences.
Belfast seemed to work manic shifts of feeling and mood and Dinah
Washington sang 'September in the Rain' to knots of soft-eyed girls
in fishnet stockings in Jim's Café on the Whiterock Road. Jim was
a handsome Italian and wore a white apron. I once saw a fellow—
a teddy boy with one lung and a flick knife—being kicked to death
there when I was eleven years old.

The old teddy boys of the 1950s had, by now, hung up their
luminous pink and green socks, the studded belts and
knuckledusters, and had settled down gratefully to pints of
Guinness and tough hard-voiced women. The macho princes had
walked into their final sunsets or so it seemed—their lean muscular
bodies clacking 78s onto turntables in maisonettes or rented
rooms, in transit, maybe, to better lives. If they were pacifists, I
would have been more frightened at a vicarage tea party. They

were sparse and hard and favoured big raw-boned dogs named
Rebel or Rover. The seagulls came like omens to the grey roofs in
the smoky mornings.

People from the Shankill drank on the Falls and nobody made
heavy weather of it. Mixed marriages were commonplace and
worked. There were unstable Jeremiahs, though, with faintly
foetid alliances. The women were largely stitchers, seamstresses,
nurses or waitresses. Most of them made their own dresses—the
cloth was bought, amongst other places, in a big Baghdad of a shop
in Royal Avenue called the Spinning Mill. From the planes at night,
Belfast was laid out like a lighted necklace in a valley. People on
the airport bus used to marvel at how beautiful the setting was as
they ploughed into the thick scent of night hawthorn and the
dark—to English cities on struggling old Viscounts.

That world of submerged violence didn't affect me in any
direct way. I was young and indifferent and, besides, London was
about adventure, new sounds, new people and places. The
Beatles, the Rolling Stones and Frank Sinatra—that master of the
pause—absorbed my interest. Also, the great sprawling
Metropolis was an emotional relief from the thin film of moral
paranoia that was Belfast.

Life on the eighth floor of Stuart House in Soho Square was
quiet. It was a law enforcement section of the Ministry of
Transport. It was cosy and urbane. Also, I was going with a girl,
Janet Hartley, a sweet girl from the genial village of Holmfirth,
outside Huddersfield.

She was the first Marxist I had ever met, but I liked her anyway.
She liked my pink face and honest eyes, she told me in a funny,
pleading accent. She lived in Jessel House at King's Cross and made
lovely strawberry jam. She was a lecturer in education at
Goldsmiths College in London. I was introduced to *A Sentimental
Education* by Gustave Flaubert and *The Loneliness of the Long
Distance Runner* by Alan Sillitoe.

My friend Gordon Winerow was from Bolton and a part-time
reserve sailor on a coastal minesweeper anchored in the Thames,
and when we got drunk we used to sing 'A Nightingale Sang in
Berkeley Square' in a kind of tuneless farce. London was a great
exuberant city then and people were generally happy.

When I thought of Belfast, it was with some kind of confused despondency and awe. It was a place of deep pain never expressed—a place of psychic battering and secrecy. The abnormal had become the normal. The dark messengers had been waiting in the woodwork and were coming out now.

This particular night, though, I was back in my own home town and going to a poetry reading in a house in the Upper Donegall Road. It was cheek by jowl with the chapel of St. John the Evangelist. A grocer's son who lived beside the Sandbanks was there with a sheaf of poems. They sounded like fizzy drinks though, and, if I may say so, I was glad when he stopped. It was a tidy street which shielded a little colony of middle-class people. One side had brick, three-storeyed houses and an attic. A few well-placed trees set the street off. Those attending were mainly humble civil servants, schoolteachers, insurance men and a few tradesmen. Like those inmost similar areas of Belfast, they wanted their children 'to get on'. There was a faint odour of sanctity and a strong lust for respectability. They were—variously—the noblest Romans of them all. At least they were humorously thought of as such by the 'low types' with a jocular brutality. They were anonymous and discreet. The relationship between the classes on the Falls Road then was both rancid and intimate in our agreed thinly veneered antagonism—the sacred and the profane as it were, but they really said nothing twice to each other in the one day. Of course, they were all Catholic in the most elastic and highly snappable sense of that word. There is always a hiss when the waters of heaven meet the fires of hell.

Conleth Ellis was from Carlow, and Fiacc had lived in New York City, in Amsterdam Avenue in the garment district of Manhattan. He had been back home in Belfast since 1947 and lived in Newtownabbey. He was a gentle soul and reminded me of a man dipped in hazel varnish who had dried out unevenly. I am uncertain whether or not he read from the *Capuchin Annual* or the *Dublin Magazine*.

At that time Marshall's Newsagents in Donegall Street was the only place which stocked literary magazines or foreign newspapers like the *New York Herald Tribune*. The Lyric Theatre, though, had a very good bookshop on the Grosvenor Road, near the Ritz Cinema, and Mullan's Bookshop in Royal Avenue was a little gem of a place. But here I was, this November night, back in my own home town, at a loose end, seeing it all anew through the bright metropolitan filter of London, where everything was available.

There was a short awkward silence, then the introductions were made and I noticed that Fiacc's right hand shuddered and he looked slightly spooky. He glanced at me furtively, perhaps to see if my face was kind—the way the Hunchback of Notre Dame did, I imagined, in the Broadway Picture House years ago, when the beautiful girl saw the heart of the Hunchback, and everybody clapped, but mostly us children in the cheap front-row seats—the soul of man under socialism, so to speak.

"Read 'Alive Alive O'," exhorted Conleth Ellis, "that's a lovely poem." A short tense silence—and Fiacc's voice crackled into a kind of bland monotone, like the hum of high cables over a cowshed on a clear country night, "Should I? Really?" There was a brief thunderstorm of nervous release which crackled around the room again, and I heard Conleth Ellis enthusing—"I love the word 'bucket'; 'bucket' is a lovely word." Fiacc wanted to be coaxed and then read—shakily:

> The altar boy from a Mass for the dead
> Romps through the streets of the town
> Lolls on brick-studded grass
> Jumps up, bolts back down
> With wild pup eyes ...
>
> This morning at twist of winter to spring
> Small hands clutched a big brass cross
> Followed the stern brow of the priest
> Encircle the man in the box ...
>
> A bell-tossed head sneezed
> In a blue daze of incense on
> Shrivelled bit lips, then
> Just to stay awake, prayed
> Too loud for the man to be at rest ...
>
> O now where has he got to
> But climbed an apple tree!

The voice swayed like a tipsy metronome in my head. There was silence and a polite little cough. Copies of *This Ripening Time* were sold at 2/6d a time. The host was a gracious and dignified man and we had another cup of tea. It was, too, a judicious act of recovery. My mind flooded with the soft purple mystery of Lent, as I had remembered it as a schoolboy in the chapel nearby. I had begun to feel an unlocated guilt, as though London had robbed something of my soul. But I had come back to this little St. Petersburg à la Dostoevsky's *The Idiot*. I was seventeen and a mixture of awe and lostness.

The year was lived season by season in Belfast, but in London the head shot forward. The heart leapt uncomprehendingly somewhere behind. I was caught between cultures, one angular and hard with a heart like a swinging brick. That was commerce. The other was poor and eschatological in its gradations of thought, feeling and mood, and blended with a city naturalism of sorts. That was Belfast specifically in time and place as I knew it, whatever the general picture might have been.

Even as young teenagers we went west—west to the Fully in the Black Mountain—west to the small town of Crumlin of the curved glen—to the airshows at Aldergrove, in the slow train—the tinny bus and corrugated grey Nissen huts, the mangled wreckages of wartime air-raid shelters, and the final incongruity of rabbits and old silver Viscounts frozen into the runways. W.H. Auden's "unimpassioned beauty of great machines".

Immediately, I sensed Fiacc's urbanity and humiliation—the poet as victim. Of what I didn't know. Although I loved Heaney's clean masculine tactile poetry in *Death of a Naturalist* and Festival Publications' *Eleven Poems*, I sensed Fiacc was closer in spirit to the fire-and-air world of the young Derek Mahon—though not a classicist in style or syntax. Clearly he was an original both as man and poet. His experiences of New York saw to that—the most sentimental of all American cities—the melting pot on the Hudson River. "Give me the moon over Brooklyn," they'd say, those American visitors with baffled disdain when confronted with the vagaries of the Ancient Quarrel.

The chamfered door opened. Somebody wanted to know where Mister Dowds, the insurance man, lived. But it was a languid and proper house and nobody was ruffled. Conleth Ellis stood up and read a poem dedicated to Padraic Fiacc, entitled 'Remembering'. The last verse of which reads as follows:

And did the heron stand as in a dream
To watch a trout against a speckled rock,
As now he stands to bring that childhood back?

A loose rambling discussion on the poetry of Gerard Manley Hopkins followed. On the lower half of the Donegall Road, people were watching *The Mountain* in the Windsor Picture House. It starred Spencer Tracy. Nobody ever called them cinemas. There was also popular enthusiasm for a film called *The Invisible Man* at the time. About seventy metres on either side of the Windsor Picture House were small mission halls, a Methodist church and the Monarch Laundry. Underneath the grey bridge ran the Belfast-Dublin railway line. There were waterhens, mallard ducks and bullrushes in the Bog Meadows.

Peggy Greer lived nearby on Donegall Avenue. She worked with my sisters in The Star—a garment-making firm. With my mother, she would shake with seismic laughter, usually about Mr. Grimble, who was finicky and straight-laced. It was a private joke, though, amongst the women.

The fire was getting low and people became restless. The bay windows caught our breath and became pimpled with fine droplets. The last poem was a sign maybe—certainly the only published poem on the event. Two years earlier I was working in Stuart House, a branch of the Ministry of Transport, in Soho Square, or the wicked Square Mile as people sometimes called it. I was catching up on spot checks in accordance with the 1960 Road Traffic Act and Mr. Thurston, the executive officer, came into the comfortable office—eight storeys up.

He was a mannered Londoner, who would smile and whistle to convey an air of nonchalance to put us at our ease. He fumbled with his umbrella and gabardine coat, before resting them in the cloakroom. The office was empty. It was 7.55 a.m. Sunlight was slipping off the tall buildings and spires of London, and shadowed angles widened.

"Brendan," he said inquiringly and quietly—aware that he

might sound petty or alarmist—"there was rioting in Belfast last night—no one hurt though, old cock."

Something about a flag and a preacher—an Elmer Gantry style figure, the type you get at Hyde Park Corner. It was the first time in a year I'd heard Belfast mentioned by anyone in the office. It existed indifferently, north of Dublin. "Rainy like Manchester," the women in the typing pool chorused abstractedly when I first started the job.

"I was at a clear up on the minesweeper with Winerow last night. Didn't hear the news, got back late from Charing Cross—they're going to France at the weekend. Some sort of drill they do. Those minesweepers have a shallow draught, it seems. They expect bad weather," I recounted in a sleepy reply.

Thurston was a happy man and he liked Winerow and me. He felt sorry for us being away from home so young. It elicited from him a kind of prudent and avuncular interest in us which was unobtrusive.

Winerow didn't appear, and I got on with my work. Thurston straightened his tie and contemplated London through the high window beside his desk. Drunken drivers and tired lorry drivers had been causing pile-ups on the M1 motorway the previous Christmas and the control car men were coming in with resolve and cold anger. It made work for everybody, not to mention the undertakers.

Strolling down Greek Street at lunchtime, I told Winerow—jaded from the previous night—that I wanted to get a copy of the *Guardian* on Shaftesbury Avenue. He had heard the news too, somehow. "Do you do examinations in sin over there?" he teased in a superior way. "I know what you mean, Winerow, but it's more complicated than that," I replied absently. "There hasn't been a shot fired in Merry England since the War of the Roses," he persisted with a grin. "Okay, Winerow, so you're the lovely people. You'll be smoking dope next and falling asleep at the wheel and the boat'll go down. No more mockers and scoffers meeting the mayors of the wee French towns." He laughed good-naturedly and waved his hand in mock disparagement. From the back page of the *Guardian* it seemed ugly enough in its own demented way. Men were playing three card tricks on cardboard boxes in Greek Street with quiet speed. It was illegal.

Fiacc's hand shuddered the teacup and broke my reverie. I didn't know whether or not I'd see him again because I'd be going back to London soon. Conleth Ellis read the last poem. It was entitled 'Belfast 1964':

Autumn came to Divis Street in splintered glass,
Twisted gratings, stones and hurleys; grass
Behind the railings of Saint Comgall's strewn
With shrivelled leaves: outside—became a tune,
A phrase, a flag can strangle rote-learned grace—
Find splintered, shrivelled heart and twisted face.
Imagining green hills the ashen breezes brushed
The glazed mill race, wide-whorled, that rushed
To find its stream, I find my path down grasses,
Over brown stones where the night herd passes,
Where only coins of light fall through leaves,
And foxes hunt, buds burst, the spider weaves.

On the Heysham boat a few Belfast lads were singing a Bob Dylan song aggressively and garrulously: "It's a haard, it's a haard, it's a haard rain that's gonna fall." I ordered a bottle of Wee Willie Dark at the bar and wondered about Belfast and the little dainty man with the hazel head and eyes. I had no answers for anything. I wearied of the loudness of the song and went up to the starry deck amongst the soldiers and the sailors. We were all sea-struck. It was quiet. Belfast was left behind in a great moonlit track of foam. I felt relieved in some sort of grave way. I was still an adolescent feeling my way between two worlds, wanting to understand what I didn't know—exactly.

Fiacc at that time in 1967 was a "bell-tossed head". His poetry was witty, vagrant and tough. He had a deft knack of slapping the sacred cows on the butt. The poems had the depth of sonic echoes. I knew then he would be mocked, because people didn't want their corners of the cobweb shaken, and a cobweb it was. They had a point, but the world of tight moral constraint was loosening and I knew that from my aviary in London.

Apart from a few poets and poems, I felt there was little to get excited about—apart from Derek Mahon's 'In Belfast', Louis MacNeice's *Autumn Journal*, some of W.R. Rodgers, Norman Dugdale and Heaney's 'Docker'—not world-shaking by any means.

From that little meeting came *Words* magazine. It looked like a film brochure. It contained poems by Michael Boyle, Michael Brophy, Seamus Heaney's 'Gravities' and work by John Morrow (who cut his literary teeth there) and an article by Ralph Bossence of the *News Letter*. Michael Emerson of the Belfast Festival was interviewed there, but it didn't see a second issue. People went to universities or lost interest.

For me, Fiacc epitomised the secret spirit and atmospherics of Belfast at the time. The third eye, so to speak. His poem 'First Movement' was an emotional flare.

Low clouds, yellow in a mist wind,
Sift on far-off Ards
Drift hazily ...

I was born on such a morning
Smelling of the Bone Yards

The smoking chimneys over the slate roof tops
The wayward storm birds

And to the east where morning is, the sea
And to the west where evening is, the sea

Threatening with danger

And it would always darken suddenly.

This was an Ancient Mariner poem—the sense of a great bruised swell of feeling bloating. Fiacc and the poets came to understand painfully the meaning of Shakespeare's lines at the end of *Love's Labour's Lost*—"The words of Mercury are harsh after the Songs of Apollo". This was the beginning of the end of a period of fatalistic aphasia. Poetry in the North began to flourish, often with rancour and weaselling.

Fiacc was the beginning—the rascal amongst the monks—the sign and the soothsayer—from Hell's Kitchen to the Dark Country—to Dante's *Inferno*, and ... finally to life lived in the shadow of the gun. He shares with Sir John Betjeman and the dogs of Belfast a love of lamp-posts and dark corners. When his autobiography comes out it will be like a Belfast version of Robert

Graves' great autobiography *Goodbye to All That*. Meanwhile, I'll not take the third light. I believe in luck and the words of William Blake: "the tigers of wrath are wiser than the horses of instruction". Imagination can create a new world—where the old one failed. Fiacc's poetry talks the language of wrath.

Perhaps the horses of instruction should take off the blinkers and listen.

Krino, No. 18 (1995)

Review of *Ruined Pages*
Selected Poems of Padraic Fiacc

MICHAEL PARKER

IN AN OFTEN PERCEPTIVE, PROVOCATIVE, BUT sometimes less than enthusiastic review of Seamus Heaney's *Field Work* back in 1980, A. Alvarez commented on what he saw as a disturbing phenomenon in English letters: how one Irish writer in each generation is elevated above his peers and selected for 'star' treatment.

While most readers would take exception to Alvarez's patronising placing of Heaney as merely "a beautiful minor poet" and the simplistic characterising of his verse as "fragile", he was certainly right to voice concern over the relative neglect that other gifted Irish writers suffer, especially when the media, the commercial world of publishing and some in the literary establishment reduce literature to a question of 'who loses and who wins; who's in, who's out'.

One Northern Irish poet whose achievement has not received the acknowledgement it deserves is Padraic Fiacc, a selection of whose work has been published by the Blackstaff Press under the title *Ruined Pages*. Though well-represented in Frank Ormsby's excellent anthologies, *Poets from the North of Ireland* (1979) and *A Rage for Order* (1992), where he is given an equal number of entries as Michael Longley, Fiacc's work is too little known outside Ireland. In the poem which provides the book's title, 'Tenth-Century Invasion', he compares Fiacc's work with that of scribes and illustrators of illuminated manuscripts in the Dark Ages, their epiphanies "written in/The shaft of the sun/In the moment on the/Margin/Never to be sung".

Born in April 1924 in Belfast as Patrick Joseph O'Connor, the future poet's earliest years were marked by tension and instability, resulting from his family's emigration to America and the fluctuations in his father's fortunes. Fiacc's mother never settled in her exile and though her husband, a former Belfast barman and IRA activist, prospered for a while in his grocery business, eventually it collapsed. Their son's earliest verses, reflections on his status and experiences as an Irish Catholic immigrant, brought him to the attention of Padraic Colum at Macmillan, and soon after, the *nom de plume*, Padraic Fiacc, was adopted. At some level this re-naming himself was to claim kinship with his important literary mentor/father, and to signal more assertively his Irishness. Not surprisingly, soon after abandoning his studies for the priesthood in 1946, Fiacc left America for Belfast, which has been his base ever since.

From the outset of this selection, 'Der Bomben Poet: Spring Song 1941', Fiacc registers in spare, seemingly dispassionate diction an engagement with the place from which he has been physically detached since the age of five. Almost inevitably the contemporary reader will detect eerie continuities in the poem, and read the lines backwards and forwards, linking its stark footage with the anti-Catholic pogroms of the 1920s, which saw Fiacc's mother's family burnt out of Lisburn, and the blazing city of recent years:

Today is my birth
-day. I am seventeen.

My home town
Has just bin
Blown up:

Dead feet in dead faces,
Corpses still alight,
Students helping kids
And old people out of

Still burning houses.

I have nothing to write
Poems about.

This is my twentieth-century

Night-life.

Those curt, clipped lines prove to be typical of the later Fiacc, whose compressing of sound and meaning may make some of his verses seem excessively austere and strained grammatically, but often generate energetic movement, sharply realised images. Particularly beautiful and potent with omen is a section called The Burning Garden from the late 1950s and early 1960s (which did not appear in print until 1969), and the collection *By the Black Stream*. In 'Two Solitudes', a poem whose analogy between the arts of baking and making predates Heaney's 'Mossbawn Sunlight', Fiacc celebrates a couple's unity in apartness, "glow with silence like the full moon", joined as they are in creative, concentrated activity; the one awaits the change of her "moth-coloured grain to golden", the other the proving of his clay into "glass pages", receptacles of clarity and light. Much of the charge in 'Burnt Orange', a kind of ode to Autumn, derives from its attempt to fuse opposites, 'malt' sea/'coral' sky, dead seaweed/new seed, rot/wean, 'blood-bloom', and also features a muted pair, separate and insubstantial as 'down', as 'smoke', and a male-speaking voice seeking closure in "The light-crazed hazel stain that/Your harvesting eyes are". That this delicate, yearning, fragile, private world is under siege becomes apparent in The Burning Garden's final poems, which find "The prayer book ... putting on fat/With *in memoriam* cards" ('More Terrorists'), the people of the little mill town "Trapped in our own shallow chill/Shadows" ('Against Oncoming Civil War'), and the garden itself succumbing to increasing acts of violence and dispossession ('Orange Man'). The latter title invites us to read the poem as an allegory for the history of Ireland, and a warning for the future, culminating as it does with the triumph of the "shrewd-eyed/Navy blue jackdaw, the brute size/Of a graveyard raven", seeing off the lonely, "tiny orange/-breasted robin" which had naïvely imagined the territory his. Interestingly, a relative of this same jackdaw featured in one of his earliest poems from the previous decade; the self-confident blatherer of the earlier poem, who relished storms and boasted of his peregrinations—his occupation of towers, 'hollow oaks', rabbit burrows and cliff-crevices—now appears translated into a pre-Hughesian thug.

Another powerful sequence also dating from the mid-1950s is East Street, in which the narrating voice remembers experiences from a broken, confused, 'brow-beaten' childhood, and rages against the pain, deprivation and repression he endured, and that "shudder no one can still" ('Haemorrhage'); a recurring image is of a 'cut head', a head full of holes, prematurely bent by Weltschmertz. Whereas in earlier, more lyrical periods in his writing career, Fiacc had often employed bird images to signify possibilities of transcendence—"I would rather have geese for their less-smooth flight/I would rather have geese for they're ugly like me" ('The Boy and the Geese'), "I am the blackbird/Of the ruined nest who sings" ('Storm Bird'), "Strong as the seedling the clay/-reared winging bird" ('Old Poet')—by the time of these later intense evocations of closed-in-on, urban Belfast, birds have acquired more sinister associations, have become yet another menacing presence, part of the place's explosive chemistry. The sequence's title poem opens and closes to "the thunder of pigeons—bombs", and at its centre draws an analogy between gulls on a pub-roof waiting "with military eyes/For the bin men" and hungry kids anticipating the arrival of their 'grub'. Given the privations maintained by the Orange state, domestic interiors also turn into battle zones, as adults in the family grind each other down in a war "us kids can't understand", where "Nothing changes", "No one wins" ('Bombay Alley'). Any wry irony accruing to the composed figure of "the grandmother with a gun/In her apron, making the Military wipe/Their boots before they rape the house" is dissipated as the focus of 'Son of a Gun' relocates to the terror-stricken mind of the young narrator, on the run still from the memory of these raids (which surface again in 'A Still Floating Child' and 'The British Connection'), from his dead father's shadow and the presence of his gun.

In giving so much space within the volume to these impressive earlier sequences, Gerald Dawe and Aodan Mac Poilin have in all hope deterred readers from seeing them merely as a preamble to *Ruined Pages*' later matter: Fiacc's responses to the recent Troubles. Given the pain seared into his own childhood, it is not surprising that in his post-'69 poems children figure prominently as victims and as objects of the poet's compassionate attentiveness. These poems hold no promise that "a terrible beauty" is being born. Rather, they confront cruelty with an "agonised directness", to use Frank Ormsby's phrase, and where they do employ ironies they leave the reader with no room for knowing superiority. 'Elegy for a "Fenian Get"' alludes to the killing of a nine-year-old, an altar boy, when the flat he has been hidden in for safety is "penetrated" by automatic fire. The poem's outrage is directed not so much at the juvenile "trigger-happy cowboy cop" responsible for the killing, as at the obscene and vicious bigotry that begat and sanctioned it. The elegy ends desolately, with nothing learnt from the tragedy, and with the next generation of little-minded children loyally intoning the previous generations' almost biblical cry, "'Burn 'im/Burn 'im, Burn the scum, Burn the vermin!'" The bitterly titled 'Victory on Ship Street' similarly connects present and past slaughters of innocents; amongst the casualties of a pub-bombing are "Two wee girls in/Hallowe'en dress/burnt/To death as witches!"

In poem after poem, Fiacc echoes Louis MacNeice's condemnation of "the intransigence of my own/Countrymen who shoot to kill and never/See the victim's face become their own/Or find his motive sabotage their motives" (*Autumn Journal* XVI), asserts the sacredness of individual human lives, and challenges the evil orthodoxies that crucify. Amongst the most effective and affecting are 'Goodbye to Brigid', 'Enemy Encounter', 'Kids at War', 'Tears'; these last three containing images of British soldiers, which show the poet re-reading and questioning received responses. In contrast to the faceless, ruthless Military glimpsed violating Catholic homes in earlier poems from earlier periods in the Troubles, the Brits of the 1970s are often presented as mere kids, "young enough to be my weenie/-bopper daughter's boyfriend" ('Enemy Encounter'), "white/-faced as young girls" ('Introit'), "grim/-faced ... hating the being hated" ('The Wrong Ones'), emotionally vulnerable, physically exposed. The two sections of 'Kids at War', for example, commemorate acts of kindness by soldiers, one a "half-kid" shot while on Lollipop Duty as he went to buy ice-lollies for a group of Irish kids which includes his future killer, the other giving up his life to save an "Irish woman and kids" when a barracks is about to explode.

A reassessment of Fiacc's contribution to contemporary Irish literature is now under way, and the publication of *Ruined Pages* makes no small contribution to this process. In the past, according to his own account, certain "fellow poets" had dismissed his writing as "cryptic, crude, dis/-tasteful, brutal, savage, bitter" ('Glass Grass'). What most often strikes me, however, about Fiacc's distinctive poetic voice is its linguistic energy and economy, its uncompromising integrity, its almost Blakean fusion of passion and compassion.

Irish Studies Review, No. 13 Winter 1995/6

Cúchulainn Cauterised
Padraic Fiacc's Twentieth Century Night-life

PAUL GRATTAN

Poetry is an exile's art. Anyone who writes it seriously writes from an exile's point of view.

—Charles Wright

READING PADRAIC FIACC'S FIERCELY ENGAGED AND often troubling poetry, it becomes obvious that here is a man who has endured far more than "Seven winters in a dark room". The phrase is John Montague's (who omits Fiacc from his *Faber Book of Irish Verse*), describing the training and duties of the bardic caste in Irish poetic tradition—and serves as a useful landmark from which to locate and extend study of Fiacc's shrouded corpus. For this is a poet who has been largely obscured, if not negated, from critical view and only Frank Ormsby has been prepared to give over fraught anthologising ground to a healthy representation of Fiacc's ruined pages.

This reputation as a 'problem' poet stems mainly from the visceral 'on the bone' nature of his verse—in relation to the violence against mind, body and soul exacted in the North of Ireland (pre and post 1969)—and his stewardship of the first major anthology, *The Wearing of the Black*, to reflect Northern poetry as product of a 'damaged' society.

If his stylistic approach to poetry was not at first or even second glance obviously 'tender', to paraphrase George Buchanan, it had—in the furore that followed the anthology's publication (waged in the *Honest Ulsterman* November '74-February '75)—"never been so truly from the heart/so treated as nothing much".

Such was the level of animosity directed against the poetry (and person) of Fiacc that it prompted these last angered words of justification on the matter:

> The bad odour surrounding *The Wearing of the Black* is the bad odour of blood and it stinks of a society that has hopelessly degraded itself and consequently degraded those of us who have to exist in it.

Perhaps the most unfortunate feature of the whole 'debate' was that relevant aspects of criticism became lost in a mounting quasi-moral tirade of abuse directed against a shibboleth—Fiacc as whiskey priest of the occupied six counties—and away from the more inflated aesthetic lapses his writing can be prone to.

Praising Fiacc's "intensity and sharp insight" in his *HU* review of *The Wearing of the Black*, James Simmons rightly highlights the first two stanzas from the poem 'Internee':

> It is not absolutely fair,
> It is not absolutely wrong,
> And is does not hurt
> To be jeered at
> When you are hanging
> Upside down,
> When hanging upside down hurts more ...

and,

> The far off neons of Belfast glint like crosses.
> I'm lying in blood, piss, pus, slime.
> My face is at the feet of the Supreme
> Victim, the people, the people who
> Are utterly lost ...

He finds the first stanza "starts off well" but that the second betrays for him a typical Fiacc flaw: "many poems tail off into hysteria, are not properly worked on".

Contrast this with the revised version of 'Internee' found over twenty years later in the selected *Ruined Pages*:

It is not absolutely fair,
It is not absolutely wrong,

And it does not hurt
To be jeered at

When you are hanging
Upside down,

When hanging upside down hurts more.

The following poem in this collection, 'Dirty Protest', has as its opening stanza: "The far-off neons of Belfast glint like crosses./I'm lying in, lying in, like my own slime./My face is at the feet of the Supreme/Victim, the People. The people, men/boys, who...".

Fiacc has undoubtedly 'worked on' these poems, splitting the '74 version into two separate wholes—a formal decapitation which weighs 'Internee' with the precision of an executioner—the *strappado* effect achieving three short two-line stanzas followed by a single longer line which keeps the eye dangling after meaning to the poems close.

'Dirty Protest' is an overfamiliar return to the Christ-crucified complex which haunts Fiacc's work, although the inarticulate disgust which mires the '74 version of the second stanza in melodrama and lame repetition is subsequently exchanged for Ancient Mariner-like imagery of man's "life in death and death in life" fall. I'm sure yon particular critic, no stranger to civic protest over the sanitary nature of his own poetic couplings, would approve of Fiacc's more measured and concentrated reprise.

Of particular interest are the omissions and revisions that take place with the selection of poems from the 1973 collection, *Odour of Blood*, that appear in the selected poems of 1994's *Ruined Pages*. Where Montague renames the loaded, 'Auschwitz, Mon Amour' as the more reflective, 'A Welcoming Party', Fiacc's changes of face are less textual than stylistic. Although, 'The Other Man's Wound' appears in the later volume stricken of its second part, most of his reshaping occurs between the lines, in the stanza breaks themselves—as if: "the hiatus and spaces intended for the person who wishes to breathe while reading a poem aloud" were no longer visible in the later versions of 'Gloss', 'Haemorrhage' and

'Alive Alive O'—poison will, it seems, no matter how high the apple tree you climb, reclaim the lungs.

Poetry wars aside, uncomfortable truths and fictions rebound throughout Fiacc's work and it is with Montague again that illuminating parallels may be drawn. Both share an Irish/American experience of estrangement and uprooting through cultural contexts and historical forces that seem at times bent on consuming identities of person and place. They are acutely aware of the attractions and repulsions of childhood—like another New York exile of the late twenties and early thirties, Lorca, whose deep songs of urban solitude affirmed a pivotal dichotomy:

> Yes your childhood: now a fable of fountains.
> Strange soul, tiny and adrift, ripped
> from the emptied space of my veins—I must look until I
>   find you.

Montague's epic, *The Rough Field* contains in its fifth section, 'The Fault', the elegy for his father, 'Stele for a Northern Republican' (anthologised by Fiacc) and seems to resonate with the conditions of the latter's own internally inscribed conflict with the familial and menacingly unfamiliar branches of his Arbres Morts:

> Little enough I know of your struggle,
> although you come to me more and more,
> free of that body armour
> you tried to dissolve with alcohol ...

Like Montague, his poetry seems continually absorbed in a permanent revolution of revision and reformation—a process which evokes the natural selection of words evolving rather than imposing meaning *sub specie aeternatus* or after the fashion of ideological conceits. Compare the former's shocking portrait of the rape of an old woman in, 'The Wild Dog Rose' with the first crazed line of Fiacc's, 'Dark Night of the Mill Hag'— both enclosed worlds of immanent physical, mental and spiritual collapse pushed towards their final solutions: "the asylum from/childhood to childhood, in a world/-womb to womb: to womb removed."

A tortured tautology reveals the dialect of this tribe—necessarily discordant and disrupted, although perhaps less palatable than other 'hollow-sounding liberal papist notes'.

In an early poem from the 40s, 'Jackdaw', we are already confronted with issues of moral ambiguity. The bird's testimony, "That storm is good", is in itself an unsettling one. A poetic that insists on invoking the instability and flux of its surroundings—of raking among the ashes in that denuded, annexed corner of the Garden of Ireland—must indeed provoke nervousness, if not nightmares amongst those who may prefer a more ordered, landscaped approach to the imagination. Dig among the debris of fingers and thumbs and expect more than cracked nails, blisters or cold shoulders from honest Ulster men and women is perhaps Fiacc's reply. Affinity with the victims of a politically parenthesised, necrotic state where "(these civil wars are only ever over on paper)", drives the poet towards an ugly confrontation with his own role and motivations. 'Glass Grass' is at once an expression of confession, conspiracy and confrontation, challenging assumptions and assertions—of right and wrong, moral or ethical behaviour—in the repeatedly battered face of this "too-near-to-the-knuckle disaster ... "

A clear and comfortless epiphany crawls out from under this relentless self-scrutiny: that sectarianism is not an abstract concept of the 'other'—which limits its appeal to the diseased minds of mad dogs and monsters—for "The Black is in my lungs now, and in my poems."

Realisation that even redemption is a suspect device leads first to aporia: "(Here, how did all this happen inside and behind time, And why so often?)"—and finally to bathos: "I am on the same anti/-depressants as the backstreet/kids and their young mothers!"

If Fiacc's attempts to say the unsayable, name the unnameable appear pointless, we should remember the counsel of another poet, Keith Douglas, who was faced with the futility of writing about and in another long war:

> To be sentimental or emotional now is dangerous to oneself and to others. To trust anyone or to admit any hope of a better world is criminally foolish, as foolish as it is to stop working for it. It sounds silly to say work without hope, but it can be done; it's only a form of insurance; it doesn't mean work hopelessly.

Whether he remains in his own time and his own place Northern poetry's internal émigré, Padraic Fiacc's bells of reckoning, awakening and alarm will continue to sound—like the birds of Autumn passage—their particular dolorous promise to:

Bring back the bone-buried
Dog-eared old shoe of the heart
And out of it make

Out of a 'sow's lug'
A work here and there
Of ground-hollow art

And bridle, bridle the teeth
Of brutal night-life with

The bit of love.

FET supplement, *Padraic Fiacc: Poet of the Pagan City* (1999)

Fiacc's America
To Hell's Kitchen and Back

CHRIS AGEE

TEMPESTUOUS, HARROWING, WORRISOME, troubled, fantastic, black, pungent, out-of-kilter, disconcerting—all adjectives applied to the poetry of Padraic Fiacc. They and their like are part and parcel of what has been said of him often enough: that, more than any other Northern poet, he is inside the psychic space of the Troubles—its sulphurous reek, its icy intolerances, its immutabilities and resiliencies. Put another way, it could be also said of him, as Ralph Ellison once said apropos Black American writers, that he has never flinched from 'fingering the jagged edge'.

The jaggedness in question is, of course, the Northern version of Ireland's 'cracked looking-glass', the proletarian world into which he was born: irredentist or loyalist, poor, angry and debased. Shards under the sectarian tawse: what Hegel called the Rabble, the dispossessed of industrial society who, lacking the privileges of the legal order, have no reason to feel any loyalty to it. It is a Belfast that even now most of those higher up the food chain, of whatever national persuasion, would wish, or shoo, away. When it imploded in the late sixties—the time-lag echo of the Southern Civil War—Fiacc was still there, by the roundabout route of a returned emigrant; and much of the bite of his work descends from the fact he speaks from the midst of that whirlwind of dark forces that so afflicts "the bogpit waste we've made of this place/Ourselves by just running away from it."

Not everyone's cup of tea—it can, at first glance, seem

ungainly—the elliptical terseness of Fiacc's style is nonetheless a sophisticated instrument for registering the storm and stress of his territory. The clanking, Latinate partitions of his titles; the jarring nuances of colloquial speech; the pared-down rhythms, sense-jinks and syntactical hiccups; the apparent roughness of enjambment and word-splits; the disjointed image- and line-movement; the snatches of street dialect—all this may take some getting used to, but for the sympathetic reader it can encompass many subtle effects, and achieve a catching, discordant, anti-aesthetic music. It has, overall, a kind of cubist passion. Like Tony Harrison, Fiacc strives for the authenticity of various registers of educated and common speech; like Ginsberg, he plumbs a colloquialism of syntax, ear-music and inner stenography.

After all, how is a poet to treat the ugly and the violent? Is there not the danger, the unfaithfulness, of aestheticising violence with the magisterial or classical? Allowing for too much of the inevitable crack between the distancing of art and brutal fact? Questions of this kind seem to inform the way he puts a formal squeeze on the immemorial gap between the two. Moreover, hearing him read is a revelation: much of the initial effort required by the printed page falls away, and an impressive fit of sense and sensibility, style and vocal tone, hits home. Rendered in his nasal American accent, a poem like 'Crucifixus'—"In all the stories the Christian Brothers/Tell you of Christ He never screamed/Like this … "—has an instant melancholy power, and is not easily forgotten.

Memorable work, then, by any sensitive reckoning. So why does Fiacc seem the perennial odd-man-out in Northern poetry? Given the amount of critical attention accorded poets here due to the political turmoil, it might have been expected that his forthright obliqueness in the uncomfortable thing would have gained a bit more literary centrality—if not by his compatriots, then by his literary peers. Or, the suspicion dawns, is the opposite more likely the case? When was the truly uncomfortable ever popular? He himself notes in a 70s poem: "my fellow poets call my poems 'cryptic, crude, dis/-tasteful, brutal, savage, bitter'". And if he has been the butt of some opprobrium, how much of it was based on a honest assessment of his achievement? Talent, of course, is decisive, if not in the short-term then the long. But with

Fiacc's poetry, I do think we are strongly into the sociology of reputation—in his case, the way literary judgments can transpose deeper social and political mindsets. It is not hard to see how Fiacc's poetry runs up against a number of obvious and powerful Northern taboos that, in turn, impact on its appreciation.

One of these is speaking about the political heart of the Troubles directly and bluntly. For a quasi-outsider like myself, a striking feature of the culture here is the reticence about talking of politics or religion in any context that might be construed as non-intimate or public. For obvious reasons: whatever you say, say nothing. But something analogous can be glimpsed in the varying degrees to which Northern poets inhabit, imaginatively, the actual psychic space of the Troubles. Whereas Heaney and Carson often address this space directly, in others, like Muldoon and McGuckian, there is more of a distancing effect; indeed much has been made critically of poetic strategies for keeping the Troubles, as it were, at an imaginative arm's length. Of course, there is no right approach. A poet's duty is simply to the language and his or her deep-level sensibility. Nonetheless, in registering with starkness and passion the sickening core of the conflict—for he is the poet of victims par excellence—Fiacc transgresses the Northern code; and, to the more delicate literary palette, his work might well seem as 'unaesthetic' or 'unpoetic' as the mean streets of "Bitch Belfast" so dreaded on the political front.

Closer to home, it is telling that his poetry has never been capable of being dragooned into service by the *soi-disant* republican movement. On the surface, he would seem an ideal candidate: he has always spoken for the "poor, bare, crossed in grain," eye-level with a working-class reality pummelled by loyalist murders as regular as storm-darkenings over Belfast Lough. Yet, reading him, it does not take long to see that he holds not the slightest consolation, cultural or political, for the mindset of the 'ethnicised' republican: his imagination is just too antithetical to the two-tradition reductionism on which Ulster's deep provincialism thrives. (Ethnicised because militarised, militarised because ethnicised: the sort for whom Tone rolls nightly in his grave.) Stylistically, he is not only streets, but whole townlands, ahead of what Jack Holland once called the "Ulster fry school" of writing—the green parochialism that so mars the literary effusions of Adams and Morrison. Not for him the trashy idyll of Falls life in the Wee Six.

Politically, he is even less palatable to the cult of "hard-on guns"; unlike most of the talking heads here, he is especially attentive, as a matter of both intellectual honour and shared *mea culpa*, to the transgressions of his 'own side'. Hardly remarked upon, amidst the justified celebration of his poetic peers, is the fact that much of *Odour of Blood* and *Missa Terribilis* constitutes perhaps the most directly enunciated poetic critique of armed politics to have emerged from the Troubles. For Fiacc's great theme is Christ glimpsed in the face of the murdered, and the attendant duty of remembrance; an insight for which there can be no sub-clauses or preconditions. A soldier, a boy, a girl, a bomber, an informer ... all the same:

> It seemed such a cheap
> Stage effect of reality that Death,
> Hiding in the wings
> On a foundry roof
> Sniping at soldiers, should,
> Like a childless woman,
> Snatch away
> A wee chalk-faced boy
> Playing marbles in the mud.

In the shadow of this sort of atrocity, how can an ethical republicanism remain deaf to the plea: free us from their Egypt!

Finally, Fiacc's poetry runs counter to the insular, even xenophobic, atmosphere of Northern life. No surrender to the outside perspective! It is a culture in love with the narcissism of small difference. In contrast, Fiacc has cultural bifocals. On the one hand, almost all his later work fixes its gaze on Ireland, and above all on his life in Belfast and its life in him; on the other, that gaze has been profoundly marked by his youthful experience of America. (He emigrated with his family at age five, and returned, in 1946, when he was 22). No doubt some of the ethnic essentialists among us, unfamiliar with global terms like 'transnational' and 'dual-place identity', will struggle with the idea of someone being fully Irish who grew up mainly overseas. "My formative years were spent in Hell's Kitchen," he writes in his memoir of the same name, "the then black heart of the worst part of New York". Even though he came to hate America, the severed self of the small immigrant child and "the uncouth slum adolescent" cannot but be the father to the man. "What was this dreadful wound New York inflicted on us," he remarks in the same memoir, "or was it simply the twentieth century?"

That American "wound" strongly suggests that the traumatic jolt of a forced immigration lies close to the heart of two characteristic features of his poetry: a special feeling for the world of childhood; and a knack for universalising the sordid, mean, pinched, vicious sectarianism of a Belfast riven by the Troubles. Anyone who reads Fiacc at length will notice his passionate alertness to the bat-soul of the child, its fragility and innocence, especially in the midst of ugliness; indeed, "the non-dead child/Buried in the man" is a recurrent theme. The Ireland of his early years is simply the universal of childhood enchantment, the streets "wombstones", however grim the surrounding hardships; the Ireland of the native son returned, a painful place where life is a long fall "all the way from childhood". Behind this temporal partition, one senses a childhood razored by an upheaval into the sweltering poverty of immigrant tenements; torn from its first world, and thrown into the brave New World of Depression New York. Perhaps that is why, back in the Old World, childhood is so often counterposed to the murderous, as in 'Midnight Assassination', when a child's-eye view of the moon prefaces the killing and evokes the final atrocity of ending, along with the man, the child within.

But New York, by Fiacc's own account, was not all sad and bad; it was "exciting and scintillating, like the last glimpse of the Hudson as we climbed the stairs down the basement entrance". His was the New York of the inter-war immigrant stew, half American, half European, where greenbacks might live cheek-by-jowl with Black Americans and the great art galleries of Manhattan—the New York immortalised by Alfred Kazin, the chronicler of American life and literature, who grew up in the cocoon of a Russian Jewish district of Brooklyn. Likewise Fiacc, amidst the heavily Irish ghetto of Hell's Kitchen: he notes that it was not until mid-adolescence, when he moved upstate, that he first met "the real honest-to-God

American". And New York then, more even than after the War, was, in its own eyes and the eyes of the world, the new century writ large. It was a life, and therefore a perspective, that could not fail to shape his poetic outlook—to inflect it with a trans-Atlantic whiff of "twentieth-century night"—when he came to trade in the Big Apple for the Lilliput of the North. Is it not pure Fiacc to begin a poem about the British connection with "In Belfast, Europe ... "? Or to link, through a sense of the *mea culpa* shared by all, the victims of the Troubles with the far-off crucifixion at Hiroshima?

"A distinctive culture," wrote the great Irish essayist Hubert Butler, "cannot exist without cultural intercourse." That is why the culture here now desperately needs huge infusions of outside influence and perspective: to fracture the reductionism of the 'two traditions' and the lacerating provincialism it has engendered since Partition. Like a kind of Kaliningrad on the Irish Sea, Ulster is cut off, marooned in political failure and enmeshed in a series of Pyrrhic culture wars that seem ever more opaque and antiquated to the outside world. Final normalisation will surely be as much a matter of the deconstruction of the two traditions as an accommodation between them. Yet this cannot be achieved without much greater cultural intercourse—as if Ulster could remain some psychic autarky. Part of the significance of Fiacc's poetry is that it embodies and illustrates the truth of this. From way back, he has dented the mould of the contending myths—"womb small as mouse-dropping black"—an achievement not unrelated to his time in the old Irish diaspora of New York. And that, as we all know, is no mean feat. It should be prized.

first published in Fortnight Educational Trust supplement,
Padraic Fiacc: Poet of the Pagan City (1999)

Man Tortured by Water
Where Does Padraic Fiacc Belong?

DAMIAN SMYTH

IT WOULD BE TOO MUCH TO describe Patrick Joseph O'Connor as the owl of Minerva, flying at dusk and bringing wisdom. But it is not too much to say that the publication of Padraic Fiacc's selected poems, *Ruined Pages* (Blackstaff Press), in 1994, and of his subsequent volume *Red Earth* (Lagan Press) in 1996, brought to public view a life's work the aesthetic of which is at once rarified and accessible.

Despite having remained strenuously outside the starry 'establishment' of northern Irish verse—Heaney, Mahon, Muldoon, Longley *et al*—Fiacc has always had his uncomfortable admirers. "When I think of Fiacc," Paul Muldoon said in 1994, "I think of good news. He represents something about the condition of being a poet that many, including me, shy away from. I admire him for that and for what he's done and for what he represents."

"I've always found him personally entertaining, but also a disturbing presence," said Michael Longley. "Although, on occasions, I've felt like turning on my heel and walking away, I've always realised that if I turned my back on Padraic Fiacc, I'd probably never write another poem. In a way, he is the custodian of the spirit of poetry."

But the fact is Fiacc hasn't always been well received. When I came to Belfast from Downpatrick as a student in 1980, Fiacc's was not a presence in the thriving literary scene, which then still had

Paul Muldoon at its core. He was not rated as a poet, was patronised as a person, was the subject of gossip by the gossipers; importantly, his work was not taught at Queen's. As Longley's qualified praise implies, he is a tempestuous and curmudgeonly figure; but his complex biography has too often served as a flag of convenience for neglect by peers and successors. Fiacc does not fit into the mould of the Poet as Civic Figure; still less does he fill the role of the Poet as Custodian of Domestic Certainties in Time of Trouble. The arc of his career—from a start in the Lower Falls, to studying for Franciscan orders in the United States in the 1940s, to his final incarnation as the bearer of witness to military, communal and paramilitary violence—encompasses a unique range of cultural influences which placed his work only on the margins of the Beautiful Ulster Lyric, which is really an English one with a very English sense of civic and aesthetic order.

Fiacc's 1973 volume *Odour of Blood* was the work of a poet twenty years older than the celebrated 1960s group of northern poets. (Was anything less '1960s' than that group? More Barber, Bilk and Ball to Fiacc's Captain Beefheart.) The collection set off charges in the careful ethic of that generation, which was in many ways less adventurous than that of their elders. His 1974 anthology of 'Troubles' verse, *The Wearing of the Black*, shocked many people, but struck at the heart of the writer's role in times of violence.

Fiacc, the 'war poet', introduced a baldness of expression which, while it sometimes founders into reportage, often succeeds memorably in producing poetry which is unsurpassed in its unmediated seizure of the frightened, violent moment:

The Military, white
-faced as young girls ...

'We're all going to be blown
To hell's gates' cries
The Welsh one: 'The bomb is

Going off at the gasworks!'
A sudden ball of orange
Spurts over the black

-board sky of chalk

Houses, and old ladies and
Soldiers shake like flowers

Crying 'Christ!' and 'Fuck!'

—'Introit'

The controversy over his work turned on the aesthetic value of
direct confrontation with the brutality of violence: the consensus
was that the poems were, as Fiacc quotes in his poem 'Glass Grass',
"cryptic, crude, dis/-tasteful, brutal, savage, bitter". The virulence
of the attack on Fiacc—for attack it was, sustained in the *Irish
Times* and the *Honest Ulsterman* and by other reviewers singing
from the hymn sheet—is scary still. Edna Longley saw *The
Wearing of the Black* as "vampirically bloated" (*Irish Times*, 15th
January, 1975); James Simmons wondered "how most of these
poems ever managed to find themselves between the covers of a
book", referring to the "scrappy incoherence of the verse" and
"indulgent rawness of the content" (this is James Simmons,
remember); John Jordan spoke of Fiacc as "an extreme case of
almost total and uncritical identification with Northern Catholics"
(*Hibernia*, 2nd November, 1973). Consistently, aesthetic hand-me-
downs about the Well-Made Poem and the Emotional Distance
Proper to Poetry—postures in literature which are not absolute and
which have their provenance in the pretensions of English
prosody—take on such fierce moral weight that Jordan's
observation about Fiacc's Catholicism could pass casually as a
comment of literary criticism and not draw the opprobrium its and
others' sectarianism deserves and which they sought to heap upon
Padraic Fiacc.

For Aodán Mac Póilin, who co-edited *Ruined Pages* with Gerald
Dawe, these criticisms have an obvious subtext: "A lot of the
reaction was expressed in aesthetic terms, but it had an ideological
basis. He is a poet who has impinged on the nationalist community,
among the non-readers of poetry. His work is sometimes seen as
expressing openly nationalist sympathies."

God forbid. But it is clear that the venom directed against Fiacc
was perhaps as much in defence of the conservative and unionist
literary politics then in the ascendant as an assault on the
destructive and disruptive practice of the 'Catholic nationalist'

poet—volumes reviewed at the same time include Michael Longley's *An Exploded View* and James Simmons' *The Long Summer Still to Come* and *West Strand Visions*. Jordan, indeed, found time also to find John Montague's *The Rough Field* "heavily in favour of Catholics and Nationalists"; to condemn Thomas Kinsella's *Butcher's Dozen* as "convenient sectarianism"; and to praise these lines from Simmons' *pièce de résistance* of languorous self-exculpation, 'Bloody Sunday':

> When speakers dissipate their breath
> demanding basic inalienable rights
> I know we are in for a boring night
> and morning paper headlines of death.

If only that were the worst some of 'us' were in for, Mr. Simmons. The point is that non-engagement was in vogue; under the cover of the Distance Proper to Poetry, sectarians could hide and wait to see who won. It is clear from Fiacc's poetry, in which there is not a single prejudiced comment which can be ascribed to himself, that it was not he who was biased. He certainly did not feel it incumbent upon him not to speak about what he saw in favour of a supposed civic duty to defend order. He opposed the order. He was not Albert Speer. He did feel it incumbent upon him, however, to project a truly cold and moral gaze on randomness and suffering and evil, preferring not to believe the liberal nostrum that it was all boring and inevitable.

Such reviewing and poetic crudity is amazing: yet it does give an indication of what exactly was felt to be at stake. Edna Longley found "a certain bias" in and "rather object[ed]" to the way *The Wearing of the Black* "literally wears its heart on its sleeve—the cover brandishes an orange and green heart, jaggedly riven and swathed in a mourning band". It is one step from there to the dismissal of the anthology as a whole: "a total absence of aesthetic and stylistic considerations". Some total.

It is easy to see how Fiacc set the teeth on edge. In 'Elegy for a "Fenian Get"', dedicated to 'Patrick Rooney, Aged Nine', the boy shot by ricochets from the gun of "some trigger-happy cowboy cop", the poet asks:

> O holy Christ, why?

'Well, it's like this:
Fenian gets out of hell are spawned in
Filthy Fenian beds by Fenian she-devils
                 will
Bloody not take the pill!'
                    The other
Little children altogether shouted:

'Rats, pigs (nits make lice!)—Burn 'im
Burn 'im, Burn the scum, Burn the vermin!'

Fiacc's critics were and are wrong and, moreover, are culpable of deliberate vilification, misrepresentation and injury to poetry. But it is not surprising. What is interesting, though, is that the taproots of Fiacc's aesthetic were, in many ways, unfamiliar to those writers. The first to note is the influence of French authors on his work; the second is the deep morality of his poetic values. Fiacc's themes are loneliness, pain, the little splinters of joy that stick in the skin and remind that one is alive, love and death:

The prayer book is putting on fat
With *in memoriam* cards.

                    —'More Terrorists'

He provides no mottoes for and draws no lessons from the moments of distress he relives in his work. He is, however, excruciatingly aware of the effects of even the smallest action on the lives of others, and that is where ethics has its place:

My little girl, my Lamb of God
I'd like to set you free from
Bitch Belfast as we pass the armed

-to-the-back-teeth barracks and
Descend the road into the school
Grounds of broken windows from

A spate of car-bombs, but
Don't forgive me for not.

           —'Goodbye to Brigid/an Agnus Dei'

His anxiety about people and his recognition of the inability of words to match the horror links him to Pablo Neruda, for whom children's blood ran in the streets "like children's blood". And Fiacc's poems disturb in their frankness and bluntness as do those of Paul Claudel and John of the Cross; but it is with the French poets Baudelaire and Verlaine that his work is most at home—a down-at-heel, rag-and-bone moral code that begins and ends—in the most unlikely way—with God:

> The monastery on the mountain
> In the cloud is no haven
> To take from what I should give
> God ...
>
> —'Prayer'

What *Ruined Pages* and *Red Earth* reveal is the consistency of Fiacc's work. The imagery most associated with the 'Troubles' poetry is right there from his earliest writings in the 40s and it displays what is Fiacc's most evocative strength.

For Fiacc is an intensely Catholic poet—a clean, intelligent, brave and generous morality which registers the pain of the individual and the people in the context of imagery steeped in the great reservoir of Catholic ritual. It is no surprise that one of his early mentors was the great short-story writer, the late Michael McLaverty—another heavily influenced by French literature and obsessed by the problem of Catholic writing in the modern world. Both McLaverty and Fiacc significantly chose to draw their models from French culture, rather than from the insipid or embittered figureheads of 'English Catholic' culture, like Greene or Waugh.

Most importantly, Fiacc's ethos, like McLaverty's, is not exclusive, but reaches out to embrace all the dead as an intimately personal loss. 'Midnight Assassination', which conveys the ordinariness before murder, directs the reader to the level of involvement (beyond boredom) which implicates us all in grief:

> Now how many loves
> Have we lost—sharp, quick
> -silver gulls, glinting in
> The dawn-dark sky, like knives?
>
> The dead are lying dead in my gut.

Such poems which deal with identifiable deaths show Fiacc at his most careful. There is no sense of exploitation, just of a kind of justice being done to the sorrow of individuals, avoiding scrupulously any hint of using the deaths to make 'larger' points. Fiacc's eye never wavers from the sad wounded and dead. His style is spare, careful, economical, hesitant, sometimes explosive, often beautifully lyrical, even with the most uncongenial themes.

The English poet Ian Duhig believes that "Catholic existentialism informs part of Fiacc's work and explains why so many have missed the ground on which he is figured." He sees Fiacc's work as "a process of selection of the fragments left after an explosion. He is like Spinoza: everything is a version of what we cannot see and we have no place to stand to see it all. Ultimately, he courts the break-up of his poem—all those ellipses. And it works."

This was a view prefigured by John Hewitt in his notice for *Odour of Blood*: Fiacc "constructs his poems with scrupulous craftsmanship, weighing every syllable. He suppresses the connections of normal narrative. For it is this control of the words and their placing which controls his deep emotion, modulating his bitterness, his pity." 'Scrupulousness', 'craftsmanship', 'suppression', 'control'—not words his detractors would have us associate with Padraic Fiacc. Paralleling Hewitt's cussed Protestant civic protest, Fiacc brings to northern poetry a peculiarly Catholic intonation.

This may or may not be a desirable thing—but it gives Fiacc a language and a myth which enables him to write with authority, without cheap demonisation, and with deep compassion of the blowtorches, the drills, the shootings and the odour of blood:

> The young father is able himself to carry
> The immaculate white coffin but
> Stains it with a dirty-faced boy's
> Fist-smudged tears
>   then suddenly cries
> Out like a man being tortured by water.
>
> —'Tears'

FET supplement, *Padraic Fiacc: Poet of the Pagan City* (1999)

'Credo Credo', 'The Kickers', 'The British Connection'

MICHAEL PARKER

PADRAIC FIACC IS A POET WHOSE direct, painful, 'jagged' texts exist at a far remove from the formally neat, more emotionally restrained lyrics of Hewitt, Heaney, Mahon or Longley. Either consciously, because of an inability or unwillingness to accommodate his stark aesthetic, or through ignorance of his work, critics have tended to write Fiacc out of Northern Ireland's literary history. Yet his work merits attention for its linguistic energy and economy, its passion and compassion, and its resolve to face up to the fragmentation he perceives around and within himself.

'Credo Credo' voices the outrage and hurt defiance of the Falls, depicting the curfew as a vain attempt by the British Military to suppress an enduringly resistant native culture. Presented metonymically through references to "rifle butts", "bullets" and "hob-nailed boots", the soldiers assert their dominance over the subject people by defiling their icons rather than by means of direct physical violence, though the latter is not ruled out. Action and allusion simultaneously link them with the iconoclasts of the Reformation, and with the Nazis—hence the stress on the Child as "Jewish"—whilst the reference to the "Machine" marks them as representative of a culture, which, though advanced in economic terms and in terms of military technology, remains crude, brutal and primitive in practice. In describing how:

... When you found our guns

You got down on your knees to them
As if our guns were the holy thing ...

Fiacc translates the soldiers' actions into a rite of obscene obeisance, and pits against these latter-day heretics the adherents of the Old Religion. Possessors of "a richer dark", worshippers of the "ancient, hag-ridden, long/-in-the-tooth Mother", they place their trust in a dubious paradox, their faith in a Pearse-like cult of failure. By deploying such words as "swarthy" and "ugly" to describe the Catholic mother and child, the text mirrors colonial discourse, which typically fixes both the Other and their icons in these terms; Fanon, for example, talks of how the coloniser views the native as "the deforming element, disfiguring all that has to do with beauty or morality".

In its presentation of Northern Catholics as an impenetrable text to outside readers, 'Credo Credo' bears some affinities with Heaney's 'Broagh', with its "*gh* the strangers found/difficult to manage." Yet where Heaney's poem constructs an opposition between Britain and northerners from both communities, and gestures towards a reconciliation founded on shared words and sounds, Fiacc's reflects that impulse within the nationalist community to read the contemporary narrative as a continuation/repetition of earlier 'history' in which its allotted role is victim.

The curfew also haunts the third section of 'The Kickers'. This opens with a reprise from 'Credo Credo': "It was our icons not/our guns you spat on", before striking forward with its spare, immediate narrative. The narrating voice warns the reader that though what happens may seem to come from "Far away in the night", in reality it is "never all that far". Suddenly we find ourselves in the present continuous, confronting force conveyed aurally through partial consonance ("kicking"/"kitchen", "guns"/"coffins"), repeated use of velars ('k', 'g', 'n'), and, to a lesser extent, stops ('b', 'd', 't'):

The Military and/or Police
Are kicking down the door

Of a small kitchen house
Holding your babies
by the feet

Shaking them for guns
Turning the dead over
in their coffins

For the speaker—as for the people in the Falls—collaboration between the Army and RUC has rendered them indistinguishable. Punctuation, grammar and lexis stress the irresistibility of their authority, contrasting it with the powerlessness of those trapped in domestic spaces; seemingly, the kitchen houses are occupied only by the vulnerable—infants, the old and the dead. The 'security forces' are the capitalised subjects of the poem's sole sentence and perform each of its disturbing acts. In at the birth of a new, and at times deadly coercive policy, the soldiers are presented as cruelly and crudely misappropriating the roles of midwives and undertakers. Fiacc's poem alludes here to what *Sunday Times* reporters refer to as a "baseless and gothic rumour that in searching the house in Balkan Street, the troops had lifted a dead child from her coffin". Interestingly, 'The Kickers' concludes not by maintaining division between abusers and abused, but, with a Lear-like simplicity, lamenting humanity's collective failure to evolve. Socially and morally, "we all still are/Kicking in the womb", senseless "poor brutes" like Poor Tom. And yet, while the closing image of the womb accords the poem a degree of universality, it also repeats a traditional nationalist trope of representing Ireland as feminine and the British military as its sadistic antithesis.

The spheres of sexuality and political violence intersect again in 'The British Connection'. For the North's repressed communities in which masculinity and cultural identity appear under threat, the gun has acquired the status of a fetish, a charm against impotence. Reverence for and resistance to the Act of Union have generated a frenzy of desire, "Almost as many hard-on/Guns as there are union jacks". The poem breaks with preceding ones in stressing the ferocity of residents' responses to the arms raids. Whereas in 'Credo Credo' and 'The Kickers' the householders are invisible victims, and spoken for, in 'The British Connection' they articulate for themselves a rage for redress. That fundamental questions about political identity have been triggered by Westminster's, Stormont's and the military's actions since late 1969 is apparent from the outset. By locating the action "In Belfast, Europe", instead of 'Northern Ireland', 'the United Kingdom' or 'Ireland', the narrator indicates his own withdrawal of consent from current constitutional arrangements. This is swiftly followed by a more overt and striking example of the new mood of defiance. In order to prevent the Army searching his house, "your man"—a tenant in the Shankill—threatens violence:

> 'Over my dead body
> Sir,' he said, brandishing
> A real-life sword from some
> Old half-forgotten war ...

The melodramatic gesture and archaic language may encourage one to view him as a comic figure, like Corporal Jones from *Dad's Army*, a quaint relic of "some ... half-forgotten war". However, the "real-life sword" authenticates the resentment and danger he embodies. Raised, it serves as a signal for the explosion of violence that ensues. The remaining stanzas are given over to a bizarre litany of weapons now being deployed to sever or sustain the connection:

> And oldtime thrupenny bits and stones
> Screws, bolts, nuts (Belfast confetti),
>
> And kitchen knives, pokers, Guinness tins
> And nail-bombs ...

The scale, intensity and invasiveness of violence in people's lives are reflected also in the multiplicity of domestic hiding-places ("the docker's tea-tin", "the scullery larder", "the oven grill") and intimate items ("the french letter", "the spinster's shift") in which weapons are stashed. One of the last locations mentioned as an arms store is "the broken-down rusted/Merry-Go-Round in the Scrap Yard". By capitalising those phrases unnecessarily, Fiacc draws attention to them; they represent the present run-down state of the province, a place for scraps and faction fights.

from *Northern Irish Literature 1956-2006: The Imprint of History*
(Macmillan)

Odd Man Out

GERALD DAWE

PATRICK JOSEPH O'CONNOR WAS BORN ON 15 April 1924 in Elizabeth Street in the Lower Falls district of Belfast. His early years were spent in the house of his maternal grandparents in East Street in the Markets area of Belfast. On both sides of his parents' families the political impact of the Irish Civil War, the backdrop of his own birth, was immediate and long lasting.

His mother's family, the McGarrys, had been driven from their home in Lisburn, their furniture (and piano) burned. His grandfather never recovered from the ordeal. His grandmother, like his own mother, would loom large in the young boy's imagination as powerful figures of spirited resistance. His father, Bernard, came from a prosperous family of shopkeepers from County Cavan. Like many before and since he went to Belfast to make his own way, working as a barman, and became active in the IRA. In the late 1920s, in the tense and economically insecure atmosphere of post Civil War, partitioned Ireland, exhausted by almost two decades of political upheaval and military campaigns, the father, again like thousands of others at the time, emigrated to America, to New York. He was reluctantly joined in 1929 by his wife, Annie Christina, and their three sons, including the eldest (and first surviving child) Patrick, who was five.

The family made headway to begin with; as the father's grocery business prospered another son and daughter were born, but with the fall-out of the Great Depression and the ensuing slump in the

1930s, the O'Connor business collapsed, and with it the fabric of the family life started to unravel with tragic results. The father began to drink heavily, his wife turned her vengeance on 'America' and yearned for home, identifying with her eldest son an intense and romantic sense of 'Irishness' mediated through her reading of Yeats's poems to the impressionable boy.

From these early experiences, first in Manhattan and eventually in Hell's Kitchen, Patrick Joseph O'Connor was schooled locally and started to write poetry and verse drama. Under the influence of the Irish literary revival's iconic figure in America, Padraic Colum and his wife Mary, the poet 'Padraic Fiacc'—O'Connor's chosen *nom de plume*—was born, modelling his work, to quote his editor, Aodán Mac Póilín, "on the technique and style of Gaelic poetry, although much of his early work was written in an identifiable idiom".

By 1941 Fiacc, now a somewhat precocious teenager, studied for the priesthood at the Franciscans in St Joseph's Seraphic Seminary in Calicoon, upstate New York. He left St Joseph's partly as a result of a disagreement over a sequence of poems which he wrote in memory of a fellow student who had drowned, but continued his studies with the Irish Capuchin Order at Holy Oak, Delaware. His time there lasted for five years when in 1946 he left America, returned to Belfast, and worked as a night porter in the Union Hotel, a well known (and somewhat shady) hotel at the back of the City Hall.

The voyage home (abroad the Swedish *Grispholm*) was through the still-mined Atlantic waters. The twenty-two-year-old Fiacc was by this time carrying within the experience of his New York years—the cosmopolitan, modernist, bulging, exuberant city; the 'ghetto'-world of ethnic districts, the clerical and spiritual exercises of a seminarian conversant in several languages; the post-war 'shock and awe' and the bravado of victory (his brother, however, had returned from war profoundly damaged by the experience); and with a sense of fulfilling his own mother's desire to return home. Quite a lot to handle for a twenty-two-year-old.

The Belfast which Fiacc returned to had itself experienced at first hand the terror of the Nazi aggression. In 1941 Belfast had been blitzed with the loss of almost a thousand lives and the destruction of well-known and familiar districts, particularly in the centre, north and east of the city. Brian Moore's *The Emperor of Ice Cream* (1965) dramatically recaptures the mood of the city at this time. Ironically, while Fiacc was making his re-entry into the city, the Belfast novelist Moore was in the process of leaving it for good, by emigrating to Canada.

In post-war Belfast, as thousands of soldiers from Protestant, Catholic and other religious and cultural backgrounds returned to civilian life, Fiacc started the long and, one might say, 'tri'-located struggle to establish himself as a poet. The trouble was where he was really from—brought up in Belfast, he was, like James Joyce, a British subject; in New York he was an American citizen, but he also viewed himself as Irish and a citizen of the (relatively) new state of Éire. These contradictions would have been apparent to him in post-war Belfast. Indeed, he renounced his American citizenship in an effort to simplify the situation, but the contradictions would resurface and ultimately propel Fiacc into an emotional and intellectual turbulence that anticipates, by quite some way, the contemporary theoretical preoccupations of postmodernist interest in hybridity and issues of national identity.

For Fiacc in the Union Hotel in Belfast in 1946, such matters were part and parcel of his life. In a fascinating interview conducted by John Brown and published in Brown's collection *In the Chair: Interviews with Poets from the North of Ireland*, Fiacc recalls that the 1950s were 'a kind of natal depression':

> W.R. Rodgers, like MacNeice, left for the BBC in London; Robert Greacen left too … and I left in the middle of the decade for New York [.] To my mind, Brian Moore's *The Lonely Passion of Judith Hearne* (1955) was a great novel of the 50s; it testified to the depression found in the North of Ireland.

Fiacc was however beginning to be recognised as a poet in Ireland, publishing poems and reviews with the *Irish Bookman*, the *Irish Times*, *Poetry Ireland* and *Rann*. The breakthrough came with the publication in America in 1948 of *New Irish Poets* (Devin-Adair)—a really significant anthology of its time and historically. Fiacc at twenty-four was the youngest poet included in the anthology. The inclusion was to change the course of his life.

In 1950 his mother died, the same age as the century. Fiacc upped sticks and returned to New York to care for his young sister and his father who had found a job in the New York subway and had become a militant trade unionist. The domestic arrangement did not work. In various public interviews and in private correspondence Fiacc makes it plain that these years he spent in New York (1952-1956) caused him great distress and may well have stored up the kind of internalised anger and damage that was to be released in his writing fifteen years later.

As a result of reading the poems of his included in *New Irish Poets* a Detroit-based painter, Nancy Wayne, started to correspond with Fiacc. This would lead to their marrying in Belfast in August 1956 where they settled in Glengormley, a satellite village in the relatively prosperous upper northside of the city. A bus ride from the city centre, on high Antrim ground overlooking Belfast Lough and coastline, part countryside, part suburb, part dormitory town, Glengormley was new territory. Here Fiacc and Nancy planned to put down their roots. Their daughter, Brigid, was born in 1962. In his interview with John Brown, Fiacc memorably describes the period:

> [W]hen I came back in the 50s, and tried to live in the suburbs in Glengormley, I guess we were trying to get out of a ghetto mentality. Even in the 60s there was still a certain amount of hope—we planned kids, O'Neill met Lemass [the Irish Prime Minister, in January 1965], all that kind of thing. Nancy and I were very much in love.

Many historians and cultural commentators see the 1960s as the make-or-break period for the Unionist administration in Northern Ireland. A slim chance existed (but a viable chance, nonetheless) to transform the political landscape, democratise its institutions and, in so doing, to avert the whirlwind of appalling violence that would engulf the province. As we know now that was not to be. Fiacc, ever mindful of "bad omens", recalls:

> There were bad omens, though, I remember two wee blackbirds getting trapped between the nylon drape and the window and fluttering madly, not able to get out; as I released them the sky darkened, a shadow came across the window just as they escaped. I'm a poet who believes in omens ... Things conspired against us. I started getting migraines. Nancy got ill too. All that medical stuff is in the poems—haemorrhage and

migraine. The doctors told Nancy my problem was not physical, so it had to be mental; they put me away for ten days or so in the hospital. Of course, I told all the people there to 'get up out of their beds and get on with it, for this was all just a conspiracy by the lunatics against us', until they had to let me out.

Even in the early 1960s, Belfast, in keeping with other cities throughout Britain, Europe and North America, witnessed an opening-up, a generational shift in cultural self-expression and confidence. In Belfast, as in the northern province as a whole, this window of opportunity was to last barely a decade. The civil rights campaign, and the loyalist reaction to it, was superseded by a vicious war of attrition, involving ghastly acts of terrorism enacted by and against fellow citizens, paralleled by state repression. In Fiacc's language, Belfast became 'Hellfast'. But in Glengormley in 1962 or 63 the idyll was still very much alive. Fiacc was increasingly acknowledged as an important 'new' figure in the literary landscape at home. Having won the prestigious AE Award in Dublin in 1957 for his (unpublished) collection, *Woe to the Boy*, Fiacc struck up friendships with other writers and his Glengormley home became a hospitable port of call for writers visiting Belfast, such as John McGahern, and local poets, including Derek Mahon—one of whose earliest and much acclaimed poems, 'Glengormley', was originally dedicated to Fiacc.

Fiacc's connection with one of the last living figures of the Revival, Padraic Colum, would certainly have preceded him. But his contact with John Hewitt—living in Coventry since March 1957 in a form of self-exile from his home town until his return in 1972—and other senior figures such as Michael McLaverty, the short story writer and novelist, placed Fiacc in the privotal early moment of what was to become known worldwide as the 'Northern Group'—Seamus Heaney, Michael Longley, Stewart Parker, James Simmons and Derek Mahon.

These and other poets were by the mid-Sixties publishing their own first collections of poetry—Seamus Heaney's *Death of a Naturalist* and *Door into the Dark*, *Night Crossing* by Derek Mahon, *No Continuing City* by Michael Longley, James Simmons's *Late but in Earnest* and *In the Wilderness*, new publications from Stewart Parker and, intriguiningly, *Astral Weeks*, the first solo album of a young Belfast musician and singer-songwriter, Van Morrison. Heady times indeed.

Now 45 years old and their senior by some twenty years or so, Fiacc, the New York Irish ex-seminarian, husband and father, who had met Thomas Mann in New York, knew Padraic Colum, seen at first hand Picasso's work, lived for years in the greatest city in the world, survived the 30s and the Second World War, weathered the storm of the 50s, knew Belfast from the doldrums to the new shoots now appearing, he too published his first collection, *By the Black Stream*. The collection came out in 1969 from Dolmen Press, the leading Irish publisher of the time, bearing a haunting, foreshadowing epigraph taken from James Joyce's poem, 'Tilly':

> I bleed by the black stream
> For my torn bough!

This is how Brendan Hamill, a friend and long-standing supporter of Fiacc's, recalls this period in his marvellous, locally-turned memoir, 'The Troubles He's Seen: Fiacc and Belfast, 1967'. Belfast, Hamill writes, "was a quiet city—full of sullen repressed raw energy and clotted with hard men who asked you with fierce eyes, 'Who the fuck do you think you're lukin' at?'—to which the reply was a derisory 'Nothing much', and then you ran for dear life." He continues:

> People from the Shankill drank on the Falls and nobody made heavy weather of it. Mixed marriages were commonplace and worked. There were unstable Jeremiahs, though, with faintly foetid alliances. The women were largely stitchers, seamstresses, nurses or waitresses. Most of them made their own dresses—the cloth was bought, amongst other places, in a big Baghdad of a shop in Royal Avenue called the Spinning Mill. From the planes at night, Belfast was laid out like a lighted necklace in a valley.

Hamill goes on to recount a poetry reading in "a house in the Upper Donegall Road" before homing in on Fiacc's presence. "I sensed Fiacc's urbanity and humiliation—the poet as victim. Of what I did not know. Although I loved Heaney's clean masculine tactile poetry in *Death of a Naturalist* and Festival Publications' *Eleven Poems*, I sensed Fiacc was closer in spirit to the fire-and-air world of the young Derek Mahon—though not a classicist in style or syntax. Clearly he was an original both as man and poet." Fiacc "epitomised", according to Hamill, "the secret spirit and atmospherics of Belfast at the time. The third eye, so to speak, an emotional flare."

In the five years that followed, between the publication of *By the Black Stream* in 1969 and Fiacc's second collection, *Odour of Blood* in 1973, the 'Troubles' had overtaken, and taken over, public life in Northern Ireland. Fatalities increased daily with bombings and shootings and the militarisation gathered momentum with the inevitable deterioration of civic society. (The statistics of fatalities make for grim reading: 1969: 19; 1970: 29; 1971: 180; 1972: 497; 1973: 263; 1974: 304; 1975: 267; 1976: 307). No one in their wildest dreams (or worst nightmares) thought that the conflict would last another twenty years and more, for such is what happened.

In the inter-regnum between *By the Black Stream* and *Odour of Blood*, Fiacc's marriage had broken up and he suffered the first bout of a recurring nervous condition which was to blight his life for the next two decades. Notwithstanding these travails he maintained an open house for other writers, following on from the hospitality of the late 50s and 60s. A hospitality that would last into the mid-1970s as poets, myself included, visited Fiacc in his Glengormley home, were 'fed and watered' and then navigated the often perilous way back home through what was fast becoming an occupied city, dangerous to traverse at night. By the time I had left Belfast in 1974 Fiacc was, in the Glengormley home, like a man living on borrowed time. And so it turned out to be as the life he had known for almost twenty years, with a wife and family and visiting friends and writers, was pitched into tragedy in 1975.

To quote Aodán Mac Póilín again, since the "civil disturbances that had blighted his parents' lives in the 20s erupted again", the effect upon Fiacc's personal life was simply "devastating". From this time too (the mid-1970s) Fiacc's reputation took a critical pummelling, first with the overwhelming critical rejection of *Odour of Blood* (1973) and then with the controversial anthology, *The Wearing of the Black*, which he edited the following year, 1974. It was launched in December 1974 with a party in Fiacc's Glengormley home, attended by many of the younger writers in the anthology. For several it was their first publication.

Excitement was high, an expectation and uncertainty given voice by the youngest poet included in the anthology, Gerry McLaughlin. There was a feeling, naïve as it may well have been, that something had been done, some artistic marker laid down, some local response in the teeth of the madness. While the anthology became ensnared in controversy about the ethics of writing 'about' violence and victims, in a matter of months after its publication, Gerry was murdered one April morning in a sectarian assassination. He was 20 years old.

Fiacc never recovered from the loss of his young friend, such a promising and eager young man, reminiscent perhaps of himself when he (Fiacc) had started to first write poems as an Irish emigrant in the New York of the late 30s and early 40s. Fiacc's poems from this point on in the mid-1970s can be read as an 'In Memoriam' to the death of that one young spirit, but also to the symbolic loss of hope Fiacc felt as increasingly more vicious acts of violence took place throughout the province. Fractures in his own temperament were opened further as the depressive illness that dogged his life threatened to turn into a fully-fledged neurosis.

Fiacc however suvived. The work he would publish during the next quarter of a century is a testament to that fact. Fiacc's poetry can be read as an interior monologue with different parts of his self melodramatically involved, as he sifts through the emotional and moral damage. Or his work can be read as an inner history of what it felt like to live at the 'cutting edge' of the 'Northern Troubles'— a political and constitutional disaster that lead (if we need reminding) to the deaths of over 3000 people and the scarring of many hundreds and thousands of lives throughout Ireland, Britain and continental Europe as terrorism took root alongside the noxious weeds of sectarianism. The books Fiacc published during this time tell this story in a shocking and unforgettable way, offending many with their often barbarous and tortured utterance, but lit through, bizaarrely, with black irony and gallows humour which brings to mind that great Irish fatalist, Samuel Beckett.

Odour of Blood had preceded *The Wearing of the Black* by barely a year. Read together, Fiacc's seemingly shocking change of tone and shift away from the Gaelic idioms and mythologies of *By the Black Stream* troubled and outraged critics. What followed confirmed his growing isolation from the mainstream. *Nights in the Bad Place* (1977); the retrospective *Selected Padraic Fiacc* (1979) (which included the ground-breaking 'defence' of Fiacc by literary critic and cultural historian, Terence Brown), and *Missa Terribilis* (1986) were barely noticed in the major media outlets of broadsheet newspapers and literary journals, or else they were discounted as the work of a poet who had clearly become unhinged by the events taking place in his native city.

The chaotic underground lifestyle seemed to underpin a descent, as he moved from rented rooms to rented rooms, haunted by the past and what might have been, victim on occasion himself to the violence of the streets, and alienated by (and alienating) the literary establishment while embracing a scandalous life for the one-time seminarian. The exterior was a defence mechanism that sought to shore up a lifetime of difficulty. Unlike most other contemporary writers who had grown up in stable and comfortable surrounds, Fiacc had experienced the life of an exposed and vulnerable emigrant, uprooted from his family home and all its familiar and known securities (and insecurities).

He embodied the 'Diaspora' condition in an intense and clearly unreconciled form. In the cultural circles of the time he was fast becoming an odd man out. In Prague or California, New York or Paris, Fiacc would probably have found an alternative counter-culture with which to identify. In the puritanical, militarised and ghettoised class-conscious world of Belfast, however, he became something of an outcast, often viewed by the nationalist 'side' with suspicion and distaste (not the 'Republican' voice that either the moment or the movement required) and, with equal measure, as an unfathomable, somewhat frightening presence in the wider community. Those close to him knew the difference and the extent to which Fiacc was fulfilling a self-lacerating role, a kind of anti-hero in the throes of a tragi-comic society the likes of which Belfast had not seen played out since Carol Reed's cinematic version of F.L. Green's novel, *Odd Man Out* (1945).

Some forms of recognition began to emerge—Arts Council awards, the *Poetry Ireland* Award (1981) and his election to the Irish academy of creative artists, Aosdána. In the early 1980s Paul Muldoon produced for BBC Northern Ireland two important radio programmes scripted by Fiacc on his American experience. Somewhat later a documentary devoted to Fiacc's life was produced for German television.

Fiacc gave occasional readings in Ireland and elsewhere, enthralling and perplexing audiences with his strange mid-Atlantic accent and ironic self-deprecation. By the mid-1990s Fiacc was reclaiming some of the recognition which had deserted him. He was acknowledged as a significant 'Irish poet' but his work remained critically very much in the shadows. In 1994, to mark his 70th birthday, *Ruined Pages*, a new and complete revised selected poems, was published in Belfast. Further individual volumes of his poetry appeared – a pamphlet version of the original 1957 prize-winning collection, *Woe to the Boy* (1994), *Red Earth* (1996) and *Semper Vacare* (1999).

Padraic Fiacc has been described by poet James Liddy as the "first of a European species to appear in Irish writing: a Holocaust child, whose mental cast is formed by the milieu of violence." Fiacc himself has spoken of 'his' generation in similar terms:

> Our generation, almost as old as this [20th] century, has been voided from a womb-culture into a bomb-culture: 20th-century schizophrenia in which the individual is not split in two, but, torn asunder, exploded and disintegrated into fragments.

He translated this perception in his own writing, as the poems become physically broken, torn asunder on the page, and aurally explode into conflicting voices, snatches of local dialect; a disintegrating form that only becomes coherent through the spoken voice. Fiacc's intelligence, masked by a kind of grotesque role-play that also afflicted his slightly older contemporary, Patrick Kavanagh, is telling in the following offhand remark he makes to John Brown:

> Both Picasso and Klee do everything in fragments, and so do I. I believe our century is in fragments, or smithereens as the Irish call it – fragments resulting from blows. Wars, though, throw up strange twists that neither poets nor painters bargain for.

Fiacc's 'European' sensibility, drawn from the French poetry he read and admired as a young man in New York (such as Baudelaire and Rimbaud), his indentification with Dostoyevsky's work, also take him outside the customary English literary conventions within which Irish writing has traditionally been viewed, and still is, more or less, to the present day. His Catholicism—a fundamental defining point of his identity—is also not of the traditional kind, as he states it in an interview of 1988:

> I'm an unorthodox Catholic and my Catholicism is tainted with Calvinism. [Northern Ireland] is a very Protestant society and the Catholic living in it is bound to be Protestantised up to a point.

Not the sort of statement that would endear Fiacc to the *status quo*, but in 1988, Fiacc was clearly in advance of most cultural commentators of the time in saying such things publicly. Fiacc's Catholicism provides the emotional and metaphorical centre to his poetry, as Chris Agee has identified it:

> Hardly remarked upon, amidst the justified celebration of his poetic peers, is the fact that much of *Odour of Blood* and *Missa Terribilis* constitutes perhaps the most directly enunciated critique of armed politics to have emerged from the Troubles. For Fiacc's great theme is Christ glimpsed in the face of the murdered, and the attendant duty of remembrance ...

Hardly surprising then that that fine English poet of Irish parentage, Ian Duhig, has seen in Fiacc's writing a 'Catholic existentialism' which "explains why so many have missed the ground on which he is figured". Duhig continues:

> [Fiacc's poetry] is a process of selection of the fragments left after an explosion. He is like Spinoza: everything is a version of what we cannot see, and we have no place to stand to see it all. Ultimately, he courts the break-up of his poem.

Similarly, Fiacc's sense of himself as a poet in the period immediately after the break-up of his marriage and the vagrant life he was to live in the ensuing two decades or so, finds a sympathetic record in Robert Johnstone's astute portrait of Belfast, *Images of Belfast* (1983), when he describes Fiacc in the following manner:

> [Fiacc] performs a salutary function as a presence on the margin of the largely middle-class poets, pouncing on hints of complacency amongst

them, and taking on him the huge task of confronting the Troubles head-on in his verse.

Whereas for Paul Muldoon speaking in 1994 and understandably weary of the (exhausted) notion of "confronting the Troubles head on", Fiacc becomes a figure representative "of the condition of being a poet that many, including me, shy away from. I admire [Fiacc] for that and for what he's done and what he represents."

It is worth pointing out the obvious here: that those who have responded to Fiacc's work with most generosity and insight are poets. This is the (uniquely positive) response of Fiacc's fellow Belfast poet, the notoriously anti-modernist, John Hewitt, as he runs his eye over Fiacc's *Odour of Blood* in 1973. Fiacc constructs, according to Hewitt, "his poems with scrupulous craftsmanship, weighing every syllable. He suppresses the connections of normal narrative. For it is this control of the words and their placing which controls his deep emotion, modulating his bitterness, his pity."

Most of the well-established readings of Irish poetry, and in particular northern Irish poetry, either studiously avoid Fiacc or dispatch his poetry with a patronising gesture here and there, before dismissing its claim to be part of the canon. Editors of contemporary anthologies have more often than not followed suit. While academic and critical trends gravitate towards the familiar well-trodden centre, Fiacc's work poses awkward distracting questions about, for instance, cultural and artistic influence beyond the Anglophone priorities of much literary criticism of Irish writing. Fiacc's relationship with American and European modernism is a case study all to itself and opens up challenging critical and historical perspectives on the Irish tradition as a whole.

Whatever we as readers may ultimately make of it all, his achievement is much more diverse and challenging than is presently credited. We should be in a position to make up our own minds. Yet the historical and critical record remains incomplete and inadequate so long as Fiacc's presence is viewed as an enigmatic, strange, self-defeating side-show. It may also be the case that Fiacc's artistic and existential experience is itself 'historical', a significant part of the history of modern Ireland, encoded in the broken bits and pieces of his writing life. The violence, the emigration, the shock of the new world, the loss of the old, the struggle to pursue the American Dream, the life found vulnerable, the return home, the momentary "possibility of a possible life" in the 60s and the painful readjustment to private and public breakdown—all these and more are caught in Fiacc's poetry.

For the contemporary theoreticians of literature Fiacc is actually a godsend. For those who need authorising precedents, he follows in an uneasy and provocative manner the footsteps not of Yeats (the early master his mother read from in those early displaced years in New York), but of Beckett. Recasting language, dragging it into the gutter, away from 'irrelevancies' of 'Grammar and Style' (the terms are Beckett's), taking the poems apart in a last ditch attempt to preserve the faith that writing does, after all, matter, was Beckett's aim. Beckettian in their bleak physicality and intensity, tragi-comic, anti-heroic, counter-lyrical, indeed anti-poetic, Fiacc's poetry is utterly unlike anything else produced by an Irish poet during the last half-century.

Poetry Ireland, July 2005

A new edition of *Ruined Pages: Selected Poems* by Padraic Fiacc, edited by Gerald Dawe and Aodán Mac Póilín, is in preparation, for which the above essay is the introduction.

Darker Than Sundown
A one-man show based
on the writings of Padraic Fiacc

PADDY SCULLY

PADDY SCULLY IS A BELFAST-BASED actor and writer. He has written plays and shows on the comedian James Young, the Belfast novelist Brian Moore, the local memoirist Alexander Irvine as well as one-man shows based on the writings of Flann O'Brien and James Joyce. *Darker than Sundown* is an orchestration of the poetry and prose writings of Padraic Fiacc with some additional expository material from the playwright.

Darker Than Sundown

Yellow lights trail, the last of daylight
On oily curling Lagan water
Crossing the town with keening Pancho
Dogging my staggering heels, gurning
And cursing me—Flash back! New world
Raucous laughter, a sundown of the mind

The New York Night

Hailing a cab
I black out on tar
Am slapped back awake
By the cop nagging
'Do you know who you are?'

My first poem—I think—the beginning

Der Bomben Poet
Spring song 1941

The Beginning

Today is my birth
-day. I am seventeen.

My home town
Has just been
Blown up:

Dead feet in dead faces,
Corpses still alight,
Students helping kids
And old people out of

Still burning houses.

I have nothing to write
Poems about.

This is my twentieth-century

Night-life.

Ancient memories of childhood ... Belfast, East St, the Markets. In the rain, running on sweaty cobblestone to this or that mill girl hoping she was Mother. Daisy Fox with the bun on top, Kitty who? McKnight who nursed me and Aunty Mary, the eternal. But Mother? No. She was always somewhere else with someone else, giving suck to brother Rory on the Sands in Bangor her long black hair streaming with the wind from the sea, an Irish Sea. At night she would come in and shower me with kisses but her scent betrayed her—she was going out about, down the town. Still, we had our moments, Mam and I

TWO SOLITUDES
The salmon leaping in our breast
Is the one breast.
—John Marshall

AMERICA MOM

You are baking bread.
I am making a poem.

We glow with silence like the full moon.

We are both obliged to wait then
For the ring of cindering bone ...

You are baking bread until it sings.
I am baking clay until it glazes.

Time is an oven—

You for your moth-coloured grain to golden
Me for my glass pages.

I was the oldest, the first born alive. Daddy went off early to America and became an American barman. He had to get out because they were killing Catholic barmen in Belfast whether they were involved in the 'Troubles' or not. My mother was a fierce Republican and there was no way she was going to get out of her own country—well except for Daddy—she followed him across the water, trailing us children with her.

ALIVE ALIVE O

The altar boy from a Mass for the dead
Romps through the streets of the town
Lolls on brick-studded grass
Jumps up, bolts back down
With wild pup eyes ...

This morning at twist of winter to spring
Small hands clutched a big brass cross
Followed the stern brow of the priest
Encircle the man in the box ...

A bell-tossed head sneezed
In a blue daze of incense on
Shrivelled bit lips, then
Just to stay awake, prayed
Too loud for the man to be at rest ...

O now where has he got to
But climbed an apple tree!

Me? An Altar Boy? Hard to imagine isn't it. But at one time it was true. My self same piety of imagination would lead me up to all sorts.

SON OF A GUN

Woe to the boy for whom the nails, the crown of thorns,
the sponge of gall were the first toy.
                    —*François Mauriac*

Between the year of the slump and the sell out, I
The third child, am the first born alive ...

My father is a Free Stater 'Cavan Buck'.
My mother is a Belfast factory worker. Both

Carry guns, and the grandmother with a gun
In her apron, making the Military wipe

Their boots before they rape the house. (These
Civil wars are only ever over on paper!)

Armed police are still raping my dreams
Thump-thud. Thump-thud. I go on nightmaring

Dead father running. There is a bull
In the field. Is Father, am I, running away

From the bull to it? Is this the reason why
I steal
time, things, places, people?

Barman father, sleeping with a gun under
Your pillow, does the gun help you that much?
I wonder

For the gun has made you all only the one
In of sex with me the two sexed son (or three

Or none?) you bequeathed the gun to
Still cannot make it so. I can

Never become your he-man: shot
Down born as I was, sure, I thought

And thought and thought but blood ran ...

I was five when we went to New York.
Like most of the wanting Irish we were always going to

America, us kids, to meet our 'Daddy' Ben, as if for the first time, maybe it was—for I was never sure who my father was—and we were told when we got there not to say we'd wash our 'hawns' any more, but wash our 'hens'. And we musn't say 'Och-aye' any more, only' Yeah sure OK'.

People in Belfast all came down to say their goodbyes at the docks and 'Auld Lang Syne' was sung. Leaving seemed permanent, forever. We landed at Halifax. We had such a good time on the boat but on arriving we would have gone back in an instant. We'd been told so much about New York—and I really wanted to see it—but at Halifax there was another brick wall, an even bigger one; my stupid Daddy had missed the train to the boat to meet us, to clear immigration so we sat disappointed beside our bags waiting until some fireman or policeman—or somebody or other—came to help us.

STANDING WATER

Putting into Nova Scotia
Nineteen and twenty-nine, girl
Mother's delph face creaks, cracks ...
(I'm breaking in two myself at five!)

Goodnight all from the beginning
Goodbye 'cobblestones' but
A backstreet womb wall won't
Let me climb out over it.

We stare at the brick Hal
-ifax sky. A yellow wolf cold
Sits on the leaden Atlantic:
A new world horizon ... Old

Morning, you are the night of life:
The Russian Orthodox priest who
Has a beard, is the Bogey Man
Will put me in his bag

Is 'America' the Bury Hole he'll
Put me in if I cry?
On the tiny (it stops tangoing)
'transoceanic motor-ship'

New York was full of bright lights and yellow taxis and movement. I loved the brightness and the noise of everything, any kid would. I was excited. But as I was very close to my mother I knew that she did not want to go to America and it was no surprise that she came to hate it. And so did I—I came to hate every part of New York—even the brightness and excitement—because my mother hated it—she never saw how glittery it was.

Dad on the other hand fulfilled the American Dream and rose from bartender to someone who owned his own grocery stores, one in Harlem and one on Amsterdam Avenue. He said the blacks paid their bills, but not the Irish, How it happened I can't remember but no sooner did he soar to the peaks than he lost all.

After a long time.

Dad finally got a job as a subway clerk. I helped him with fractions and maths until he passed his civil service exams. Mother still hated America but not as much as she used to. She is beginning to hate life itself. She rarely goes out.

We are hanging out of the front-room windows on pillows. We face Broadway. The cars and buses, bumper to bumper, are streaming down town to Time Square.

"So many cars," I groan.

"It's only the world passing by," she sighs.

And reads Yeats to me.

"A person would be better off dead." She complains of existence; she never saw Ireland again. How I Love Mother and How I Love Dad but I must get away. I can't cope with or bear their unhappiness any longer.

Mum and Dad were to die in New York.

GOODBYE TO OUR FATHER

Father asleep in Central Park without
A hole to hide in you're dead now but

Not inside. Inside it is still
Old nineteen twenty wirelesses

Jangle glass beads;
Ay, you steal back
For the cop to beat you over the head

With the night stick for 'drunk as sin'
Singing the Red Flag again
but nobody
Cares: It's not an insult any more.

Things bare teeth back to gums and skull

Grins to privates.
I see your bone-naked
Face scrutinising 'Injustices' still!

Never bother! You have a hole to hide
in now:

Hide in the bogpit waste we've made
of this place
Ourselves by just running away from it.

SOLDIERS

The altar boy marches up the altar steps.
The priest marches down. 'Get up now
And be a soldier!' says the nun
To the woman after giving birth. 'Get up now
And march, march: Be a man!'

And the men are men and the women are men
And the children are men!

Mother carried a knife to work.
It was the thorn to her rose ...

They say she died with her eyes open
In the French Hospital in New York.
I remember those eyes shining in the dark

Slum hallway the day after
I left the monastery: Eyes that were
A feast of welcome that said 'Yes
I'm glad you didn't stay stuck there!'

'Would you mind if I went to prison
Rather than war?'
'No, for Ireland's men all went to prison!'

At the bottom of a canyon of brick
She cursed and swore
'You never see the sky!'

A lifetime after,
just before
I go to sleep at night, I hear
That Anna Magnani voice screaming
Me deaf 'No! No, you're not
To heed the world!' In one swift
Sentence she tells me not to yield
But to forbear:
'Go to prison but never
Never stop fighting. We are the poor
And the poor have to be 'soldiers'.

'You're still a soldier, it's only that
You're losing the war

'And all the wars are lost anyway!'

Then I joined a seminary.

Yes, seminary. ME! I did study to be a priest. Of course, I fucked that up. I was never totally interested in becoming a priest. The nuns at my first school told me not to go to Haaren High School because it was in Hell's Kitchen. The nuns also said to 'Go to any school that teaches Latin' and with Haaren being the only school nearby to teach Latin I wrote and applied when I was thirteen or fourteen. 'Ah, Te-Tum, hum-ah-hum-ah-hum.' 'E-TAL-E-AN?' 'LATIN?' About as good as getting yourself an Alsatian dog! My mother's side of the family were not that religious, but on my father's side I'd my Aunt Mary who took me to do the Stations of the Cross. I could never understand, though how Christ as the Son of God could allow those bastards to torture him. And yet, that's complicated for the image came with my awareness of sex and death; I'd look at the soldiers, at those centurions with their muscular legs, and at the time—I was thirteen—I had just started reading Dostoyevsky's *The Brothers Karamazov* where Father Zosimas's body gives off a smell when he dies. He was supposed to be a saint but he gives off a foul odour. Dostoyevsky talks truth and faces reality. God, even a big horsefly came out of the saint's body!

But sometimes I felt trapped in the monastery. I used to jump up and down on my glasses and smash them to get home. I remember an old priest who was sympathetic to the Irish climbing the hill to the monastery and meeting me in a yellow shirt and black jacket and tan boots, and he stops me and asks: "What are you doing in that get-up?" And so I told him I didn't want to end up looking like a penguin but, of course, he made me climb the hill and put on a black suit. They were strict. You see, I just didn't have the habits of a monk. I had to leave the regimental orders. I left in 1945.

ABANDONING STUDIES

I do not know
What salmon do

After they leave their young
In a cloud of milk

Or where they go
Or why lovers die

And I do not want to.

All the sages wrote
Their names in sand

Watched the mystery wash
'I do not understand'

With wave on wave
of wind.

I am content to be
brave as blind.

I first left New York in 1943. I said goodbye to New York, goodbye forever, at least seven times in thirty years. Dog to heel. The last time was because a relative had committed suicide. For a long time I lived in hope that I'd never see her bright lights and noisy company again. But how can you escape New York?

In 1948 I renounced my American citizenship in Belfast.

Five years in a post-war Belfast smouldering in bombed-out ruins, fuel shortages, clothes and food rationed and no work.

Two years back in Ireland and with my Irish passport that says Belfast, Eire, I'm targeted as the biggest nut of the day. Aunt Mary drags me down to the dole people—but she can't keep her mouth shut.

"This gentleman is under three flags!"

The dole clerk freezes. "I know that, I know that, but what is he—Irish, British or American?"

Even I don't know. The cops won't give me a permanent ID card. Somehow I frighten them but not as much as they frighten me. Long black coats and even longer faces.

In Belfast I wrote poems for magazines. I was included in *New Irish Poets* in the late 40s. I gave them poems and my Aunt Mary took me down to the photographer and stood behind him shouting, "Stop grinning! Only fools grin." And so I was included— grinning—as the youngest poet and it was those poems that Nancy (later to be my wife) read ten years later when she was working in a bookshop in America. She began to write; she fell for those poems, their innocence, hook, line and sinker, and I was amazed. I guess we were both religious and romantic, even if I was a manic depressive. Nancy linked in with the religious element in the poems. Look at 'chaunt rann of a singer', such innocence.

In Belfast, I renounced my American citizenship. I would now be—what? An Irish poet?

GLOSS
Nor truth nor good did they know
But beauty burning away.
They were the dark earth people of old
Restive in the clay.

Deirdre watched Naisi die
And great King Conor of himself said
'Did you ever see a bottomless bucket
In the muck discarded?'

And comradely Dermot was destroyed by Fionn
Because of the beauty of a girl

Because of the beauty of a girl
The sky went raging on fire

And the sea was pushed out into rage.
They were the dark earth people of old
And Deirdre pitched herself into the sea.
Turn the page. Turn the page.

TENTH-CENTURY INVASION

Doves beat their wings
Against their breasts

Bloodying their wings
Bloodying their breasts ...

Bells ring throughout the book
At the bottom of the lough

Gold running over the
Ruined page

Drowned
Emerald and lilac ink

From the song written in
The shaft of the sun

In the moment on the
Margin
Never to be sung.

Family deaths and crises called me back to New York and Hell's Kitchen throughout the 40s and 50s. When I met and married Nancy in 1956 she came with me to settle in Glengormley.

I suppose that coming back to the North brought back my childhood, which I'd tried to avoid. I had been born into the Civil War here when they were just making Northern Ireland. Although I was only a child, I knew there was something wrong. My grandmother was burned out of her house in Lisburn and she went mad and delusional. Even as a child I could sense her paranoia about me wandering off, the way children do. One day wandering off into Lagan Street one day and seeing these two kids blurtin' and pointing to a man who was whipping a horse. I went over to ask him not to whip the horse, calling him a 'bad baste' and he turned and asked, "Do you want me to whip you?" He meant it.

ONCOMING CIVIL WAR

Salmon silvering grey to die
The summers of the past day

Trapped in our own shallow chill
Shadows, then slowly a whole season's

Twilight bleeds like a blue blood's at
The least scathing, opens out

The silk cloud's spider-fingering pine
Against the going away to sea sky

Cannot be wrenched back nor hoarded
But given only as the black ever

-greens go on living high up over
The mountain hill wall, high up over

This little mill town, the mornings
Growing darker than sundown.

So when I came back in the 50s, and tried to live in the suburbs in Glengormley, I guess we were trying to get out of a ghetto mentality. Even in the 60s there was still a certain amount of hope—we planned kids, O'Neill met Lemass, all that kind of thing. Nancy and I were very much in love. There were bad omens, though. I remember two wee blackbirds getting trapped between the nylon drape and the window and fluttering madly, not able to get out; as I released them the sky darkened, a shadow came across the window just as they escaped. I'm a poet who believes in omens. There was news that Nancy's brother, who was schizophrenic, had killed himself; there was the 'Troubles'. Things conspired against us. I started getting migraines. Nancy got ill, too. All that medical stuff is in the poems—haemorrhage and migraine. The doctors told Nancy that my problem was not physical; they put me away for ten days or so in the hospital. Of course, I told all the people in there to 'get up out of their beds and get on with it, for this was all just a conspiracy by the lunatics against us' until they had to let me out.

SAINT COLMAN'S SONG FOR FLIGHT
for Nancy and Brigid—flown

Run like rats from the plague in you.
Before death it is no virtue to be dead.
The crannog in the water, anywhere at all sure!
It is no virtue and it is not nature
To wait to writhe into the ground.

Not one in the Bible could see these dead
Packed on top of the other like dung
Not the two Josephs in Egypt
But would not run!

And Christ's blessing follow
(It is not a blessing to escape storm?)

Pray to old Joseph not a witless man
Who had the brains not to want to die

But when his time came only and at home in bed,
The door shut on the world, that wolf outside
Munching the leper's head ...

The secret of my work is my wife Nancy, her leaving me—the loss. I was left on the ground when she left with our beautiful baby daughter. The troubles, and my marriage breakdown became fused in my mind.

GOODBYE TO BRIGID/AN AGNUS DEI

I take you by the hand. Your eyes,
Mirroring the traffic lights,
Are green and orange and red.

The Military lorries by our side
Drown out your child-heart
Thumping tired under the soot

-black thorn trees these
Exhaust-fumed greasy mornings.

My little girl, my Lamb of God,
I'd like to set you free from
Bitch Belfast as we pass the armed

-to-the-back-teeth barracks and
Descend the road into the school
Grounds of broken windows from

A spate of car-bombs, but
Don't forgive me for not.

INTIMATE LETTER 1973

Our Paris part of Belfast has
Decapitated lamp posts now. Our meeting
Place, the Book Shop, is a gaping
Black hole of charred timber.

Remember that night with you, in
-valided in the top room when
They were throwing petrol bombs through
The windows of Catholics, how
My migraine grew to such
A pitch, Brigid said 'Mummy,
I think Daddy is going to burst!'

We all run away from each other's
Particular hell. I didn't
Survive you and her thrown
To the floor when they blew up the Co
-Op at the bottom of the street or Brigid
Waking screaming after this
Or that explosion. Really,
I was the first one to go:

It was I who left you ...

"Odour of blood when Christ was slain/Made all Platonic tolerance vain/And vain all Doric discipline." I put Yeats and Lawrence at the front of the book, talking about blood and Joyce talks about "bleeding for his torn bough ... by the black stream" inside the book which takes you back to the crucifixion. That Yeats quote is one of his deepest and darkest perceptions. It's a bloody book. Don't leave that book on the coffee table. Tolerance and just about everything else, including philosophy, goes out the window when crucifixions start happening. Christ is the enemy in the book and in a century as dark as this one. He is the enemy.

CHRIST GOODBYE

I
Dandering home from work at mid
-night, they tripped Him up on a ramp,
Asked Him if He was a 'Catholic' ...

A wee bit soft in the head He was,
The last person in the world you'd want
To hurt:
His arms and legs, broken,
His genitals roasted with a ship
-yard worker's blow lamp.

II
In all the stories that the Christian Brothers
Tell you of Christ He never screamed
Like this. Surely this is not the way
To show a 'manly bearing'
Screaming for them to PLEASE STOP!
And then, later, like screaming for death!

When they made Him wash the stab
Wounds at the sink, they kept on
Hammering Him with the pick
-axe handle; then they pulled
Christ's trousers down, threatening to
'Cut off His balls!'
Poor boy Christ, for when
They finally got round to finishing Him off
By shooting Him in the back of the head

'The poor Fenian fucker was already dead!'

The poet is alone, the "wolf outside munching the leper's head".
'Christ Goodbye' was a harder poem to write than 'Glass Grass' and

I don't understand—I still can't understand—why they would want to torture someone like the innocent old Protestant man I had dinner with in Rathcoole. I often wonder what happened to him. I tried to get near to the killer mentality in this book and Father Des Wilson says he still can't understand the sentiments in it. Behind the book is the murder of Gerry McLaughlin, a poor innocent boy, who used to come visit me in Glengormley and bring some chips and beer and keep me company while we weeded the garden. God, we didn't even use weedkiller. One day you switch from classical music to Radio Ulster and you just find out they murdered him. I'd seen too much when I came to write that book. I was, I still am bitter. I just can't understand—I just can't understand.

THE DITCH OF DAWN
for Gerry McLaughlin

How I admired your bravado
Dandering down the road alone
In the dark yelling, 'I'll see
You again, tomorrow', but

They pump six bullets into you.

Now you are lying in a mud
Puddle of blood, yelling.

'There is no Goodbye',
No 'Safe Home'
In this coffin country where
Your hands are clawed ... '

How can I tell anyone
I'm born, born lying in
This ditch of a cold Belfast dawn
With the bullet-mangled body of
A dead boy
and can't
can't get away?
A young
Brit soldier wanders

Over to my old
donkey honk
Of bitter Miserere of
Dereliction on the street:

'What is it mate, what is it?

WHAT'S WRONG?'

INTERNEE

It is not absolutely fair,
It is not absolutely wrong,

And it does not hurt
To be jeered at

When you are hanging
Upside down,

When hanging upside down hurts more.

ENEMIES

At the Gas and Electric Offices
Black boats with white sails
Float down the stairs

Frightening the five-year-old
Wee Protestant girls ...

'Nuns, nuns,' one of them yells,
'When are yez go'n to git
married?'

II *Lullaby*
When the ricocheting bullet bites into
The young child wanted to walk
In her mother's high heels to push
The doll's pram, she
Gives out a funny little 'oooh!'

And lets the blood spill
All over the bright new bib ...

ENEMY ENCOUNTER

Dumping (left over from the autumn)
Dead leaves, near a culvert
I come on
a British Army soldier
With a rifle and a radio
Perched hiding. He has red hair.

He is young enough to be my weenie
-bopper daughter's boyfriend.
He is like a lonely little winter robin.

We are that close to each other, I
Can nearly hear his heart beating.

I say something bland to make him grin,
But his glass eyes look past my side
-whiskers down
the Shore Road street.
I am an Irish man
and he is afraid
That I have come to kill him.

I am aware that, in compiling this anthology, I might be accused of a cynical exploitation of what is, it is hoped, a transient situation. It is self-evident, however, that the violence, division and hatred that, in their present acute phase, disfigure the face of Ireland, have roots that run deeper and spread wider than the events of the past six years. Whether or not any of the poems in this anthology have the mark of greatness is for a future generation of readers to judge. But there is a time to keep silence and a time to speak; at the very least there is nothing in this anthology that did not cry out to be said, and that is surely more than enough to justify its existence.

So then I was accused by some of carrying on a vigorous guerrilla campaign against the earnest Honest Ulster Establishment of pee-the-bed Pyjama Poets. I plead guilty. I'm hostile to what they stand for.

I know three Faber poets personally and they all have in common an 'odour of sanctity'. Talking to any one of them is always like talking to a holy picture. They answer back like old-time students for the priesthood and the wee-est one of them all talks down his nose to you like a Bishop. Why is this? The answer is because getting published by Faber is canonisation in one's own lifetime. It means 'Who's like me since Leather Arse died?'

Well, what's wrong with a little puffed-up play-acting triumphalism anyway? Everything's wrong with it. Poetry and religion ought not to be kept locked away in a watertight compartment by the cozy select few. Poetry and religion belong to the people; not to some whiter than white clique, some monopoly or other, baptising themselves as the elite, pushing towards the maximum regimentation of the arts and religion because their frightened greed demands a bank-like military security. They lock themselves up in craftily wrought, but sterile, facades of versifications, like hiding in some well-furnished pub lounge. It's the life inside the shell that matters.

GLASS GRASS

Try to
understand that you yourself
are guilty of every atrocity
howsoever far from you
it seems to be happening.
—Gunter Eich

The scorched-cloth smell of burnt flesh
From morning, a bomb in one of the parked cars,
The gulls, glinting like ice on asphalt in April,
The sun, in a smog of cheap petrol exhaust
Fumes: All bring on the sinusy migraine.

Trudging against an east wind from the cement
Factory (awful bad for the chist!), I wade
Through broken glass in a yellowing black smoke,
Through steel-smouldering street. There's
Broken glass in my wedding shoes
(I wore them for luck!).

Crossing the shadow-deflected town that burns,
Crossing the always-takes, never-gives man,
Crossing our bone-sieves, crossing our stunted lives.
Crossing the starlings with football-kicking kids
Who make the telephone cables do a war dance,

Once I sipped at your wanton wonder like wine;
Now everything taken from us is reflected back in
-to this Chinese-lacquered black aubade
Like piano music in a French film breaks
Into bits of staccato shooting from an M1.

Ducking flying glass from the workers cleaning
Up afterwards, I take to the middle of Royal Avenue
On my way in gold-rimmed Polaroids to give
A poetry reading in Ballymurphy: clutching at
Ragged editions of my own poems, like clutching at

Strands of grass to hold you up from falling
With the crashing debris down the mountainy ware
-houses and hotels! I promised John Hewitt and Des
Wilson, otherwise I wouldn't venture forth again
Into this too-near-to-the-knuckle disaster ...

Tired of trying to pretend I am not this frightening
Freak has something in common with the terrorist
Of women and children, I read my poem about
The 'icons and guns' and ask 'Now is
That 'sectarian'? '
'We're all 'sectarian' here!'

Some honest person replies. In the discussion after
-wards Des Wilson says 'I'm frightened of poets.
I'm frightened of their perceptions!'
He wants me to answer.
'Can you put yourself into the mind
Of the man who kills?'
'No.' I lie to the priest. 'I can't',
But I can, I'm polluted

With the poison of violence, born and bred into it:
I'm dying of those dark looks I get from boy
Soldiers from slits in 'pigs', and I try to rub
The hatred from my eyes but it's deeper than 'looks':
The black is in my lungs now, and in my poems.

Interview with Padraic Fiacc

JOHN BROWN

You were born in Belfast in 1924. Was your family background an important influence?

My family were a big influence. My mother and father were mad rebels in the 1920s. My grandmother was madder. She kept a gun in her apron; she ruled the whole of East Street in Belfast. She would tell the military: "Don't you dare come through that door, I've just washed the floor." I come from folks who are not terribly sane. My grandmother would march you up and down East Street shouting, "You wee hussies! Get in and wash your hair! Go in and mind the weans!" I still don't know who my father was. He went off early to America and became a barman. He had to get out because they were killing Catholic barmen in Belfast whether they were involved in the 'Troubles' or not. My mother was a fierce Republican but there was no way she was going to be sent out of her own country. I was the oldest, the first born alive. As the eldest I was conscious of my father not being there from an early age, although he sent my mother home costumes from America—she was a flapper—and after he left in 1927-28, we moved to East Street. Even though we all called our grandfather 'da', I knew he wasn't. In the very early years I grew up on Elizabeth Street on the Falls. *Elizabeth* Street? Now, how's about that? I've only the briefest memories of my father: he used to come home from work and kiss me and I'd run my fingers through his black, curly hair and I remember like all children I was conniving—asking him one day to hold me up to look over the big blind wall at the back of the house. And what was on the other side of the wall? Just a hungry dog gnawing into the bin. The poetry in life, eh?

Why did your father leave?

He had to get out. He left in 1927 just in time for the American depression. At a joint reading with John Montague he pointed out that we shared a liking for Patric Collins; I pointed out that we shared fathers who had sweated working in the New York subways. After my father left we moved from Elizabeth Street to East Street to live with my grandmother.

You left Belfast at an early age for New York. What were your first impressions of New York?

I was five when we went to New York. People in Belfast all came down to say their goodbyes at the docks and 'Auld Lang Syne' was sung. Leaving seemed permanent, forever. We landed at Halifax. We had such a good time on the boat but on arriving we would have gone back in an instant. We'd been told so much about New York—and I really wanted to see it—but at Halifax there was another brick wall, an even bigger one; my stupid father had missed the train to the boat to meet us, so we sat disappointed beside our bags waiting until some fireman or policeman—or somebody or other—came to help us. Joyce calls the Atlantic an "abyss of tears"; it is for anyone who crosses it as an Irish immigrant. There is that sense of loss. Recently I wrote a poem about the flight from Toronto to London; it's now just a single night flight and I needed St. Augustine in the poem to slow the flight down, but in my mother's day America was exile. My first impressions of New York were that it was full of bright lights and yellow taxis and movement. I loved the brightness. I was excited. I was very close to my mother and I knew instinctively that she did not want to go to America. I came to hate every part of New York— even the brightness—for no matter how glittery it was I was determined to hate it because my mother hated it. I went to Commerce High School and there was all that standing up every day to do 'God Bliss A-mer-ic-a'—awful, hypocritical—and it left you, as it probably did many immigrant children, trapped somewhere. Everyone in America in the 30s was fighting the

Spanish Civil War in the kitchen, even at Thanksgiving dinners, but I'd just do wash-up with my mother and she'd listen to them talking and she'd say, "Shit, shit, and more shit—and sugar on the top of it." We'd do the washing up and let them fight in the Spanish Civil War.

When did you start writing?

I started writing in the late 30s, the early 40s, in New York. I had this teacher—a Jewish, forcefully leftist Communist—who encouraged me; he thought I had a flair for words. Of course he was up against it, with Franco being a Fascist and me being a Catholic, but he needed someone to argue with so I cut my teeth on him as a writer. I'd get up in class and ask him to 'forgive me', just before I'd set off to wind him up. My first real poem was 'Der Bomben Poet' from 1941; it is the first poem in *Ruined Pages*. "This is my birthday. I have just turned seventeen. My home town has just been blown up." I was riding a bus through Hell's Kitchen and I saw this newspaper headline: 'Belfast Bombed'. Ah, I couldn't believe it. It's a good poem though: "Dead feet in dead faces". It's therapeutic, mad. I remember thinking about my home town and family. I was frightened for them.

You studied for the priesthood and your early poems repeatedly refer to 'sanctuary', 'monastery' and 'psalm'. What is your attitude to Catholicism? Why didn't you become a priest?

Who are you talking to? Of course, I fucked that up. I'm a Catholic, but I was never totally interested in becoming a priest. The nuns at my first school told me not to go to Haaren High School because it was in Hell's Kitchen. The nuns also said to "Go to any school that teaches Latin" and with Haaren being the only school nearby to teach Latin I wrote and applied when I was thirteen or fourteen. "Ah, Te-Tum, hum-ah-hum-ah-hum." "E-TAL-E-AN?" "LATIN?" About as good as getting yourself an Alsatian dog! My mother's side of the family were not that religious, but on my father's side I'd my Aunt Mary who took me to do the Stations of the Cross. I could never understand, though, how Christ as the Son of God could allow those bastards to torture him. And yet, that's complicated for the image came with my awareness of sex and death; I'd look at the soldiers, at those centurions with their muscular legs, and at the time—I was thirteen—I had just started reading Dostoevsky's *The Brothers Karamazov* where Father Zosimas's body gives off a smell when he dies. He was supposed to be a saint but he gives off a foul odour. Dostoevsky talks truth and faces reality. God, even a big horsefly came out of the saint's body!

The suggestion, though, has been made that you parted company with the seminary and a vocation because you wrote morbid poetry?

Sometimes I felt trapped in the monastery. I used to jump up and down on my glasses and smash them to get home. I remember an old priest who was sympathetic to the Irish climbing the hill to the monastery, and meeting me in a yellow shirt and black jacket and tan boots, and he stops me and asks: "What are you doing in that get-up?" And so I told him I didn't want to end up looking like a penguin but, of course, he made me climb the hill and put on a black suit. They were strict. The story is that I left the monastery because of the morbidity of my writing, but I remember writing a play called *Fire* about St. Patrick, where he was supposed to meet the King of Ireland's wife. Mickey Maloney, a real arm-wrestler from the Bronx, insisted on playing the Queen in high heels—he wasn't too hot on historical accuracy—and came in click, click, clicking across the stage and he says he "do believe in St. Patrick". Of course the priests were outraged and laughing into their sleeves. The corpse that was supposed to be dead on the stage came awake; it was tragedy gone into a farce. You see, I just didn't have the habits of a monk. I had to leave the regimental orders. I left in 1945.

You submitted an early volume of poems, Inisfail Lost, *to Padraic Colum at Macmillan. What influence did he have on your subsequent work?*

Colum was a little old priest. He got hold of the New York poems like 'Inisfail Lost'. Although he thought poems like 'Master Clay' were nasty, he did see something in the poems and he helped me move from verse that was sweet and twee into a new phase. The poems I wrote at this time were nasty, wonderful and full of terrible longing. Padraic advised me: "Write of your own people. Dig in the garden of Ireland." He gave me Gaelic literature and folklore and myth and that became important in my work. And, of course, the more I dug, the more I was horrified. Colum was trying to take me off the streets of New York and I guess I was flattered that an older, established poet was interested. In New York even if you want to escape reality you have got to face it for it just keeps coming and coming at you—there might be five or six murders a night every night in Manhattan. You see, I had this terrible longing for Ireland and Padraic nursed that in me; there are the translations of early Irish literature but these poems are not about escape. Look at Deirdre who "pitched herself into the sea. *Turn the page. Turn the page.*" She's the Deirdre who is the "gold albino" who would "eat the spokes out of the wheel". You might say I was trying to escape the niceties of my early verse. This early Irish literature is supposed to be about men—I was trying to write about men but I came to realise that all those women are ferocious and they take over so the men don't get a look in. "And great King Conor of himself said/Did you ever see a bottomless bucket/In the muck discarded?" How New York can you get? The link between early Irish poetry and New York is that both force you to face reality.

Does Cúchulainn interest you as mythic character?

Cúchulainn does interest me as a mythic character. He's masculine, an Irish King Kong, a pampered, rugged, destructive little shit—the opposite of Deirdre, who was also cursed in the womb from birth, but at least she spent her early years in a garden like the Buddha; she did not experience violence early, unlike Cúchulainn who was trained in arms early on. Cúchulainn is stubborn and macho, and having been around men all my life I know how they behave like children, so there is a link in my head between Cúchulainn and men in twentieth-century Ireland. Conor fell in love with Cúchulainn and made him his Hound of Ulster, so he defends Ulster against Medbh all over the head of a lousy cow and he kills his own son and falls into a depression—and so he should. He's a man who never grew up.

'Gloss': that sense of poetry as re-translation, a re-injection of old truth in new language, implies that poetry is trans-cultural, that it can translate. Is that important in your work?

Yes. The Benedictine monks who came to Ireland were

influenced by post-Reformation thinking when they came over here. Like the Jesuits they had a lot up top. And they dug into and dug up Irish mythology. I know this Irish literature like a Benedictine monk. The Scots and Welsh know these stories too and the Scottish are Celts and the Welsh are Celts and the northern English are Celts. This place should not be called the British Isles but the Celtic Isles.

Religion, though, in its contemporary Ulster variety, is surely a barrier against 'gloss' or translation. Look at Seamus Heaney's poem 'The Other Side'. The rosary goes on inside a Catholic farmhouse and the Biblical Protestant farmer stands outside; the poet is uncertain whether he can talk to the man about everyday things like the "weather" or "the price of grass seed".

Yes, but I'm not an orthodox Catholic. French Catholicism and Jansenism have always had a big influence in Ireland and a lot of priests here trained in France. Spain would have been better. Here in Ulster you get Protestantised. In the monastery in America they taught us that Protestants wanted individuality and Catholics were for a universal conscience. I wanted, of course, to be more individualistic than Protestants. You know I even think Paisley has a sense of humour and I think I've probably more in common with him than I have with many middle-class Catholics. Recently, when I was in hospital, after I was beaten up, this guy, who was lying across from me, says: "You're that poet fellow who writes about killing Catholic babies." And that's sad. Just Catholic babies? I include every baby, every single one. I love kids. I'm a good babysitter and I've written poems about, and for, kids. Did he not know I'd written poems for the Protestant minister, James Parker, who kept a toll of the dead in Belfast? Did he not know that poem about those wee Protestant girls who meet the nuns and ask them when they are "gonna get married"?

You left New York for Ireland in 1946 and returned to New York in the early 50s. Why?

Well, the move back to Ireland from New York was a choice between enlisting in the American army and going back to Belfast. I found a man who could get me a passport back. Padraic's wife Mary told me I was mad: "What do you wanna be going back to

Ireland for?" she asked. "There's no work there." I boarded a Swedish liner, though, the *Grispholm*, and got to the far end of the boat to get away from everybody waving bye-bye to the Statue of Liberty. I met this woman who lived in a studio in Paris that Verlaine and Rimbaud had lived in—they were both lovers and I loved Rimbaud—so I didn't need to be down the far end of the boat when I could talk Rimbaud with her. In Belfast I wrote poems for magazines here. I was included in *New Irish Poets* in the late 40s. I gave them poems and my Aunt Mary took me down to the photographer and stood behind him shouting, "Stop grinning! Only fools grin." And so I was included—grinning—as the youngest poet and it was those poems that Nancy read ten years later when she was working in a bookshop in America. She began to write; she fell for those poems, their innocence, hook, line and sinker, and I was amazed. I guess we were both religious and romantic, even if I was a manic depressive. Nancy linked in with the religious element in the poems. Look at "chaunt rann of a singer", such innocence. I don't think I could write that kind of poem now. I went back to New York in the early 50s, even though I hated it, to look after my kid sister when my mother died. My mother was dark, tempestuous, Spanish, beautiful. I loved her. My brother had come back from World War II permanently damaged, unrecognisable, and even my father (who was far gone on whiskey) recognised that something was wrong. There was no alternative but to stay and look after my sister and father. I did his washing and ironing and tried to be my mother to him. I got a job as a typist with IBM on $42 a week. In the evening, when I was playing mother, I wrote those tough-guy poems of the early 50s—the sort of poems you would write if you never took a cigarette out of your mouth.

New York in the 50s was different from New York in the 20s?

Yes. New York had become an American city. It was now full of immigrants and black people and Puerta Ricans and people with different sexual preferences. They were all hated, especially if they were suspected of the sexual perversity of Communism. I'd a German friend and I'd use my finger as a make-believe moustache to pretend I was Hitler until I found out later that Hitler really was a madman who didn't know his arse from his elbow. I'd a Jewish teacher who, like many Jews, gave himself a simpler name when he arrived in America. He chose Maidman. He was asking for trouble and my friend Bubbles changed one syllable on the blackboard to make him a madman, too. America paid for freedom and its many races in paranoia and materialism. You know, I remember helping the mothers undress the kids to go to the wading pool in the little green oasis that was Central Park—I love kids—and my own father even accused me of sexual perversity. Ah, that's terribly sad.

Your sexuality, though, is a subject for speculation and dirty gossip in Belfast.

Well, folk want me out of the cave and into some other closet. I know they say I'm homosexual but naturally I love both men and women and that's what you are supposed to do. Edna O'Brien says that "Women are the valleys and men are the mountains." And she's right. That's the way God made us. I was conscious of that in Swansea recently, the valley of the swan. I am fond of men. I have had five or six close physical relationships with men; I love their bodies but I'm vulnerable because men pick on my feminine side; whilst I try to accommodate everybody, I'm only a human being. I'd gladly give in to a man but I'm Catholic, so I would have to make confession to the priest; there would be a hell of a lot of Hail Marys. As a priest once said to me, "You have always got to think of the other guy."

You were in Belfast in the early and late 50s? How would you describe that time?

The 50s were a kind of natal depression; I've written about this. W.R. Rodgers, like MacNeice, left for the BBC in London; Robert Greacen left too—although he continued to write letters—and I left in the middle of the decade for New York. W.R. Rodgers's second poetry collection *Europa and the Bull* came out in the early 50s and there was John Montague's *Poisoned Lands*, which was well named. There was McFadden's long and chilling poem, 'Elegy for the Dead of the Princess Victoria'. To my mind Brian Moore's *The Loneliness of Judith Hearne* was a great novel of the 50s; it testifies to the depression found in the North of Ireland. In Belfast, PEN meetings took place in the Union Hotel at the back of the City Hall after the American troops, who had been stationed there during the war, had gone. I worked as a night-porter in the dump. I would see writers, like John Hewitt, ensconced between the palm trees before their meetings. In Cork, *Poetry Ireland* was edited by David Marcus. John Hewitt was a guest editor of an Ulster edition; although he found my poems disconcerting (with their Gaelic words like 'leifer' or 'chaunt-rann'), he wrote from Coventry later asking for poems to print in Mary O'Malley's *Threshold* and he used a long one. I dedicated 'Jackdaw' to him, because of his love of the Glens of Antrim, and he dedicated 'The Scar' to me. I didn't know McFadden until the 70s when we met in Michael McLaverty's home, where I also met Seamus Heaney.

Let's talk about specific literary influences in the writing. You preface poems with quotations from Mauriac and Baudelaire. Critics such as James Liddy and Terence Brown suggest that your poems use syntactical disruptions, internal rhymes and sentences that spill over the line so that technique encounters the shock of real life. Were you influenced by French literature in this?

Ah oui. And si. Terence Brown understands me, my work. French and Spanish writers influenced me to a very bad degree and American poetry with its new freedom. I use words broken by hyphens, sentences that brake and swerve in the middle. Padraic Colum's wife Mary gave me a copy of Rimbaud, a beautiful translation of *The Drunken Boat* (*Le Bâteau Ivre*). Rimbaud was the nasty wee boy I wasn't allowed to be. I was the oldest; I ended up looking after my father and taking the kids to Central Park. There's darkness in Rimbaud, the ability to make real life more real. He's dangerous. Internal rhymes? I'm a poet and it's just a matter of giving myself licence; while this is in French literature (and in Irish literature, too) it doesn't mean that there is no composition. John Hewitt said that in my poems "even the very syllables count" and they do. That's oriental. The Japanese and Chinese wrote poems on rice paper, hung them on trees, and let the wind blow them where it would; I think that's beautiful. Li Po says that when he woke up in the morning to a whole lot of noisy people and commotion, it was "only the lamentation of monkeys".

He could compress a lot. Chinese and Japanese poets attract me because they are saying less is more. Of course, this means that the more poems I've written, the less I've written.

Which American poets do you admire?

Robert Lowell. Lowell refused to serve in the army and I admired that. "Why do you love me if I am not a man?" Lowell wrote in one poem. "I am bleak bone with survival." I understand that too. Walt Whitman, who was homesexual and went around kissing everyone. Emily Dickinson, too, wrote the most beautiful poems; she was enclosed but wrote wonderfully; she had no social occasions to shine at. I like Hemingway too, his great style. I identify with the Americans because of their individualism and materialism.

Have English language poets from England influenced you?

Only in so far as you write in the English language are they an influence. They are the Romantics like Shelley, Keats, Wordsworth and Coleridge—I like his nasty habits—but they are not a direct influence. Poetry is not a rigged card game anyway, a case of knowing all the cards or literary influences. The bad social vibes, the violence that happened on the streets of Hell's Kitchen, and my own way of making it up out of cheesecloth break in. Shostakovich did the same in music. I'm a manic depressive, perhaps even schizophrenic, and that is important in my poems; and there is also the unpredictable in life and what happens there.

Surely there is also fatalism in your work, a determinism which closes off doors, which makes the womb a prison that ejects us forcibly into what Hopkins called "the blight that man was born for"?

The fatalism—I am fatalistic—comes from French writing. I do believe in destiny. There's that Arab way of seeing which knows that "the desert is the garden of Allah"; that's understood by the French and Spanish and it came into Europe from North Africa—for the Mediterranean is not a sea, it's only a wee river between north and south Europe—so that the desert enters French thinking from the Arabs. What it amounts to is that suffering is part of my vision. Some people tell me that not everyone suffers but I do not believe that; I think everybody does.

You returned with Nancy to live in Belfast in 1956. How important was your relationship with Nancy for the poems?

The secret of my work is my wife Nancy, her leaving me—it's loss. I was left on the ground when she left with our beautiful baby daughter; even the dog she left chewed up my shoes when I was upstairs watching TV. I suppose that coming back to the North brought back my childhood, which I'd tried to avoid. I had been born into the Civil War here when they were just making Northern Ireland. Although I was only a child, I knew there was something wrong. My grandmother was burned out of Lisburn and she ended up mad and ever in childhood I could tell she was paranoid about me wandering. I remember wandering off into Lagan Street one day and seeing these two kids blurtin' and pointing to a man who was whipping a horse. I went over to ask him not to whip the horse and called him a "bad baste" and he turned and asked, "Do you want me to whip you?" He meant it. So when I came back in the 50s, and tried to live in the suburbs in Glengormley, I guess we were trying to get out of a ghetto mentality. Even in the 60s there was still a certain amount of hope—we planned kids, O'Neill met Lemass, all that kind of thing. Nancy and I were very much in love. There were bad omens, though. I remember two wee blackbirds getting trapped between the nylon drape and the window and fluttering madly, not able to get out; as I released them the sky darkened, a shadow came across the window just as they escaped. I'm a poet who believes in omens. There was news that Nancy's brother, who was schizophrenic, had killed himself; there was the 'Troubles'. Things conspired against us. I started getting migraines. Nancy got ill, too. All that medical stuff is in the poems—haemorrhage and migraine. The doctors told Nancy that my problem was not physical, so it had to be mental; they put me away for ten days or so in the hospital. Of course, I told all the people in there to "get up out of their beds and get on with it, for this was all just a conspiracy by the lunatics against us" until they had to let me out.

Belfast is central in the poems. By the Black Stream *(1969) and* Odour of Blood *(1973) capture a black, bleak, rainy, sectarian and violent town. Why did you leave New York and choose Belfast?*

I call it 'Hellfast'. I was asked by a journalist from Dublin about leaving New York and I told her, "I couldn't breathe in New York. Next question." She asked why I'd come to Belfast and I told her, "I like it OK, but it's Hellfast." She wrote about 'what would he call it if he didn't like it!' Belfast is not love-hate, though, for I do love the place and I couldn't tell you why. It smells of tar, chimneys, cooking grub and the boneyards. There's that poem from the bad days in the 70s where I call it a "beaten, sexless dog". You'll get what I feel about its suffering in 'Glass Grass'. Why do I love it? God knows. In my darkest and bleakest book, *Nights in the Bad Place*, it's a place where the "dead stick in your gut"; you can't live here without being poisoned. There is something else here too, though. I remember coming down over the mountain one evening in a car with John Hewitt and Roberta and driving back home and thinking about the street names—gorgeous names like Violet Street—and about how beautiful the place seemed. I love flowers—my grandfather was a gardener for the Quaker School in Lisburn—and even in Wellesley Avenue I could grow geraniums in the window box. But look at the place now. I can understand them wanting to kill a taxi driver the odd time—I've even wanted to myself—but not literally, not one or two every night. God, what a sweetheart of a place!

Is your poetry political? Should poetry be political in the context of Northern Ireland?

No. In America it was all politics and politics there is religion: you have to take one side or another. I don't like taking sides. Here I try to keep my mouth shut, difficult though that is. I suppose we could have Northern Ireland and that other shitbag of a neighbour together—a bit like England and Scotland and Wales—but the whole question of a united Ireland depends on people. Even Jimmy Connolly knew there was no point in having a united Ireland unless the people were united in wanting it. Connolly talked of a unity of Catholic, Protestant and Dissenter. I guess that whatever the answer, I'd be a dissenter.

Odour of Blood was published in 1973. How would you describe that volume?

"Odour of blood when Christ was slain/Made all Platonic tolerance vain/And vain all Doric discipline." I put Yeats and

Lawrence at the front of the book, talking about blood and Joyce talks about "bleeding for his torn bough ... by the black stream" inside the book, which takes you back to the crucifixion. That Yeats quote is one of his deepest and darkest perceptions. It's a bloody book. Don't leave that book on the coffee table. Tolerance and just about everything else, including philosophy, goes out the window when crucifixions start happening. Christ is the enemy in the book and in a century as dark as this one, He is the enemy. Do you know that the colour of red appears in all my books. I was anaemic as a child; I could hardly look at a bowl of tomato juice without fainting (let alone blood), so I'm facing up to a deep fear—the fear of death—in the book. I remember, when I went to school in New York, they gave us red ties as part of the uniform and when I asked why, they said it was because we were all now martyrs for Christ. I don't want to be a martyr. Do you know that early poem 'Trying to Study Philosophy'? I wrote it in New York; it's about a blackbird singing down Belfast Lough, its song from its lovely "black bell" singing from the twelfth century when Finn McCool brought the blackbirds here from Norway. The last two lines ask: "What is true?/What is beautiful?" And the only thing that is ... is the bird's song; I'm saying you can experience and imagine that but you can't build philosophy out of it. The birdsong is the only concrete thing in the poem and the abstracts give way to that. In *Odour of Blood*, I'm saying that poetry is the enemy of philosophy. "I can't love the furled flag on the responsible street".

If poetry is not philosophy is "a poem a prayer"? You quote Samuel Beckett, saying this in the introduction to one poem. And yet you say, in another poem, that you want "pagan words". Surely there is a contradiction? You also admire the painter Francis Bacon who thought, like Beckett, that man's existence was an accidental act, a "game without reason". Bacon would probably have gone as far as saying that God was dead. Would you agree?

No. I don't agree with that. Bacon and Beckett could get carried away sometimes. Beckett, though, is right in saying that "a poem is a prayer". The only problem is that I need "pagan words" sometimes. I'm contrary—but this has been a brutal century and the poems are about human beings and experience and that is contradictory in itself. Poetry, painting and music are all pagan. Beckett, though, is so deadly serious. He picked up Socrates's notion of life as a tragic joke, a black farce, and I'd say, too, that the loneliness in life is the wildness in life. Yes, the loneliness in life is the wildness in life! Let the poets explore that. You know I was supposed to go and meet Beckett once. I went along to this café in Paris but he just up and died, so he didn't turn up. Now, what a contrary thing to do! Ain't life just one big bowl of cherries.

In the mid-70s you edited an anthology called The Wearing of the Black, *which attracted a storm of criticism. What motivated you to do this anthology? Would you still defend it?*

I met a student after doing *The Wearing of the Black* and he asked if I was the poet Pad-rage Fiasco or Out-raged Franco or something and I told him, "Sure, you're getting warm." The anthology drove folks mad and I loved every minute of it. I must have been a sadist and a masochist to do an anthology of 'Troubles' writing. I'm an American and an outsider. The critics wanted to crucify me. Even the funders were annoyed. I was motivated by my own sense of outrage. I watched a Canadian interviewer talking to poets from here and commending them for their "lovely cadences from such a troubled place", but I wanted to tell how raw this place really was. The Europeans loved this book; it was taken up by a European underground. Of course, I was producing a book that went right in the teeth of the funders and good taste. All the bards have had sharp tongues.

Nights in the Bad Place *is also no picnic. In poems like 'Christ Goodbye' a man's genitals are "roasted with a ship/-yard worker's blow lamp". Has the poetry been "swamped by brutality"? How do you react to the criticism that in being too close to experience you forget to analyse it?*

Experience in good poems is analysis. This book came in the wake of Nancy leaving and in the face of the 'Troubles' and, even more than *Missa Terriblis*, it is my bleakest and blackest and darkest book. The poet is alone, the "wolf outside munching the leper's head". 'Christ Goodbye' was a harder poem to write than 'Glass Grass' and I don't understand—I still can't understand—why they would want to torture someone like the innocent old

Protestant man I had dinner with in Rathcoole. Ratcool! I often wonder what happened to him. I tried to get near to the killer mentality in this book and Father Des Wilson says he still can't understand the sentiments in it. Behind the book is the murder of Gerry McLaughlin, a poor innocent boy, who used to come visit me in Glengormley and bring some chips and beer and keep me company while we weeded the garden. God, we didn't even use weedkiller. One day you switch from classical music to Radio Ulster and you just find out they murdered him. I'd seen too much when I came to write that book. I was, I still am bitter. I just can't understand—I just can't understand—why people would kill each other over religion and politics here.

Is there a difference between the poem that is crafted and the poem that is given? The poem is born, not made? Or the poem made, not born?

Only academics make these kind of distinctions. I think poems are spontaneous; there is a great deal of luck in writing. Even if poets are born, poems still need revision and I remember Nancy asking me why I'd go over and over poems, but you have to work at it. Take 'First Movement', which dreams itself over from America to Ireland on drifting clouds—I loved watching clouds when I was a kid—where there's the yellow of the poem's opening before your expectation darkens suddenly as you experience coming home. It appears spontaneous, and it is, but there's also composition.

What is the relationship between painting and your work?

I understood painting long before I understood poetry. I started off painting like the Surrealists in the monastery and it frightened the priests. When I did an art class in Hell's Kitchen, I did everything that was bright in pastels. Yellow is my favourite colour. I didn't have the discipline for it, though. I remember doing a 'Madonna with the Child Teething'. It was beautiful. I myself know (laughs). I was influenced by religious art even if you can't imagine me with da Vinci. There was a time when I was knocking Madonnas out all over the place. Raphael's are best of all. During the Second World War, the treasures of European painting went over to New York and I used to go to the galleries and museums there. I loved El Greco; he's in one poem. I remember winding up Padraic Colum's circle of admiring young girls when he gave me colour plates of El Greco by telling them the artist had only elongated everybody and should not be allowed to get away with that. Picasso was influenced by El Greco and I love Picasso. I love him saying that "soldiers are donkeys" and I agree with him in the poems I've written about soldiers. 'Guernica' was an important painting in my day (even if we fought the Spanish Civil War sitting on our asses) and the Second World War darkened my writing; it permanently damaged my brother and I knew many Jews, a humorous and lovable people in New York. Hiroshima? It's in that poem where the child asks its mother why it is so dark. Picasso is the war artist. It was terribly apropos that I used his 'Guernica' on the cover of my *Missa Terriblis* because he's organic and so are my poems. If Picasso found a seashell—or something that he needed for his art—on the beach, the girlfriend went out the window. Both Picasso and Klee do everything in fragments, and so do I. I believe our century is in fragments, or smithereens as the Irish call it—fragments resulting from blows. Wars, though, throw up strange twists that neither poets nor painters bargain for. The BBC reporter I wrote about, who broke down on the screen when the bomb went off on Corn Market? I met him later when I was shopping in Marks & Spencer but he would not forgive me for the poem I wrote about this, even when I asked. The soldier who saved the woman and children in another poem? I found out later that his wife had sold the VC because he had left her poor. Wars use soldiers who are poor and women and children suffer—my mother knew that.

In your last poem in Red Earth *(1998) you tear up an image of yourself in a poem and a painting.*

The first painting Nancy made of me was of this very suave, sophisticated, guy smoking a cigarette in a Picasso moods. In a second painting, which she did after we split up, the whole jawline had changed. I could hardly bear looking at myself. She had captured me in a totally disruptive image; I nearly had to give up babysitting when a child looked at the painting and pointed at me and said, "da da". The poem and picture are made from torn strips; the romance has gone.

Modernism's "fragments ... shored against ... ruin". Does Eliot's
The Waste Land strike you as an important poem?

Eliot, Klee and Stravinsky were all interested in working with
the kinds of fragments I work with. I understood Eliot. I came
across his work early on and read it again in the 70s. I think he is,
perhaps, one of the greatest poets of the century. He's certainly
more highly educated than I am. Education does not necessarily
make for good poems, although in Eliot's case it did. With all his
learning he spoke out for the lonely, the lost, the sick, for those on
the operating table and I can't help but admire that. Eliot talks
sense about the deadliness of existence; in the most perfect way he
was a true existentialist.

Your last volume of the twentieth century was Semper Vacare
(1999). What are you saying in this volume?

The volume goes back to my relationship with Nancy of twenty
years. She would have been a Benedictine nun had she not met
and married me; having left the order to be with me, I came to St.
Benedict and the order through her. Benedict is everybody's saint,
a Catholic-Protestant monk who is accepted by Anglicans, and he
insisted that the monks drank wine with their dinner—which is
civilised. Nancy was fond of saying the Benedictine Latin phrase,
'Semper Vacare'—always make space, make room, make distance.
It was something that happened in our relationship—our marriage
fell apart—but it is also a deep spiritual saying about how to relate
to the world. I'm trying, too, to give each poem space in this book
and to still allow the mind 'to protect itself' in the face of 'pathos'
(as Hugh Buckingham says in the preface to 'Your Man'); so there
are poems about loving the blackbirds and poems about torture
and you try to keep your mind intact by trying to write about both.
I visited my cousin's son in the Royal Victoria Hospital, after he was
injured by a bomb in Armagh, and in 'Your Man' I'm looking at his
injuries and bringing him toys, "Making him/Unwrap the paper
bags himself/To gauge the amount of brain damage". It's a book
about toys in the hospital, about the fact that even though suicide
is deeply attractive we must go on to bring toys to the hospital
because there is no other alternative.

The 'spoiled' book is recurrent in the work. There is the "gold" that runs from the "ruined pages" in the book found at the bottom of the lake and the cuckoo that shits lime on the page.

Birdshit on the page? Why not? In France there were two writers and one of them, Jacques Maritain, found himself and his book under attack from the other and he had to fight for his life in defending his book. I loved what he said in his defence: "It's only a book." How many books have I written? Nine? It's all rien. And that's all there is to it. Rien. You'd think by the cover on some books that the writer is supposed to be God. Does it mean the writer is God? Rien. Rien. Rien. Rien. Rien.

first published in
*In the Chair: Interviews with Poets
from the North of Ireland* (Salmon Press, 2002)

Notes on Contributors

Chris Agee is a poet and editor of the journal *Irish Pages*. His most recent collection is *Next to Nothing* (2008). He has also edited *The New North: Contemporary Poetry from Northern Ireland* (Wake Forest, 2008).

John Brown is a poet and critic. His debut collection of poetry was *As the Crow Flies* (2003). He is also editor of *Magnetic North: The Emerging Poets* (Verbal Arts Centre, 2006).

Terence Brown is a critic and lectures at Trinity College, Dublin. His books include *Ireland's Literature: Selected Essays* (Lilliput Press, 1988) and *Ireland: A Social & Cultural History* 1921-2001 (updated edition 2004).

Maírtín Crawford was a poet and editor. At the time of his early death in 2004, he was working on a film documentary on Padraic Fiacc, *Stormbird*. His *Selected Poems* were published posthumously in 2005.

Gerald Dawe is a poet and critic, currently lecturing at Trinity College, Dublin. With Aodan Mac Poilin, he is co-editor of *Ruined Pages: Selected Poems of Padraic Fiacc*. His most recent collection of poetry is *Points West* (2008).

David Gilligan is a critic, currently teaching in Japan.

Paul Grattan is a poet. His debut collection is *The End of Napoleon's Nose* (2002).

Francis Hagan is a novelist and critic.

Brendan Hamill is a poet, reviewer and friend of Padraic Fiacc. He currently lives in Belfast.

Henry McDonald is a journalist living in Belfast. His most recent book is *Gunsmoke & Mirrors: How Sinn Féin Dressed Up Defeat as Victory* (Gill & Macmillan, 2008).

James Millar is an artist living in Belfast.

Michael Parker is a Professor of English Literature at the University of Central Lancashire. He most recent book is *Northern Ireland Literature: The Imprint of History* (Macmillan, 2007)

Damian Smyth is a poet, playwright and critic. His most recent collection of poetry is *The Down Recorder* (2004).

Paddy Scully is a Belfast-based actor and playwright.

Des Wilson is a priest in Belfast and a columnist with the *Andersonstown News*.